Energy Law in Nigeria

Energy Law in Nigeria

Yemi Oke

This book was originally published as a monograph in the International Encyclopaedia of Laws/Energy Law.

Founding Editor: Roger Blanpain
General Editor: Frank Hendrickx
Volume Editors: Kurt Deketelaere & Bram Delvaux

Wolters Kluwer

Published by:
Kluwer Law International B.V.
PO Box 316
2400 AH Alphen aan den Rijn
The Netherlands
E-mail: lrs-sales@wolterskluwer.com
Website: www.wolterskluwer.com/en/solutions/kluwerlawinternational

Sold and distributed by:
Wolters Kluwer Legal & Regulatory U.S.
920 Links Avenue
Landisville, PA 17538
United States of America
E-mail: customer.service@wolterskluwer.com

ISBN 978-94-035-3887-7

e-Book: ISBN 978-94-035-3897-6
web-PDF: ISBN 978-94-035-3907-2

The Author

Prof. Yemi Oke earned his *LLM* and *PhD* degrees from Osgoode Hall Law School, York University, Canada; *LLB* from University of Ilorin, Nigeria; *BL* from the Nigerian Law School, Abuja.

He is a professor of Energy/Electricity Law and a pioneering specialist and leading expert/scholar in Oil & Gas, Energy and Electricity Law in Africa. He has authored several books on these subjects. He is an internationally renowned scholar and has authored numerous other legal writings under various headings of Energy Resources, including Electricity Law and Regulation, International Environmental Law, Climate Change Law, Oil & Gas and Minerals and Mining Law.

Prof. Oke is the author of 10 law books including monographs, and about 100 published foreign and local academic and professional articles in his areas of specialization.

At various times in the course of his legal training, he was the 'Best Performance Award Winner', Department of Public Law University of Ilorin, Nigeria; 'Best Performance Award Winner', Department of Private and Property Law, and was also awarded several prizes in other law subjects in the same University. For his postgraduate education, he was a recipient of the prestigious 'York University Scholarship for Academic Distinctions' and 'Peter W. Hogg Award' (for exceptional students with demonstrable leadership potentials) at Osgoode Hall Law School, York University, Ontario, Canada and the 'Willard Z. Estey Fellowship for Research and Teaching Excellence' among other scholarship/fellowships by the same institution.

He was, at various times, counsel in leading law firms in Nigeria including Chief Rotimi Williams' Chambers; Babalakin & Co; Olaniwun Ajayi and KPMG Nigeria. In the course of his graduate studies, he taught at York University and Ryerson University both in Ontario, Canada before joining the Faculty of Law, University of Lagos.

E-mail: yemioke@msn.com, yoke@unilag.edu.ng, Tel.: 234- 802-314-8096; 803-463-0227.

The Author

Table of Contents

List of Abbreviations

ALSCON	Aluminum Smelting Company of Nigeria
CAMA	Companies and Allied Matters Act
CFRN	Constitution of the Federal Republic of Nigeria
CGT	Capital Gains Tax
CITA	Companies Income Tax Act
DEOPs	Decentralized Energy Options
DGSO	Domestic Gas Supply Obligations
DPR	Department of Petroleum Resources
EC	European Community
ECN	Electricity Corporation of Nigeria
EEZ	Exclusive Economic Zone
EFCC	Economic and Financial Crimes Commission
EIA	Environmental Impact Assessment
ELP	Escravos-Lagos Pipeline
EMEP	European Monitoring and Evaluation Programme
EPIC	Electric Power Implementation Committee
EPSR	Electric Power Sector Reform
ET	Education Tax
FDI	Foreign Direct Investment
FEED	Front End Engineering and Design
FEPA	Federal Environmental Protection Agency
FID	Final Investment Decision
FIRS	Federal Inland Revenue Service
GGA	Good Governance Africa
GGFR	Global Gas Flaring Reduction Partnership
GMP	Gas Master Plan
GNL	Gaslink Nigeria Limited
HEDPAC	Hydro-Electric Power Producing Areas Development Commission
ICCPR	International Covenant on Civil and Political Rights
ICEED	International Centre for Energy, Environment and Development

List of Abbreviations

ICESCR	International Covenant on Economic, Social and Cultural Rights
IDSL	Integrated Data Services Limited.
IGST	Institute of Geosciences and Space Technology
IJVs	Incorporated Joint Ventures
IMO	International Maritime Organization
IOC	International Oil Companies
IPP	Independent Power Producers
ITC	Investment Tax Credit
JOA	Joint Operating Agreement
JVA	Joint Venture Agreement
LFN	Laws of the Federation of Nigeria
LIA	Lagos Industrial Area
MDGs	Millennium Development Goals
MNOC	Multi National Oil Company
MOPI	Ministry of Petroleum Incorporated
MOU	Memorandum of Understanding
MPR	Ministry of Petroleum Resources
NAFCON	National Fertilizer Company of Nigeria
NAOC	Nigerian Agip Oil Company
NDA	Niger Dams Authority
NDDC	Niger Delta Development Commission
NEEDS	National Economic Empowerment and Development Strategy
NEITI	Nigerian Extractive Industries Transparency Initiative
NEP	National Energy Policy
NEPA	National Electric Power Authority
NEPP	National Electric Power Policy
NERC	Nigerian Electricity Regulatory Commission
NESCO	Nigerian Electricity Supply Company
NESREA	National Environmental Standards and Regulations Enforcement Agency
NGC	Nigerian Gas Company
NGP	National Gas Policy
NHT	Nigerian Hydrocarbon Tax
NLNG	Nigerian Liquefied Natural Gas Limited
NNOC	Nigerian National Oil Corporation
NNPC	Nigerian National Petroleum Corporation
NOC	National Oil Company
NOSDRA	National Oil Spill Detection & Response Agency
NOTAP	National Office for Technology Acquisition and Promotion

NPAMC	Nigerian Petroleum Assets Management Company
NPC	National Petroleum Company
NPIRD	National Policy on Integrated Rural Development
NPRC	National Petroleum Research Centre
NREEEP	National Renewable Energy and Energy Efficiency Policy
OECD	Organisation for Economic Co-operation and Development
OEL	Oil Exploration Licence
OGEFZ	Oil and Gas Export Free Zone
OML	Oil Mining Lease
OMPADEC	Oil Mineral Producing Areas Development Commission
OPEC	Organization of Petroleum Exporting Countries
OPL	Oil Prospecting Licence
PCAF	Power Consumer Assistance Fund
PEF	Petroleum Equalization Funds
PEL	Petroleum Exploration Licence
PHCF	Petroleum Host Community Fund
PHCN	Power Holding Company of Nigeria
PIA	Petroleum Industry Act
PIB	Petroleum Industry Bill
PIGB	Petroleum Industry Governance Bill
PML	Petroleum Mining Lease
PPL	Petroleum Prospecting License
PPMC	Pipeline and Products Marketing Company
PPTA	Petroleum Profit Tax Act
PSC	Production Sharing Contract
PTDF	Petroleum Technology Development Fund
PTI	Petroleum Training Institute
PWD	Public Works Department
REA	Rural Electrification Agency
REAP	Renewable Electricity Action Programme
REF	Rural Electrification Fund
REMP	Renewable Energy Master Plan
REP	Rural Electrification Project
REPG	Renewable Electricity Policy Guidelines
RESIP	Rural Electrification Strategy and Implementation Plan
RETF	Renewable Electricity Trust Fund
SERAP	Socio-Economic Rights and Accountability Project
SNG	Shell Nigeria Gas
SPDC	Shell Petroleum Development Company

List of Abbreviations

TCPC	Technical Committee on Privatization and Commercialization
TFZ	Tax Free Zones
TPY	Tons Per Year
UNCLOS	United Nation Convention of the Law of the Sea
UNDP	United Nations Development Programme
UNECE	United Nations Economic Commission for Europe
UNFCCC	United Nations Framework Convention on Climate Change
VAT	Value Added Tax
WAGP	West African Gas Pipeline
WAPCO	West African Portland Cement Company
WHT	Withholding Tax
WSSD	World Summit on Sustainable Development

Chapter 1. Growth and Development of the Nigerian Energy Sector

§1. INTRODUCTION

1. The Nigerian energy sector had battled with identity, ownership and governance challenges for several decades largely due to colonial legacies. The period immediately before independence presented a rare opportunity for those legacy issues to be resolved for effective sector governance, as the challenge had since been brought to the fore and settled in international law.[1] The international regime of energy and natural resource ownership was remodelled to reflect the aspirations of the developing countries under the UN resolution of 1952.[2]

2. The 1952 resolution was not without some shortcomings. The criticisms levied against the resolution led to the re-wording of the ideological basis of the principle of 'permanent sovereignty over natural resources' in the 1962 UN resolution.[3] Aside from international law, global industry best practices, international environmental law, norms and conventions among others also constitute transnational regulation of the Nigerian energy and petroleum sector. At the local level, until the *Petroleum Industry Act (PIA), 2021*[4] became the *grundnorm*, the repelled *Petroleum Act* and a long list of other enactments regulating the energy sector made up the local regimes.[5] Added to the long list is the *Nigerian Oil & Gas (Industry and Content Development) Act* 2010.[6]

---

1. The notion that countries have 'Permanent Sovereignty Over Natural Resources' within their domains is traceable to two major resolutions of the United Nations General Assembly- the 1952 and 1962 editions. The 1952 resolution recognizes that 'the right of peoples freely to use and exploit their natural resources is inherent in their sovereignty'. *See* Resolution No. 626 (VII) of the United Nations General Assembly, 21 Dec. 1952.
2. *Ibid.*
3. The concept was originally proclaimed in the 1962 resolution, which provides among others that:

   > The right of peoples and nations to permanent sovereignty over their natural wealth and resources must be exercised in the interests of their national development and of the well-being of the people of the State concerned.

   See Resolution No.1803 (XVII) of the United Nations General Assembly, 14 Dec. 1962.
4. *See* the *Petroleum Industry Act, (PIA) No. 6 of 2021.* According to the Long Title to the PIA, it is 'An Act to Provide Legal, Governance, Regulatory and Fiscal Framework for the Nigerian Petroleum Industry, the Development of Host Communities; and For Related Matters'. The PIA commenced on the 16 Aug.2021.
5. *See Petroleum Act* Cap P10 Laws of the Federation of Nigeria (LFN) 2004. Aside the Petroleum Act, other relevant statutes in the energy sector of Nigeria include: *Deep Offshore and Inland Basin Production Sharing Contracts Act* Cap D3 LFN 2004, which provides fiscal incentives to oil companies operating in the inland basins and deep offshore areas of Nigeria; *Associated Gas Re-injection Act* Cap A25 LFN as amended, which regulates the re-injection of associated gas into oil wells; the *Land Use Act* Cap L5 LFN, which regulates land ownership rights and tenure system; *Environmental Impact Assessment Act* Cap E12 LFN, which makes the conduct of an environmental impact assessment mandatory prior to the development of any energy project or activity likely to have a significant effect on the environment; *Exclusive Economic Zone Act* Cap E17 LFN, which defines the limits of Nigeria's exclusive economic zone; the *Deep Water Allocation to Companies (Back In*

3. The present regime of energy resources management in Nigeria is an eclectic mix of historical, political, economic and transnational trends. The colonialist came with the predetermined objectives of trade exploitation and political domination. They overwhelmed the local apparatuses, and gradually overawed the local people by edging them out of control of their energy and petroleum resources.[7] The Western idea of energy resource ownership and management was conceived, developed and introduced as part of the strategies of the colonial administration. In nationalizing the energy resources of Nigeria, the British colonialists passed several Ordinances meant to establish firm grips on energy and other valuable natural resources of the then-colonial territory. These included the *Mineral Oils Ordinance* which provided that:

> [T]he entire property in and control of all minerals, and mineral oils, in, under or upon any land in Nigeria, is and shall be vested in, the Crown.[8]

4. By virtue of section 6(1) (a) of the *Mineral Oils Ordinance*, the grant of oil exploration and production is exclusively reserved for the British subjects, both natural and corporate.[9] This and other facts gave a British oil giant overwhelming dominance in the Nigerian energy resources sector to date.

Rights) Regulations 2003, which gives the Federal Government a back-in right into offshore oil concessions located in depths of 200 meters and beyond; *Offshore Oil Revenues (Registration of Grants)* Act Cap O4 LFN, which ensures that instruments relating to the grant of any oil lease or license are registrable in contiguous states; *Oil in Navigable Waters Act* Cap O6, which regulates the transportation of crude oil in Nigerian waters and prohibits the release or spillage of oil from any facility into the navigable waters of Nigeria; *Oil Pipelines Act* Cap O7 LFN, which regulates the construction and operation of oil pipelines. Other statutes include the *Oil Terminal Dues Act* Cap O8 LFN, which regulates the payment of terminal dues on any ship evacuating oil from terminals in Nigeria; *Pre- shipment Inspection of Exports Act* Cap P25 LFN, which regulates the inspection of oil goods before their shipment to a place outside Nigeria; the *Petroleum Profits Tax Act* Cap P13 LFN, which imposes a tax on profits of companies engaged in upstream oil activities; the *Companies Income Tax Act* Cap C21, which imposes a tax on profits of companies engaged in downstream oil activities as well as the *Education Tax Act* Cap E4 LFN, which imposes a 2% tax on the profits of oil companies in Nigeria and the *Value Added Tax Act* Cap V1 LFN, which imposes a tax on consumable goods and services.

6. *See* the *Nigerian Oil & Gas (Industry and Content Development) Act* 2010.
7. *See* generally the analysis of Battiste and Henderson on the effects of colonization on indigenous peoples and their culture, M. Battiste & J.Y. Henderson, *Protecting Indigenous Knowledge; A Global Challenge* (Saskatoon: Purich Publishing, 2000) at 13.
8. *Mineral Oil Ordinance* 1948. *See* W. McElroy, *West Africa and Colonialism* (Pt. 1–3) at 11, online at: Freedom Daily http://www.fff.org/freedom/fd0410d.asp, accessed December 2015. *See also* I. Bagudu, et al., *Oil and Gas Exploration: Reconciling Contending Issues* in Simpson & Fagbohun (Eds,) *Environmental Law and Policy* (Lagos: Law Centre, 1998) at 310.
9. *See also* the colonialist laws before the *Mineral Ordinance of 1948*. For example, the provisions of the *Colony and Protectorate Mining Regulations (Oil Ordinance) of 1907* were basically similar to the preceding *Mineral Oil Ordinance of 1914*. The significance of the later is that it exclusively reserves oil mining for British companies and related interests. Some of the clauses in the 1907 Ordinance were also retained under s. 6 of the 1914 Ordinance. It provides:

   6 (a) no licence or lease was to be granted except with the approval of the Secretary of States;

5. After gaining independence, the Nigerian regime of energy resources, particularly its ownership and management aspects, continue to reflect neo-colonialism. For example, the Petroleum Industry Act (PIA) provides explicitly, in line with the existing, entrenched colonial energy framework, thus:

> The property and ownership of petroleum within Nigeria and its territorial waters, continental shelf and exclusive economic zone is vested in the Government of the Federation of Nigeria.[10]

6. The PIA stated its objectives to include, to:

(a) create efficient and effective governing institutions, with clear and separate roles for the petroleum industry;
(b) establish a framework for the creation of a commercially oriented and profit-driven national petroleum company;
(c) promote transparency, good governance and accountability in the administration of the petroleum resources of Nigeria;
(d) foster a business environment conducive to petroleum operations; and
(e) deepen local content practice in Nigeria's oil and gas industry.[11]

7. The nature and model of energy and other natural resources governance inherited from Nigeria's colonial overloads is also reflected in other enactments beyond the PIA and the repealed *Petroleum Act*. For example, equivalents of colonial-oriented provisions like in the *Mineral Oils Ordinance* and PIA are enshrined in the local regime, including the Nigerian Constitution.[12] The constitutional provisions on

---

(b) no licence or lease was to be granted except to a British subject or a British Company registered in Britain or a British Colony having its principal place of business within Her Majesty's Dominions. The Chairman, the managing director, if any and the majority of other directors must be British Subjects.

10. *See* s. 1 of the PIA, *supra* note 4.
11. *Ibid.*, s. 2(a–e).
12. *See Constitution of the Federal Republic of Nigeria* (as amended) CFRN 1999. Section 44(3) provides:

> Notwithstanding the foregoing, the entire property in and control of all minerals, mineral oils, and natural gas, in, under, or upon any land in Nigeria or in, under or upon the territorial waters and the Exclusive Economic Zone of Nigeria shall vest in the government of Nigeria.

See also s. 1 (1) of the old *Minerals and Mining Act Cap M12 LFN 2004* (and also the 2007 Minerals and Mining Act) provide that:

> The entire property in and control of all minerals, in, under or upon any land in Nigeria, its contiguous continental shelf and of all rivers, streams and watercourse throughout Nigeria, any area covered by territorial waters or constituency, the Exclusive Economic Zone is and shall be vested in the Government for and on behalf of the people of Nigeria.

energy resources particularly adopted the colonial version almost verbatim,[13] and the same also forms the basis of energy and other natural resources management clauses under specific enactments regulating the resource sub-sectors in the country.[14]

8. The PIA has formally segmented the Nigerian petroleum industry into upstream sector on the one hand, and midstream and downstream sectors, on the other. The upstream sector is now being administered by the *Nigerian Upstream Petroleum Regulatory Commission* ('the Commission'),[15] while the midstream and downstream sectors are administered by the *Nigerian Midstream and Downstream Petroleum Regulatory Authority* (the 'Authority').[16] The PIA establishes the Commission to have primary regulatory powers and oversight over the technical and commercial activities of the upstream petroleum industry. The Commission regulates all technical activities in the upstream sector by enforcing, administering, and implementing all laws, regulations, national and international policies, standards, and practices relating to the sector. The Commission is also to enforce compliance with the conditions of all leases, licences, permits and authorizations issued to companies in the sector. The Commission regulates technical activities in the upstream petroleum industry including seismic operations, drilling operations and design, construction, and operation of upstream facilities, among others.

9. Section 29 of the PIA, however, establishes the Authority to have technical and commercial regulation functions in the midstream and downstream segments of the petroleum industry. The Authority's functions include the regulation of petroleum liquid operations, domestic natural gas operations and natural gas export operations. It is also to determine the appropriate tariff methodology for processing of natural gas, transportation and transmission of natural gas, transportation of crude

---

13. *Ibid.*, s. 44 (3) of the current 1999 Constitution, *ibid.*
14. Resource ownership and management structures under s. 44 (3) of the CFRN 1999 above is virtually replicated under most natural resource laws of the country as typified by s. 1 (1) of the Minerals and Mining Act of Nigeria, *supra* note 7 and the s.1(1) of the Petroleum Act, *supra* note 4.
15. *See* Part III, s. 4 of the PIA. It states:

> 4. (1) There is established the Nigerian Upstream Petroleum Regulatory Commission (in this Act referred to as 'the Commission') which shall be a body corporate with perpetual succession and a common seal.
> (2) The Commission shall have the power to acquire, hold and dispose of property, sue and be sued in its own name.
> (3) The Commission shall be responsible for the technical and commercial regulation of upstream petroleum operations.

16. *See* Part IV, s. 26 of the PIA. It provides thus:

> 29. (1) There is established the Nigerian Midstream and Downstream Petroleum Regulatory Authority (in this Act referred to as 'the Authority'), which shall be a body corporate with perpetual succession and a common seal.
> (2) The Authority shall have the power to acquire, hold and dispose of property, sue and be sued in its own name.
> (3) The Authority shall be responsible for the technical and commercial regulation of midstream and downstream petroleum operations in the petroleum industry.

oil, bulk storage of crude oil and monitoring the quality of service provided. The Authority is empowered to issue regulations in pursuance of its regulatory oversight.

§2. Overview of Salient Provisions in PIA

10. The explanatory memorandum of the *Petroleum Industry Act* (2021) states that the Act provides a legal, governance, regulatory and fiscal framework for the Nigerian petroleum industry, and the development of host communities.[17] Part I of Chapter 1 vests petroleum in the Nigerian State while Part II of Chapter 1 codifies the powers of Nigeria's Minister of Petroleum. Part III of Chapter 1 establishes the objectives, functions, duties and powers of the 'Nigerian Upstream Petroleum Regulatory Commission ("The Commission")' while Part IV of Chapter 1 establishes the accompanying 'Nigerian Midstream and Downstream Petroleum Regulatory Authority'. Part V of Chapter 1 establishes the 'Nigerian National Petroleum Company Limited'.

11. Chapter 2 of the Act deals with the ways and means of managing and administering petroleum resources in Nigeria. Part I of Chapter 2 highlights the objectives and management of petroleum resources in Nigeria while Part II of Chapter 2 details the legal administration of upstream petroleum operations in Nigeria, especially as they affect the environment. This part outlines the laws guiding the creation of a 'national grid system', the granting of a petroleum exploration licence, the bidding and award process of field rounds and other related administrative exercises.

12. Part III of Chapter 2 enshrines the general administration of midstream and downstream petroleum operations in Nigeria. This part governs matters relating to licence applications, licensing regulations, compensation for the acquisition of land and other related matters. Part IV of Chapter 2 deals with the administration of midstream and downstream gas operations while Part V of Chapter 2 is about the administration of midstream and downstream petroleum liquids operations in Nigeria. Parts VI and VII of Chapter 2 contain provisions on other matters relating to midstream and downstream operations and the common provisions for upstream, midstream and downstream petroleum operations in Nigeria.

13. Chapter 3 of the Act provides a legal and governance framework for the development of host communities. The objectives and regulations in this chapter speak directly to the development of oil-producing communities in Nigeria.

14. Chapter 4 of the Act addresses the fiscal framework of Nigeria's petroleum industry. Part I of Chapter 4 contains the objectives and general administration of the fiscal framework of the petroleum industry. Part II of Chapter 4 stipulates how hydrocarbon tax should be administered while Part III of Chapter 4 legally delineates how chargeable tax should be ascertained. Part IV of Chapter 4 speaks to the

17. Explanatory Memorandum, Petroleum Industry Act, 2021.

ascertainment of chargeable profits and consolidation for tax purposes while Part V of Chapter 4 deals with chargeable persons. Part VI of Chapter 4 gives a legal description of the applicability, accounts and particulars of entities that have tax liability while part seven addresses appeals-based tax liability. Parts VIII, IX and X contain provisions about the collection, recovery and repayment of tax, the offences and penalties for tax-related crimes and the application of companies' income tax to petroleum operations, respectively. Part XI of Chapter 4 contains general provisions.

15. Chapter 5 of the Act contains miscellaneous provisions, including the processes for commencement of legal proceedings, the filing of a pre-action notice, and the processes for a transfer of assets and liability to the Nigerian Upstream Regulatory Commission, among a handful of other salient provisions. More fundamental and far-reaching are the supremacy provisions of the PIA. The Act overrides provisions of all other enactment or law save for the Nigerian Oil and Gas *(Industry Content Development) Act.*[18] It states thus:

> Subject to the Constitution of the Federal Republic of Nigeria, 1999, upon the commencement of this Act, where the provisions of any other enactment or law except the Nigeria Oil and Gas Industry Content Development Act are inconsistent with the provisions of this Act, the provisions of this Act shall prevail and the provisions of that other enactment or law shall, to the extent of that inconsistency, be void in relation to matters provided for in this Act.[19]

§3. Historical Facts of Energy Exploration in Nigeria

16. The first recorded, active oil exploration began in Nigeria in the year 1908 by the Nigerian Bitumen Company, a German company whose activities stopped hurriedly at the commencement of the First World War in 1914.[20] In 1921, oil exploration rights were granted to two British companies, specifically, D'Arcy Exploration Company and Whitehall Petroleum Company Limited in the Niger Delta. Unfortunately, these companies did not record any commercial success. In 1937, Shell D'Arcy was granted exclusive exploration and production rights in the whole of Nigeria. Although the Second World War interrupted their work, upon recommencement of commercial activities, Shell D'Arcy in conjunction with British Petroleum as Shell-BP, emerged as the pioneer multinational Oil Company in Nigeria.[21]

17. Oil was first discovered in commercial quantity at Oloibiri in the Present Bayelsa State in 1956 by Shell-BP. In January 1958, the first oilfield was carved out

---

18. *See* the Nigerian Oil and Gas (Industry Content Development) Act, 2010.
19. *See* s. 309 of the PIA, *supra* note 4.
20. A. Akinrele, *Nigeria and Oil and Gas Law* (OGEL-Oil, Gas & Energy Intelligence, 2005) at p. 5.
21. *Ibid.*

with a production capacity of about 5,100 barrels per day (bpd). This ushered Nigeria into the international oil arena.[22] Shell-BP enjoyed the monopoly of exploration for a relatively long period by virtue of section 6(1)(a) of the Mineral Oils Ordinance 1914 largely due to the colonial links of Nigeria with Great Britain. The above section was a statutory monopoly which Shell BP enjoyed until it was repealed by section 2 of the Mineral Oil Amendment Ordinance No. 5 1958.[23]

18. The end of the Biafran war in 1970 coincided with the rise in the world oil price, and Nigeria was able to reap instant riches from its oil production. In July 1971, Nigeria became the eleventh member of the Organization of Petroleum Exporting Countries (OPEC) and established the Nigerian National Petroleum Company (NNPC) in 1977. NNPC is a state-owned bureaucracy and player in both the upstream and downstream sectors.[24] Actual oil production and export from the Oloibiri field commenced in 1958 with an initial production rate of 5,100 barrels of crude oil per day. By the late sixties and early seventies, Nigeria had attained a production level of over 2 million barrels of crude oil per day.

19. Petroleum production and export play a dominant role in Nigeria's economy and account for about 90% of the country's gross earnings. The dominant role of petroleum has pushed agriculture, the traditional mainstay of the economy, from the early fifties and sixties to the background.[25] Nigeria has attained the status of a major oil producer, ranking seventh in the world in 1972, and has since grown to become the sixth largest oil-producing country in the world.[26] Six oil companies – Shell, Elf, Agip Mobil, Chevron and Texaco dominate the oil industry in the country. Together, they hold some 98% of the oil reserves and operating assets. A range of fifty others have minor interests, some of which were recently acquired.[27]

20. There are three major actors in the Nigerian oil industry. They are: the Ministry of Petroleum Resources (MPR), the Nigerian National Petroleum Corporation (NNPC) and its subsidiaries, and the oil prospecting companies made up of multinational oil companies and indigenous companies[28] together with their subsidiaries.

---

22. Atsegbua L., *Oil and Gas Law in Nigeria, Theory and Practice*, Second Edition (New Era Publication, Benin City: 2004) p. 42.
23. A. Akinrele, *supra* note 20, at p. 6–7. *See also* Yemi Oke, 'Impacts of International Law and Global Best Practices on Energy Resources Governance in Nigeria' (2012) 8 *University of Ilorin Law Journal*, 156–180. *See also* Yemi Oke, *Nigerian Energy and Natural Resources Law-Notes & Materials* (Princeton & Associate Publishing Company Limited, Lagos: 2016) at 202–221.
24. Maxwell M. Gidado, *Petroleum Development Contracts with Multinational Oil Firms* (Ed-Linform Services 1999), at p. 56.
25. *See* NNPC Business Information, online at: http://www.nnpcgroup.com/NNPCBusiness/BusinessInformation/OilGasinNigeria/IndustryHistory.aspx last viewed on 24/05/14, accessed 24 Jun. 2017.
26. *Ibid.*
27. Baghebo, M. and Atima, T.O. 'The Impact of Petroleum on Economic Growth in Nigeria' (2013) 2:5 *Global Business and Economics Research Journal*, p. 103.
28. Dominic, A. 'The Petroleum Industry in Nigeria: Joint Operating Agreements, Memorandum of Understandings, Compensation and other Related Issues in Perspective' (1999). *See also* Maxwell M. Gidado, *Petroleum Development Contracts with Multinational Oil Firms, supra* note 24; Yemi Oke, 'Impacts of International Law and Global Best Practices on Energy Resources Governance in Nigeria', *supra* note 23.

§4. The Nigerian Upstream Petroleum Regulatory Commission ('The Commission')

21. One of the innovative provisions of the *Petroleum Industry Act (PIA), 2021*[29] is the establishment of the *Nigerian Upstream Petroleum Regulatory Commission* ('the Commission').[30] Under the PIA, the Commission has primary regulatory powers and oversight over the technical and commercial activities of the upstream petroleum industry. The Commission is saddled with the statutory functions of regulating all technical activities in the upstream sector by enforcing, administering, and implementing all laws, regulations, national and international policies, standards, and practices relating to the sector. Most significant is the duty imposed on the Commission to enforce compliance with the conditions stipulated in all leases, licences, permits and authorizations issued to companies in the sector.

22. Beyond specific objectives, the Commission has technical and commercial functions as clearly stipulated by the PIA. By virtue of section 7 of the Act, the technical regulatory functions of the Commission include to: (a) enforce, administer and implement laws, regulations and policies relating to upstream petroleum operations; (b) ensure compliance with applicable national and international petroleum industry policies, standards and practices for upstream petroleum operations; (c) establish, monitor, regulate and enforce health, safety and environmental measures and standards relating to upstream petroleum operations including: (i) management of petroleum reserves and installations, and (ii) exploration, development and production activities within the onshore, frontier, shallow water and deep offshore acreages of Nigeria; (d) administer, monitor and enforce compliance with the terms and conditions of leases and licences granted and permits and authorizations issued to a company in respect of upstream petroleum operations; and (e) set, define and enforce approved standards and regulations for design, construction, fabrication, operation and maintenance of plants, installations and facilities used or to be used in upstream petroleum operations including: (i) crude oil and natural gas evaluation and management, (ii) upstream natural gas gathering, (iii) natural gas treatment, and (iv) the elimination of natural gas flaring and venting.[31]

23. The need to ensure a commercial and economically viable petroleum sector for Nigeria is the primary aim of the new regime brought by the PIA. This makes it ineluctable for the vesting of specific commercial regulatory functions in the Commission.[32] The PIA provides that the commercial regulatory functions of the Commission shall be to: (a) review and approve the commercial aspects of field development plans in the upstream petroleum operations; (b) develop cost studies and benchmarks for the evaluation of upstream petroleum operations taking into

---

29. *See* the *Petroleum Industry Act, (PIA) No. 6 of 2021.* According to the Long Title to the PIA, it is 'An Act to Provide Legal, Governance, Regulatory and Fiscal Framework for the Nigerian Petroleum Industry, the Development of Host Communities; and For Related Matters'. The PIA commenced on the 16 Aug. 2021.
30. *See* Part III, s. 4 of the PIA.
31. Section 7(a–e)(i–iv) of the PIA.
32. *See* generally s. 8 of the PIA.

account petroleum industry-specific issues, including field size, reservoir depth, location of operations, technology applied, production methods and petroleum quality.[33]

24. The PIA further vests commercial regulatory functions in the Commission to include power to- (c) allocate petroleum production quotas for the purpose of curtailing the export of petroleum in conjunction with NNPC Limited and where in situ facilities or fixed or floating platforms or vessels provide for fully integrated upstream and midstream petroleum operations, the Commission shall be in charge of such integrated operations. For this purpose, petroleum operations are considered integrated where there is a joint use of utilities exclusively for the upstream and midstream operations.[34]

25. To further ensure regulatory efficiency in the petroleum sector, the PIA also vests the Commission with specific functions over frontier basin in addition to technical and commercial functions. The functions of the Commission with respect to frontier basins shall be to: (a) promote the exploration of the frontier basins of Nigeria; (b) develop exploration strategies and portfolio management for the exploration of unassigned frontier acreages in Nigeria; (c) identify opportunities and increase information about the petroleum resources base within frontier basins in Nigeria; and (d) undertake studies, analyse and evaluate unassigned frontier basins in Nigeria.[35]

I. Powers of the Commission

26. The Commission has specific powers as conferred by the PIA. A temporal reading of the provisions of the PIA on objectives,[36] functions,[37] duties and powers of the Commission as respectively listed shows that they are not intended to be used or applied interchangeably.[38] There is no homogeneity in the nature, types, context, extent and complexities of the respective statutory roles of the Commission under the PIA. This further makes it crucial that any attempt to interpret these provisions must treat and regard specific clauses as separate and distinct.

II. Special Powers of the Commission

27. The PIA confers special technical powers on the Commission to undertake a number of statutory activities and related privileges relating to its functions under

33. *Ibid.*, paras (a–b).
34. *Ibid.*, paras (c–d).
35. *See* s. 9(1)(a–d) of the PIA.
36. Section 6 of the PIA provides for the 'Objectives of the Commission'.
37. Sections 7 and 9 of the PIA provide for 'Technical regulatory functions of the Commission', 'Commercial regulatory functions of the Commission' and 'Functions of the Commission for frontier basins' respectively.
38. *Ibid.*

the Act. These powers are extensive and encompassing. Section 26(1) of the Act provides that, in exercising its functions, the Commission shall have special powers to:

(a) inquire, inspect, examine or investigate any business or activity relating to upstream petroleum operations under this Act, where it believes that illegal upstream petroleum operations are going on;
(b) conduct surveillance on crude oil and natural gas installations, premises and vessels where it believes that illegal upstream petroleum operations are going on;
(c) enter any upstream wellsite, plant, facility or place:
  (i) at which crude oil or natural gas is produced, handled or treated; or
  (ii) that is used in connection with any upstream wellsite, plant, facility or place where crude oil or natural gas is produced, handled or treated.
(d) enter at any reasonable time premises containing any records or property required to be maintained under this Act or related to the administration of upstream petroleum operations under this Act for the purpose of inspecting those records or that property;
(e) require any person or his agent, representative, partner, director, officer or employee engaged in upstream petroleum operations to:
  (i) answer any question that may be relevant to the inquiry, inspection, examination or investigation; and
  (ii) provide any required information contained in computer hardware or software or any other data storage, processing or retrieval device or system used in connection with the business or activities relating to upstream petroleum operations under this Act.
(f) take any sample or carry out any test or examination as it may consider necessary in the performance of its functions;
(g) use any machinery, equipment, appliance or thing as it may consider necessary in the performance of its functions;
(h) remove for examination and copy anything that may be relevant to the inquiry, inspection, examination or investigation, including removing any computer hardware or software or any other data storage, processing or retrieval device or system, during which copyright and trade secrets shall be properly protected;
(i) in conjunction with the Nigeria Police or other law enforcement agencies, arrest with a warrant, any person reasonably believed to have committed an offence under this Act; and
(j) exercise any other power that may be conferred on it under any law or regulation.[39]

28. In a bid to ensure effective and smooth discharge of its functions and exercise of special powers of the Commission, the Act provides that an entity, person or agent, representative, partner, director, officer or employee of that entity or person

39. Section 26(1)(a–j) of the PIA.

under investigation by the Commission shall grant access to officers of the Commission with regard to any place, website, plant, facility, upstream machinery, equipment, appliances or things that may be relevant to the investigation; and provide on request, any book, account, record, document, voucher, information and explanation relating to upstream petroleum operations as the officers of the Commission may require.[40]

29. The PIA provides for the establishment of a Special Investigation Unit (SIU) for the purpose of exercising the special powers conferred on the Commission under section 26 of the Act. The special powers of the Commission shall be exercised by the Commission or any person authorized.[41] The Act indemnifies officers of the Commission from proceedings brought against them in an official capacity. It provides that the Commission Chief Executive, a commissioner or any officer of the Commission shall each be indemnified out of the Commission Fund against any liability incurred in defending any proceeding against the Commission or brought against him in his official capacity. Such indemnity shall not cover liability incurred pursuant to wilful misconduct or negligence.[42]

§5. The Nigerian Midstream and Downstream Petroleum Regulatory Authority (The 'Authority')

30. Under the PIA, the midstream and downstream sectors are administered by the *Nigerian Midstream and Downstream Petroleum Regulatory Authority* (the 'Authority').[43] Section 29 of the PIA establishes the Authority to have technical and commercial regulatory powers over midstream and downstream petroleum operations. The Authority's functions include the regulation of petroleum liquid operations, domestic natural gas operations and export natural gas operations. The Authority also determines the appropriate tariff methodology for processing of natural gas, transportation and transmission of natural gas, transportation of crude oil, bulk storage of crude oil and monitoring the quality of service provided. The Authority is also empowered to issue regulations for the purpose of its regulatory oversight and functions as further amplified below.

40. Section 26(2).
41. *See* s. 27 of the PIA.
42. The PIA provides in respect of indemnity of the Commission's officers that: The Commission Chief Executive, a commissioner or any officer of the Commission shall each be indemnified out of the Commission Fund against any liability incurred in defending any proceeding against the Commission or brought against him in his official capacity. Notwithstanding the provisions of subs. (1), the Commission shall not indemnify the Commission Chief Executive, a commissioner or any officer of the Commission for any liability incurred as a result of wilful misconduct or gross negligence. *Ibid.*, ss 28(1) and (2).
43. *See* Part IV, s. 29 of the PIA.

I. Establishment and Objectives of the Authority

31. The objects and functions of the Authority under Part IV of the Act are strictly limited to midstream and downstream petroleum operations.[44] The objectives of the Authority are extensive[45] but similar to those of the Commission for the upstream petroleum operations in Nigeria.[46]

II. Functions of the Authority

32. The PIA provides that the functions of the Authority shall be to: (a) regulate and monitor technical and commercial midstream and downstream petroleum operations in Nigeria; and (b) regulate commercial midstream and downstream petroleum operations, including petroleum liquids operations, domestic natural gas operations, and export natural gas operations.[47] The Act also vests the Authority with the duty of determining appropriate tariff methodology, including for processing of natural gas, transportation and transmission of natural gas, transportation of crude oil, and bulk storage of crude oil and natural gas.[48]

33. The Authority also has it as part of its statutory functions to set cost benchmarks for midstream and downstream petroleum operations; provide pricing and tariff frameworks for natural gas in midstream and downstream gas operations and petroleum products based on the fair market value of the applicable petroleum products as well as advise the Government, government agencies and other stakeholders on commercial matters relating to tariff and pricing frameworks.[49]

34. The development of open access rules applicable to petroleum liquids and natural gas transportation pipelines, terminal facilities and bulk storage facilities; regulation of the bulk storage, distribution, marketing and transportation pipelines of petroleum products are vested as part of the statutory functions of the Authority. These include granting, issuing, modifying, extending, renewing, reviewing, suspending, cancelling, reissuing or terminating licences, permits and authorizations for midstream and downstream petroleum operations.[50] The Authority also monitors and enforces compliance with the terms and conditions of licences, permits and authorizations issued by it.[51] It keeps public registers of licences, permits and other authorizations issued by it as well as records of any renewals, assignments, amendments, suspensions or revocations of licences and permits.[52]

---

44. *Ibid.*, s. 30.
45. *See* generally s. 31(a–m) of the PIA.
46. *See* and compare s. 6(a–k) of the PIA.
47. *See* s. 32(a)(b)(i–iii).
48. *Ibid.*, s. 32(c)(i–iii).
49. *Ibid.*, s. 32(d–f) of the PIA.
50. *Ibid.*, s. 32(g–i).
51. *Ibid.*, s. 32(j).
52. *Ibid.*, s. 32(k)(i–ii).

35. In a bid to ensure openness and fairness, the PIA makes it part of the statutory functions of the Authority to publish decisions, directions or determinations on official issues, together with the reasons for such decisions, directions or determinations.[53] It also has it as a function under the law to promote the interests of customers with regard to midstream and downstream petroleum operations; promote the principles of economic development of infrastructure with regard to midstream and downstream petroleum operations as well as promote competition and private sector participation.[54]

36. The Authority determines the domestic gas demand requirement and the crude oil required for the domestic crude oil supply obligation and ensures that economic and strategic domestic demands are met. In doing so, the Authority regulates the supply, distribution, marketing and retail of petroleum products; administers and monitors strategic stocks of petroleum products; monitors the application of petroleum product prices, pricing formulae and frameworks as well as monitors market behaviour with respect to midstream and downstream petroleum operations.[55]

37. The Authority has other crucial institutional functions to ensure the effectiveness and efficiency of sector regulation in the midstream and downstream petroleum sector of Nigeria which include identifying, investigating and preventing abuse of dominant positions and restrictive business practices with regard to midstream and downstream petroleum operations. It also establishes, monitors, regulates and enforces technical, health, environmental and safety measures relating to midstream and downstream petroleum operations as well as develops, specifies and monitors technical and safety standards for wholesale marketing, processing plant, retail marketing and bunkering of petroleum products.[56]

38. Beyond strategic price regulatory functions, the Act gives the Authority powers to perform such other functions as may be necessary to give effect to the provisions of the PIA.[57] It also ensures and monitors performance parameters of industry players and the quality of service provided by servicing companies in the midstream and downstream petroleum industry in addition to conducting studies relating to the economy and efficiency or effectiveness of the midstream and downstream petroleum industry in Nigeria.[58]

---

53. *Ibid.*, s. 32(r).
54. *Ibid.*, s. 32(s–u).
55. *Ibid.*, s. 32(v–z).
56. *Ibid.*, s. 32 (aa–cc).
57. *See* s. 32(ss) of the PIA, *supra* note 4.
58. *Ibid.*, s. 32(tt–uu).

III. Special Powers of the Authority

39. Like the Commission,[59] the PIA confers special powers in the Authority.[60] The Act provides that an entity, person or agent, representative, partner, director, officer or employee of that entity or person under investigation by the Authority shall grant access to officers of the Authority with regard to any place, wellsite, plant, facility, midstream or downstream machinery, equipment, appliances or things that may be relevant to the investigation. The investigated entity or any regulated entity under investigation, shall also provide on request, any book, account, record, document, voucher, information and explanation relating to midstream or downstream petroleum operations as the officers of the Authority may require.[61]

40. The Act imposes penal consequences for failure of such entities to comply. An entity, person or agent, representative, partner, director, officer or employee of that entity or person who fails to comply with subsection (2) commits an offence and is liable on conviction to a minimum fine of NGN 5,000,000 or a term of imprisonment for five years, and in the case of a continuous offence, to an additional minimum fine of NGN 100,000 for each day during which the offence continues.[62] However, the PIA imposes a duty of care and due diligence on the Authority to ensure that in the exercise of its special powers, it avoids undue hindrance of entities and persons engaged in lawful midstream or downstream petroleum operations.[63]

41. The Act also creates a Special Investigation Unit for the Authority,[64] similar to another Special Investigation Unit created for the Commission[65] in a manner that may likely create confusion and unintended conflict of operations and nomenclatures. The PIA creates two Special Investigation Units, one for the Commission and the other for the Authority. This is legislative inelegance. The appropriate approach would have been to create separate units by distinct names, to avoid overlapping functions and duties in the same petroleum sector.

§6. The Midstream and Downstream Gas Infrastructure Fund

42. The Act establishes a special body, a sub-agency within the Authority named the Midstream and Downstream Gas infrastructure Fund. The Fund is a new development in the petroleum industry in Nigeria and is meant to stabilize and ensure the sustainability of the midstream and downstream petroleum industry. The Fund shall,

59. *See* s. 26 of the PIA and compare special powers of the Commission with that of the Authority.
60. *See* generally s. 49 (1–4) of the PIA.
61. *Ibid.*, s. 49(2)(a–b).
62. *Ibid.*, s. 49(3)(a–b).
63. *Ibid.*, s. 49(4).
64. *See* s. 50 of the PIA.
65. *See* and compare the provisions of s. 27 of the PIA on *Special Investigation* Unit for the Commission with s. 50 which creates another *Special Investigation Unit* for the Authority.

subject to appropriation by the National Assembly, be a body corporate with perpetual succession and a common seal and reside in the Authority as prescribed in accordance with the provisions of the PIA.[66] The Fund shall have the power to acquire, hold and dispose of property, sue and be sued in its corporate name.[67]

43. The Governing Council supervises and makes investment decisions on behalf of the Fund.[68] The Council is comprised of the Minister, who shall be the Chairman of the Council; representative of the Central Bank of Nigeria not below the rank of a director; representative of the Ministry of Finance not below the rank of a director; Authority Chief Executive; and Executive Director Midstream and Downstream Gas Infrastructure Fund. The Board also includes three independent members, who shall be appointed by the President for a term of four years and may be reappointed for another four years and no more and the Legal Adviser of the Authority who shall serve as the Secretary to the Governing Council.[69] It needs to be noted that, by virtue of the provision of section 52(17) of the PIA, the members of the Governing Council shall be paid such allowances from the funds of the Midstream and Downstream Gas Infrastructure Fund in accordance with the approved guidelines by the *Revenue Mobilization, Allocation and Fiscal Commission.*[70]

44. The Executive Director of Midstream and Downstream Gas Infrastructure Fund is the administrative head. He shall have extensive managerial, technical or professional knowledge of midstream petroleum operations, fund management or any other relevant industry with a minimum of fifteen years' post- qualification experience. His tasks shall include project management and administration of the Midstream and Downstream Gas Infrastructure Fund.[71] Like the Executive Director, by virtue of section 54(4) (f) of the Act, other members of the Governing Board shall also have extensive managerial, technical or professional knowledge of the midstream petroleum operations, fund management or any other relevant industry with a minimum of fifteen years post-qualification cognate experience.[72]

45. The statutory purpose of the Fund is to make equity investments as Government owned participating or shareholder interests in the midstream and downstream gas operations for the purpose of increasing domestic consumption of natural gas in

66. *Ibid.*, s. 52(1)(a–b).
67. *Ibid.*, s. 52(2).
68. *Ibid.*, s. 52(3).
69. Section 52(4)(a–g).
70. The ***Revenue Mobilisation Allocation and Fiscal Commission*** (RMAFC) was established by Decree No. 49 of 1989 and later amended by Decree 98 of 1993 (now ***Revenue Mobilisation Allocation and Fiscal Commission*** (RMAFC) Act, CAP R7, LFN 2004). Under s. 153(1) of the 1999 Constitution of the Federal Republic of Nigeria (As Amended), RMAFC is listed as one of the fourteen Federal Executive Bodies. It has a Chairman and Members from each State of the Federation and the Federal Capital Territory appointed by the President. There are presently thirty-five Members from the States and Federal Capital Territory. For further details on RMAFC, *see Revenue Mobilization, Allocation and Fiscal Commission* on-line at: https://rmafc.gov.ng/about-rmafc/, accessed 17 Jan. 2023.
71. *Ibid.*, s. 52(5)(a–b).
72. *Ibid.*, s. 52(6).

Nigeria. The Fund also aims at encouraging private investment through risk sharing by participating initially in selected high-risk projects and in such other equity investments that encourage investment in midstream and downstream gas infrastructure with a view to reducing or eliminating gas flare.[73]

46. The PIA provides for the appointment of a Transaction Advisor, who shall be responsible for providing transaction advisory services, including technical and commercial evaluation of proposals, defining project screening criteria and profitability targets for projects. The transaction advisor shall also perform any other duty as may be assigned by the Council on behalf of the Fund.[74] The Transaction Advisor shall he selected on a need basis through competitive and transparent criteria specified by the Council. The selection process shall be managed by the Executive Director, Midstream and Downstream Gas Infrastructure Fund, subject to the approval of the Council. In performing his or her duties, the transaction advisor shall submit a report of his findings and recommendations to the Council.[75] The PIA makes detailed provisions for the way and manner the Midstream and Downstream Gas Infrastructure Fund shall be managed.[76]

47. PIA makes it absolutely compulsory that earnings, interest and other income accruing from the equity investment made under subsection (10) of the Act shall also be paid directly to the Midstream and Downstream Gas Infrastructure Fund's Account.[77] However, interest on investment and other incomes accruing from the equity investment of the Midstream and Downstream Gas Infrastructure Fund may be re-invested in other secured low-risk investments as approved by the Governing Council.[78]

§7. Petroleum Licences and Leases under Petroleum Industry Act

48. The PIA provides for three categories of petroleum licences and leases.[79] The legal regime of petroleum licensing in Nigeria remains the same under the repealed Petroleum Act and the current *Petroleum Industry Act*, 2021. Generally, the principal legislation on the subject of petroleum and gas prospecting, exploration and mining in Nigeria is the Petroleum Industry Act.[80] The PIA provides that there shall be the following licences and leases under the Act related to upstream petroleum operations:

(a) petroleum exploration licence, which may be granted to qualified applicants to carry out petroleum exploration operations on a non-exclusive basis;

73. *See* s. 52(9)(a–c).
74. Section 52(11).
75. Section 52(13–14) of the PIA.
76. *Ibid.*, s. 52(14)(a–e).
77. *Ibid.*, s. 52(15).
78. *Ibid.*, s. 52(16.
79. *See* s. 70(1–2) of the PIA.
80. *See* PIA, *supra* note 4.

(b) petroleum prospecting licence, which may be granted to qualified applicants to:
   (i) drill exploration and appraisal wells and do corresponding test production on an exclusive basis; and
   (ii) carry out petroleum exploration operations on a non-exclusive basis.
(c) petroleum mining lease, which may be granted to qualified applicants to:
   (i) win, work, carry away and dispose of crude oil, condensates and natural gas on an exclusive basis;
   (ii) drill exploration and appraisal wells and carry out the related test, and production on an exclusive basis; and
   (iii) carry out petroleum exploration operations on a non-exclusive basis.

49. A licence or lease may be granted under this Act only to a company incorporated and validly existing in Nigeria under the Companies and Allied Matters Act (CAMA).[81]

I. Petroleum Exploration Licence

50. The PIA provides that the Commission shall be responsible for granting Petroleum Exploration Licences (PEL). The holder of a PEL shall have non-exclusive right to carry out petroleum exploration operations within the area provided for in the licence.[82] PEL is awarded for a period of three years subject to the fulfilment of prescribed conditions. The PIA clearly excludes a grantee from certain rights. A PEL licensee shall not exercise any right to win, extract, work, store, carry away, transport, export or otherwise treat petroleum discovered in or under the licence area.[83]

51. The PIA stipulates that a PEL may cover an area that includes petroleum prospecting licences or petroleum mining leases, provided that the holders of such licences or leases shall have no obligation to purchase the results of any survey conducted under the petroleum exploration licence.[84] By virtue of section 71(5) of the PIA, a PEL granted in respect of frontier acreages may include a provision permitting the licensee to select, based on the result of his exploration work and be granted one or more petroleum prospecting licences prior to the termination of the licence containing the fiscal provisions stipulated in Chapter 4 of the Act.[85] For the purpose of a PEL licence, the Commission shall have sole right and title over any acquired raw and interpreted data obtained by a licensee. However, the licensee shall be entitled to grant a data use licence to a third party subject to a written authorization by the Commission, which shall not be unreasonably withheld. The licensee is

81. *See* generally s. 70(1–2) of the PIA.
82. *See* s. 71(1–2).
83. *Ibid.*, subs. (3).
84. *See* s. 71(4) of the PIA.
85. Chapter 4 of the Petroleum Industry Act (PIA) deals extensively with the *Petroleum Fiscal Framework.*

entitled to charge a fee on a third party for data use licence granted under subsection (6) and shall remit the agreed portion of the fee to the Commission.[86] The licensed exploration activities conducted pursuant to a PEL shall be monitored and administered by the Commission in accordance with regulations made under the Act.[87]

II. Petroleum Prospecting Licence

52. The PIA creates another category of petroleum licence called the Petroleum Prospecting Licence (PPL).[88] The Act provides that the holder of a petroleum prospecting licence shall, subject to the fulfilment of obligations imposed by this Act, have:

(a) exclusive right to drill exploration and appraisal wells and non-exclusive right to carry out petroleum exploration operations within the area provided for in the licence; and
(b) right to carry away and dispose of crude oil or natural gas won or extracted during the drilling of exploration or appraisal wells as a result of production tests, subject to the fulfilment of obligations imposed by this Act.[89]

53. A holder of the PPL is not entitled to be granted an extension except as prescribed under sections 78 (4), or (9) and 79 (6) of the Act.[90] However, where a holder of a PPL fails to fulfil any term or condition of the licence, it shall not, except

86. *See* s. 71(6–7) of the PIA.
87. *Ibid.*, subs. (8). Subsection (9) however provides that the Commission shall have sole right and title to overall acquired and interpreted data from existing speculative survey agreements entered into with the Department of Petroleum Resources on behalf of the Government prior to the effective date.
88. *See* s. 72(1)(a–b), (2–6) of the PIA.
89. *Ibid.*, subs. (1)(a–b).
90. *See* s. 78(4) which provides that:

> Where a licensee considers that a discovery merits appraisal, the licensee shall submit to the Commission within one year for approval–
>
> (a) a commitment to an appraisal programme of not more than three years with a scope and nature permitting the licensee to declare a commercial discovery, where the result of the appraisal is positive; and
> (b) the appraisal area, not larger than the outer boundary of the discovery, as determined by the licensee and a zone of not more than two kilometres surrounding the outer boundary, provided that the appraisal area does not extend beyond the area provided for in the applicable petroleum prospecting licence.

Section 78(9) provides that:

> Where a significant gas discovery or significant crude oil discovery has been declared, the licensee shall be entitled to retain the area of such significant gas discovery or significant crude oil discovery for a retention period as may be determined by the Commission, which shall not

as provided in the licence, give the Minister a right of claim against the licensee or be deemed a breach of the licence, if the failure arises from force majeure. This implies that, unless it is a clear case of force majeure, the Minister may exercise right of claim against the licensee.[91] The Act provides a just and fair balance to the extent that in case of any delay by a licensee in the fulfilment of any term or condition of a PPL caused by force majeure, the period of such force majeure shall be added to the period fixed for the fulfilment of the applicable term or condition. The exception is subject to a three-year moratorium after which the licence may be terminated by the Commission or the licensee.[92]

54. The grant of a PPL is to a qualified applicant on the recommendation of the Commission. However, where the Minister does not grant the licence, the Minister shall inform the Commission in writing of the rationale of the decision. This provision notwithstanding, a PPL may also be granted under section 93 of the Act on relinquishment upon renewal or conversion of an Oil Mining Lease (OML).[93]

55. The provisions of the PIA on PPL are a sharp departure from the structure under the repealed Petroleum Act. Under section 2(1) (b) of the old Act,[94] the Minister may grant an OPL to a company incorporated in Nigeria and the holder is conferred with an exclusive right to explore and prospect for petroleum within the licenced area which shall not exceed 2,590 square kilometres. Under the old model, the holder of an OPL may carry away and dispose of petroleum won during prospecting operations, subject to the fulfilment of obligations imposed upon him under the Act (including any special terms or conditions imposed under paragraph 34 of the Schedule) or by the Petroleum Profit Tax Act (PPTA) or any other law imposing taxation in respect of petroleum.[95] In contrast, under the PIA, the holder of a PPL has the non-exclusive right to carry out petroleum exploration operations within the area provided for in the licence but could exercise the right to carry away and dispose of crude oil or natural gas won or extracted during the drilling of exploration or appraisal wells as a result of production tests, subject to the fulfilment of obligations imposed by the Act.[96]

> be more than 10 years from the day the declaration was made and with the approval of the Commission a licensee is entitled to drill further appraisal wells.

Section 79(6) of the Act states:

> Where the licensee has submitted a field development plan for the field, the licence shall continue until the process for the grant of a lease has been completed or the Commission has decided not to grant the lease.

91. *Ibid.*, s. 72(2).
92. *Ibid.*, subs. (3–4).
93. *Ibid.*, subs. (5–6). This subsections apply subject to the provisions of s. 93 of the Act on *Relinquishment upon renewal or conversion of an oil mining lease.*
94. *See* the repealed Petroleum Act, 1969.
95. *See* paras 5, 6, and 7 of the first Schedule to the Petroleum Act, *ibid.*
96. Section 72(1)(a–b) of the PIA.

III. Bidding Process

56. The PIA has mainstreamed critical issues and fundamentals of a fair, transparent and competitive bidding process as an essential part of the Act. This is against the background of challenges of open and fair bidding and award processes for petroleum licences. The PIA states that subject to the provisions of sections 71 (5), 74 (3), 81(1) and 93 (2) of the Act, petroleum prospecting licence or petroleum mining lease shall only be granted based on a fair, transparent and competitive bidding process and in compliance with the provisions of the Act, regulations made under it and licensing round guidelines which may be periodically issued and published by the Commission for each licensing round.[97]

57. The bidding process under the PIA is also made subject to section 71 (5) and other provisions of the Act. The Minister may, on the recommendation of the Commission, grant a petroleum prospecting licence or petroleum mining lease to a winning bidder in accordance with section 74 of the Act, provided that the winning bidder has complied with the requirements of the bid invitation.

58. The provisions of subsection (4) appear problematic. The author heavily criticized this provision for being subject to abuse and manipulations. It unintendedly created what the author had, at different forums,[98] described as *'Deemed grant of petroleum licence or lease'*. It says:

> The Minister shall inform the Commission of his decision within 90 days of the application for licence or lease and where he fails to inform the Commission within the stipulated time; the licence or lease shall be deemed granted.[99]

59. The author is of the view that a deemed grant of petroleum licence or lease is possible under the above provisions. Although that is not the intendment of the PIA, it may be possible to create a deemed petroleum right where the Minister fails to take and communicate a decision to the Commission within ninety days.

---

97. Section 73(1)(a–b) and (2).
98. *See* Yemi Oke, 'Understanding Petroleum Industry Act: Implementation Phases and Strategies for Managing Stakeholders' Expectations and Anxieties', Senior Management Training on PIA for former DPR, NNPC and other Subsidiaries under new *Nigerian Upstream Petroleum Regulatory Commission (NUPRC)* and *Nigerian Midstream and Downstream Petroleum Regulatory Authority (NMDPRA)*; (*Batch 'A'*) 1–2 Nov. 2021, Ibeto Hotels, Abuja, Nigeria. *See also* Yemi Oke, 'Petroleum Industry Act Implementation Phase: Managing Stakeholder's Expectations', Senior Management Training on PIA for former DPR, NNPC and other Subsidiaries under new *Nigerian Upstream Petroleum Regulatory Commission (NUPRC)* and *Nigerian Midstream and Downstream Petroleum Regulatory Authority (NMDPRA)*; (*Batch 'B'*) 22–23 Nov. 2021, Ibeto Hotels, Abuja, Nigeria.
99. *Ibid.*, subs. (4).

IV. Award Process

60. The process and procedure for awarding Petroleum licence or lease under the PIA is strictly by open bid and competitive bid to be conducted by the Commission.[100] The winning bidder shall be determined on the basis of specified bid parameters which include, for a single bid: (i) a signature bonus to be paid in full prior to the granting of the licence or lease by or on behalf of the winning bidder; (ii) a royalty interest; (iii) a profit split or profit oil split; (iv) a work programme commitment during the initial exploration period; or (v) any other parameter as may be defined specific to a bid round; and a combination of the bid parameters specified in paragraph (a) of this subsection, based on a points system assessable by the bidder in such a manner that the bidder with the highest aggregate number of points shall be the winning bidder.[101]

61. Bidding parameters may be waived or moderated to target a particular qualified investor for diplomatic reasons, particularly where there is a bilateral or multilateral agreement between Nigeria and another country. The Government may, for strategic purposes and in return for substantive benefits to the nation, direct the Commission to negotiate and award a petroleum prospecting licence or petroleum mining lease to a qualified investor identified in the agreement or treaty. This notwithstanding, a signature bonus payable in respect thereof shall be based on a transparent method for evaluating the acreage.[102]

62. The call for bids shall be based on the procedure published on the website of the Commission and at least two international financial newspapers and two national newspapers with wide coverage.[103] Call for bids shall prescribe in a regulation or guideline the minimum pre-qualification criteria of prospective bidders in terms of technical and financial requirements and previous experience. Bids may be received electronically and shall form part of the bidding process which shall be open to the public and conducted in the presence of representatives of the Nigerian Extractive Industry Transparency Initiative,[104] the Federal Ministry of Finance and the Federal Ministry of Petroleum Resources.[105]

---

100. Section 74(1) states that:

> The grant of a petroleum prospecting licence or a petroleum mining lease on a previously appraised area of a petroleum prospecting licence or a surrendered, relinquished or revoked petroleum mining lease in under or upon the territory of Nigeria, shall be by an open, transparent, competitive and non-discriminatory bidding process conducted by the Commission under section 73 (1) of this Act.

101. Subsection (2)(a)(i–v).
102. *Ibid.*, subs. (3–4).
103. *Ibid.*, subs. (5).
104. *See* the *Nigerian Extractive Industry Transparency Initiative Act*, 2007. Nigeria was the first country in the world to take practical steps to implement the EITI. It was also the first country to institutionalize the implementation of the EITI through a triple mechanism-the NEITI Act 2007; a national EITI Secretariat with full time staff, devoted entirely to EITI implementation and the provision of an annual budget for EITI implementation and legislative over-sight at the national level.

63. Licensing rounds guidelines[106] are designed to provide certain information including a model licence,[107] as a guide. The PIA also indicate that the guidelines shall include: (a) licence or lease acreages, the term and minimum work obligations; (b) requirements to be fulfilled by the bidders and the pre-qualification criteria, as the case may be; (c) bid parameter; (d) list of documents required and criteria for the evaluation of technical capacity, financial competence and legal status of interested parties; and (e) details and cost for the acquisition of relevant data and studies.[108]

64. In terms of duration and area of PPL, the PIA provides that onshore and shallow water acreages shall be for a duration of not more than six years, comprising of an initial exploration period of three years and an optional extension period of three years. Deep offshore and frontier acreages shall be for a duration of not more than ten years, comprising an initial exploration period of five years and an optional extension period of five years. Generally, however, the area provided for in a petroleum prospecting licence shall not exceed: (a) 350 square kilometres for any onshore or shallow water acreages; (b) 1,000 square kilometres for any deep offshore acreages; and (c) 1, 500 square kilometres for any frontier acreages.[109]

In 2003, Nigeria voluntarily signed up to the global Extractive Industries Transparency Initiative (EITI). The decision to accede to the EITI and establish the Nigeria Extractive Industries Transparency Initiative (NEITI) was taken in the context of the comprehensive socio-economic reform programme embarked upon by the Federal Government of Nigeria during the second term of the former President Olusegun Obasanjo administration which commenced on 29 May 2003. The reform programme, which was encapsulated in the National Economic Empowerment Development Strategy (NEEDS), focused on four main areas namely to improve Nigeria's macro-economic environment; pursue structural reforms; strengthen public expenditure management and implement institutional and governance reforms. Implementing the EITI in Nigeria by establishing the NEITI was part of the institutional and governance reforms. Nigeria joined the EITI basically to promote prudent management of revenues from its abundant natural resources to reduce poverty and ensure sustainable development. The NEITI therefore represents the Nigerian national sub-set of the global EITI. *See* Nigeria Extractive Industries Transparency Initiative (NEITI), on-line at: https://neiti.gov.ng/about, accessed 21 Jan. 2023.

105. *See* s. 74(6–7) of the PIA, *supra* note 4.
106. *See* s. 75(a–e) of the PIA.
107. By virtue of s. 76(a–h) of the PIA, the model licence or model lease for each bid round shall reflect the conditions of the licensing round guidelines for the bid round and shall in all circumstances include: (a) description of the acreage; (b) term of the licence or lease; (c) minimum work programme and minimum level of investment; (d) details of guarantees to be provided by the licensee or lessee regarding the performance of its licence or lease obligations; (e) details of obligations regarding relinquishment, decommissioning and abandonment; (f) rules for the resolution of disputes including arbitration, mediation, conciliation or expert determination; (g) applicable sanctions in the event of failure by the licensee or lessee to comply with the terms and conditions of the licence or lease; and (h) such other clauses as the Commission may deem necessary.
108. Section 75, of the PIA.
109. *See* s. 77(1–3)(a–c) of the PIA.

V. Work Commitment Duration, Commercial and Significant Gas Discovery

65. A PPL carries a statutory requirement that the licensee commit to a work programme and such other terms and conditions as the Commission shall determine. A licensee shall, during the initial exploration period and the optional extension period provided for in a PPL, commit to drilling at least one exploration well to a minimum depth specified in the licence for each period, except for frontier acreages, where the work programme during the initial exploration period may only consist of geophysical work.[110]

66. The PIA imposes a sixty-day period on the Commission to act on the approval request for the appraisal programme after its submission and a licensee shall, upon the approval of the appraisal programme and appraisal area by the Commission, promptly carry out the committed appraisal programme. Like the above implications of 'deemed grant of licence and lease', the Act imposes another 'deemed approval' in respect of the statutory sixty-day period imposed on the Commission for approval of the work programme. By virtue of subsection (6), where the Commission fails to act on the appraisal programme referred to under subsection (5) within sixty days, *the appraisal shall be deemed approved.*[111]

67. The PIA applies the provision of section 88 (3)[112] by reference to any appraisal area under subsections (5) and (6). However, upon the completion of the appraisal programme, the licensee shall declare a commercial discovery, a significant gas discovery or a significant crude oil discovery, or inform the Commission that the discovery is of no interest to the licensee.[113] Where a significant gas discovery or significant crude oil discovery has been declared, the licensee shall be entitled to retain the area for a retention period as may be determined by the Commission, which shall not be more than ten years from the day the declaration was made and shall be entitled to drill further appraisal wells with the approval of the Commission.[114]

68. The Commission shall approve an area of a significant gas discovery or significant crude oil discovery which shall not be larger than the outer boundary of the discovery declared by the licensee, including a zone of not more than two kilometres surrounding the outer boundary, provided that such area shall not extend beyond

---

110. *Ibid.*, s. 77(1).
111. *Ibid.*, subs. (5).
112. Section 88(3) of the PIA provides that:

> Every appraisal area or retention area shall be retained as provided for under this Act and where one or more declarations of a commercial discovery have been made, the petroleum prospecting licence shall be extended until all related petroleum mining leases have been granted or denied.

113. *See* s. 78(8)(a–c).
114. *Ibid.*, subs. (9).

the area described in the applicable PPL. The retention area shall also be subject to the provision of section 88 (3) of the Act.[115]

69. The Act makes it definite that if the licensee has not declared a commercial discovery after the retention period, the area declared under subsection (9) shall be immediately relinquished by the licensee.[116] The applicable petroleum prospecting licence shall expire upon the relinquishment of the retention area with the latest expiry date referred to in subsection (13). But where a licensee declares a discovery of no interest under subsection (3) or (8) of the Act, the Commission may require the relinquishment of the parcels that cover the structure of such discovery.[117]

70. A commitment by a licensee under section 78 of the PIA shall be supported by a bank guarantee, letter of credit or performance bond issued by a bank acceptable to the Commission for an amount determined by the Commission.[118] This is in addition to the statutory requirement that the licensee shall in each calendar year present an annual work programme and status report as prescribed by regulations for approval by the Commission and such programme shall as a minimum, contain the committed work.[119]

VI. Commercial Discovery and Field Development Plan

71. Distinct provisions are made by the PIA where a licensee declares a commercial discovery and for a consequential field development plan. Where a licensee under a PPL declares a commercial discovery under section 78 (8) (a) of the Act, the licensee shall within two years of the declaration, submit to the Commission a field development plan with regard to the commercial discovery together with a commitment to carry out the work described in the field development plan.[120] The Commission shall evaluate the technical and commercial terms of the field development plan (FDP) and shall only approve the FDP where it meets the technical standards required for petroleum operations based on good international petroleum industry practices among other requirements.[121]

VII. Unitization

72. Unitized development of an extended area is possible under the PIA in respect of commercial discovery.[122] The licensee or lessee shall promptly notify the Commission of any petroleum reservoir which extends beyond the boundaries of its

115. *Ibid.*, subs. (11–12).
116. *Ibid.*, subs. (13).
117. *Ibid.*, subs. (14–15).
118. *Ibid.*, subs. (16).
119. *Ibid.*, subs. (17).
120. *See* s. 79(1) of the PIA.
121. *Ibid.*, subs. (2)(a–n).
122. *See* generally s. 80 of the PIA.

licence or lease area. The Commission may, for the purpose of ensuring optimum recovery of petroleum from a petroleum reservoir, require all petroleum operations relating to commercial discovery to be carried out by a licensee or lessee on the basis of a unitized development of the applicable commercial discovery. Unitization is possible where: (a) the petroleum reservoir covered by an area to which a licence or lease relates extends beyond the boundaries of such area into an area to which another licence or lease relates and in respect of which a different person is a licensee or lessee; and (b) at least one licensee or lessee has made a declaration of a commercial discovery.[123]

73. Where notification is duly served and received by the Commission, it shall direct the applicable licensee or lessee to enter into a unit agreement to develop the petroleum reservoir as a unit, within a period of time to be determined by the Commission, which shall not be less than two years. The unit agreement shall be approved by the Commission where it is based on terms agreed by the parties and in a form that conforms with good international petroleum industry practices and contains terms and conditions as may be required by a regulation issued by the Commission for the purpose of regulating unitization under subsection (9).[124]

74. The Commission's approval of a unit agreement shall also be based on reliable technical, operational and economic considerations; setting out the proposed operator of the applicable unit and technical information regarding the petroleum reservoir subject to unitization, including structure mapping, net pay and other such engineering and geophysical information as may be required by a unitization regulation issued by the Commission. A joint development consultant may be appointed where parties are unable to reach an agreement in respect of unitized development.[125]

VIII. Petroleum Mining Lease

75. The Petroleum Mining Lease (PML) is the central nerve of petroleum exploration and production. The provisions of the PIA on PML are radically different from OML under the repealed Petroleum Act. It provides that a petroleum mining lease shall be granted for each commercial discovery of crude oil or natural gas or both, to the licensee of a petroleum prospecting licence (PPL) who has satisfied the conditions imposed on the licence or the licensee and received approval for the

123. *Ibid.*, subs. (1) and (2)(a–b).
124. *Ibid.*, subs. (3) and (4)(a–b).
125. *Ibid.* Section 80(6) of the Act provides for a practical option to be adopted where parties re unable to reach an agreement on unitised development.

applicable field development plan from the Commission.[126] A PML shall be granted under sections 70 (2)[127] and 74[128] of the Act, where a prospective lease area contains a petroleum field with suspended wells or continuing commercial production, where the corresponding petroleum mining lease has been revoked or has expired.[129]

76. A licensee shall propose that a separate petroleum mining lease be granted for each commercial discovery to which a petroleum prospecting licence relates prior to the expiration of the applicable petroleum prospecting licence but shall comply with the requirements of section 81(7) of the Act.[130] Notwithstanding any grant of a PML under subsection (4), the applicable PPL shall continue for the remaining area to which that licence relates for the duration provided for in that licence.[131]

77. The PIA restricts a PML to an area not less than one parcel or where a parcel has been subdivided under section 69 (5) of the Act,[132] less than one subdivision of such parcel. Like PPL, by virtue of subsection (11), a PML may also be granted for a beneficial diplomatic relationship between Nigeria and another country pursuant to sections 74 (3)[133] and 93[134] which provides for relinquishment upon renewal of an Oil Mining Lease. This notwithstanding, the PIA makes it compulsory that where a lessee makes a separate commercial discovery underneath the area of a PML in shallower or deeper formations, the lessee may present a development plan for such discovery and upon approval of such plan the lessee shall be granted a separate lease for such commercial discovery.[135]

---

126. Section 81(1)(a–b) of the PIA.
127. Section 70(2) of the PIA provides that 'a licence or lease may be granted under this Act only to a company incorporated and validly existing in Nigeria under the Companies and Allied Matters Act'.
128. Section 74 of the PIA.
129. *See* s. 81(a–b) of the PIA.
130. *Ibid.*, subs. (3). This provision is made subject to subs. (7) which states that:

> The Commission shall approve the proposed area, which shall contain every parcel within the outer boundary of the field based on oil-water contacts, spill point, intersection of planned development wells with the reservoirs or other reservoir limits, including a zone surrounding the boundary consisting of all parcels that are in whole or in part within one kilometre of such outer boundary, provided that such area shall not contain parcels:
>
> (a) outside the original licence area from which the lease is derived;
> (b) in areas relinquished by the licensee; or
> (c) in an existing petroleum mining lease.

131. *Ibid.*, subs. (5).
132. Section 69 (5) of the Act gives the Commission power to subdivide parcels into equal units of one hectare or such sub-units as it may deem appropriate.
133. *See* s. 74 (3).
134. *See* s. 93 of the PIA.
135. *Ibid.*, s. 81(12).

IX. Exclusive Right to Conduct Operations

78. A PML confers the exclusive right to carry out the development and production of the petroleum with respect to the formations under the lease area as defined in the lease including the exclusive right to drill exploration and appraisal wells in the lease area and the non-exclusive right to carry out petroleum exploration operations.[136] During the term of a PML, the Commission shall: (a) verify the implementation of the work commitments by the applicable lessee and its compliance with the applicable field development plan; (b) monitor capital and operating costs incurred by the applicable lessee; and (c) ensure that upstream petroleum operations at all times are carried out to conform with the standards required by the Act and by regulation made under it.[137]

X. Duration and Renewal of Leases and Licences

79. The PIA provides that a petroleum mining lease shall be granted for a maximum period of twenty years,[138] which term shall include the development period prescribed under subsection (4).[139] The PIA guides against redundancy in the reformed petroleum sector. It states that where a PML does not initiate regular commercial production within the stipulated development period prescribed under subsection (4), the Commission shall recommend to the Minister to revoke the lease or licence at the end of the stipulated development period. The PML stands revoked unless the lessee or licensee can provide or furnish the Commission with a valid and substantial reason to make it recommend an extension of the development period to the Minister.[140]

---

136. Section 82(1–2) of the PIA. However, subs. (3) further provides that:

> A petroleum mining lease for conducting upstream petroleum operations shall only be granted on the basis of a commitment from the applicable lessee to:
>
> (a) develop and produce the commercial discovery of crude oil or natural gas in the area to which the lease relates in accordance with the applicable field development plan; or
> (b) restart or continue petroleum production in the area to which such lease relates.

137. *Ibid.*, subs. (4)(a–c).
138. Section 86(1) of the PIA.
139. The above is subject to the provision of subs. (4), which states that:

> The development period for a petroleum mining lease granted under section 81 of this Act shall be the period established in the field development plan under section 79 (2) (n) of this Act and where development period is not stipulated, the development period shall be:
>
> (a) five years for an onshore lease; and
> (b) seven years for a lease in shallow water or deep offshore or a lease in a frontier acreage.

140. *Ibid.*, subs. (3).

80. Where a PML is revoked under subsection (2), the applicable acreage shall vest in the Government and be controlled and administered by the Commission and may become subject to a new PML granted in accordance with section 81 of the Act. The acreage in respect of an expired or revoked PML shall be subject to a new bidding process under section 73 of the Act where commercial production is still possible unless the term of the PML has been extended.[141] A PML that continues to produce in paying quantities may be renewed by the Commission in accordance with section 87 of the Act. The renewal shall be for one or more successive additional terms of not more than twenty years each, provided that the field continues to produce in paying quantities and all rents, royalties, taxes and other applicable fiscal obligations stipulated under the Act shall continue to be applicable, subject to section 87 of the Act which provides condition for renewal of PML.[142] The Act lists conditions and requirements for a lessee of PML to renew the lease. The Act provides under section 87 for renewal of PML.

81. A PML that ceases to produce in paying quantities for a period of not less than 180 days may, except for force majeure or any other reason acceptable to the Commission, be revoked by the Commission. It is absolutely compulsory for a lessee of a PML who intends to suspend production for more than 180 days and to resume production at a later date, to submit to the Commission a specific shut-in plan and a commitment to restart production in accordance with the shut-in plan.[143]

XI. Relinquishment and Surrender of Licences and Leases

82. A licensee shall, prior to the expiration of the initial exploration period of three years or of the optional extension period of three years under section 77(1) of the Act, relinquish every area that is not an appraisal area, retention area or lease area based on parcels or sub-parcel under section 69 of the Act which deals with a national grid system.[144] Prior to the expiration of the initial exploration period of five years or of the optional extension period of five years under section 77 (2) of the Act, a licensee shall relinquish every area that is not an appraisal area, retention area or lease area on parcel or sub-parcel subject also to the provision of section 69 of the Act.[145]

83. Voluntary relinquishment is provided under the Act to the extent that a licensee of a PPL may voluntarily relinquish parcels and sub-parcels under section 69

141. *Ibid.*, subs. (5).
142. *Ibid.*, subs. (6).
143. *Ibid.*, subs. (7) and (8).
144. *See* s. 88(1) of the PIA.
145. *Ibid.*, subs. (2). *See* and compare subs. (3) which provides that:

> Every appraisal area or retention area shall be retained as provided for under this Act and where one or more declarations of a commercial discovery have been made, the petroleum prospecting licence shall be extended until all related petroleum mining leases have been granted or denied.

of the Act provided the licensee has complied with the obligation in the PPL. The shape of a relinquished block shall be approved by the Commission to maintain acreage of shape that is viable for an award in a future licensing round.[146] In the case of a PML, after ten years of the commencement of a PML, the applicable lessee shall relinquish all parcels which do not fall within the boundary of a producing field. Any formation deeper than the deepest producing formation shall be relinquished, and shall vest in the Government.[147]

84. Upon the expiration of any significant gas discovery retention period in respect of a PPL, every area relating to the significant gas discovery retention area shall be relinquished, unless the applicable licensee has declared a commercial discovery in such significant gas discovery retention area.[148] A relinquished area or zone shall be vested in the Government to be administered by the Commission.[149] The licensee or lessee shall not be entitled to a refund of any rent paid in respect of relinquished area or zone and shall be without prejudice to any obligation or liability imposed by or incurred under the applicable licence or lease.[150] This is without prejudice to the rights of third parties in respect of overlapping petroleum rights which shall be handled by recourse to a cooperation protocol based on good international petroleum industry practices as provided under subsection (9).[151]

85. In respect of the surrender of licence or lease, the PIA provides that a holder of a PPL, PEL or PML may surrender part or the whole of the licenced or leased area, provided that the licensee or lessee has complied with obligations imposed by or incurred under the applicable licence or lease and given three months' notice in writing to the Commission prior to the surrender.[152] Any rent or fee paid prior to a surrender shall not be refundable and such surrender of a licence or lease shall be without prejudice to any obligation or liability imposed by or incurred under the applicable licence or lease.[153]

---

146. *Ibid.*, subs. (4)(a–b).
147. *Ibid.*, subs. (5)(a–b).
148. *Ibid.*, subs. (6).
149. *Ibid.*, subs. (7).
150. *Ibid.*, subs. (8).
151. Subsection 9 provides that:

> Where the deep rights have been relinquished and subsequently granted to a third party under subsection (5) (b), the Commission shall ensure that the licensees or lessees of the overlapping petroleum rights shall enter into a cooperation protocol based on good international petroleum industry practices, dealing with matters such as non-interference measures, location of wells, construction of gathering lines, unauthorised production from reservoirs, notice of dangerous operations, joint emergency response, joint use of certain facilities and pipelines, land and water rights and such other matters as the Commission deems required for optimal petroleum operations pursuant to regulations.

152. Section 89(1)(a–b) of the PIA.
153. *Ibid.*, subs. (2).

XII. Marginal Field under the PIA

86. Prior to the enactment of the PIA, discretionary awards of OPLs to indigenous companies became a deliberate policy of the Government under the repealed Petroleum Act, to encourage local and indigenous players to participate in the upstream sector of the petroleum industry through special contractual arrangements. The concessions granted were those that were relatively easy to exploit based on seismic and other data. The second contractual arrangement which involves indigenous companies is that of the grant of marginal fields. The term 'marginal field'[154] as commonly understood in Nigeria means an oil field in a concession that is held by a major oil company not containing a significant discovery or due to certain reasons.

87. Marginal fields in Nigeria evolved from the Petroleum Amendment Act 1996, which introduced paragraph 16A into the First Schedule to the now repelled Petroleum Act. The amendment provides that the holder of an OML can farm out any marginal field which lies within the OML. Also, under the amendment, the President may cause the farm-out of a marginal field which has been left unattended for a period of not less than ten years from the date of the first discovery of the marginal field. For there to be a valid farm-out, there must be the consent of the President of the Federal Republic of Nigeria.

88. The new *Petroleum Industry Act* (PIA) has altered or brought above a complete overhaul of the administration of marginal fields in Nigeria.[155] The management and administration of marginal fields under the PIA is a radical departure from the norm under the repealed Petroleum Act.[156] It categorizes existing marginal fields under two broad categories based on whether the marginal field is a producing field or a non-producing field.[157] The PIA imposes durational restrictions for the purpose of definition of marginal fields and their operational structures, farm-outs.[158] The

---

154. The term marginal field is defined in the Petroleum (Amendment) Act 1996 No 23 (Now para. 16A of the first schedule to the petroleum Act) as 'such field as the President and Commander-in-Chief of the Armed forces may from time to time identify as a marginal fields'. For other features of a marginal field *see* para. 5 of the Guideline for Farm-Out and Operation of Marginal Fields issues in August 2001 by the Office of the Presidential Adviser on Petroleum and Energy.
155. Section 94(1–9) of the PIA makes details provision for marginal field.
156. *See* Dentons, 'Administration of Marginal Fields under the PIA: Assessing the Legal and Commercial Impact on Farm-out Arrangements', on-line at: https://www.jdsupra.com/legalnews/administration-of-marginal-fields-under-8542424/, accessed 13 Jul. 2022.
157. PIA defines a marginal field as: 'a field or discovery which has been declared a Marginal Field prior to 1st January 2021' or which has been lying fallow without activity for seven years after its discovery prior to the effective date.
158. Section 94(8)(a) and (b) provide thus:

    For the purpose of this section–

    (a) 'marginal field' means a field or discovery which has been declared a marginal field prior to 1st January 2021 or which has been lying fallow without activity for seven years after its discovery prior to the effective date; and

objective of the PIA is to create a direct or semi-direct relationship between the marginal field holder and the Nigerian Government ('Government') by creating a mandatory conversion of the marginal field to either a Petroleum Prospecting License (PPL) or a Petroleum Mining Lease (PML), depending on whether the marginal field is producing or not.

89. Section 94(1) of the PIA provides:

> A producing marginal field shall be allowed to continue to operate under the original royalty rates and farm out agreements, but shall convert to a petroleum mining lease under this Act, with terms applicable under sections 267 (b), 302, and other provisions under the Act within 18 months from the effective date.[159]

90. The PIA also provides that no new marginal fields will be declared under the Act[160] and that existing marginal fields will be transitioned under two main categories namely: (a) producing marginal fields; and (b) non-producing marginal fields. This is further classified into non-producing marginal fields declared before 1 January 2021 which have been transferred to the Government, and non–producing marginal fields which have not been transferred to the Government by the holder of an Oil Mining Lease ('OML') within three years of the effective date of the PIA[3] ('Effective Date').[161]

XIII. Producing Marginal Fields

91. Under this category, a holder of a producing marginal field is permitted to continue operations based on the original royalty rates and terms of the existing farm-out agreements entered with the farmor of the marginal field but is mandatorily required to convert to a PML ('Conversion') within eighteen months of the Effective Date ('Conversion Period') to benefit from the new fiscal regime. It needs to be pointed out that under the new regime, while all existing OPLs and OMLs would be automatically converted to PPLs and PMLs upon their expiration, the PIA however allows holders of OPLs and OMLs under the current regime to voluntarily covert them to PPLs or PMLs, within eighteen months respectively.

92. A Farmee may opt to convert to a PML at any time within the conversion period provided by PIA. However, unless the Farmee elects to voluntarily convert

---

(b) 'farm-out' means an agreement between the holder of a petroleum mining lease or petroleum prospecting licence and a third party, which permits the third party to explore, prospect, win, work and carry away any petroleum encountered in a licence or lease area during the validity of the licence or lease.

159. *See* s. 94(1) of the PIA.
160. *See* s. 94(9) of the PIA.
161. Dentons, *supra* note 156.

during the statutory windows, the marginal field will automatically be converted to a PML at the lapse of time as to the conversion period. It is anticipated that players would seize the opportunity of the incentives provided in the fiscal regime of the PIA which reduced headline tax rates from 85% to around 47.5% for the purpose. Under the PIA, a producing marginal field that is converted to a PML may benefit from special status which entitles it to a lower hydrocarbon tax rate of 15% compared to the 30% rate applicable to OMLs converted to PMLs.

XIV. Non-producing Marginal Fields

93. The PIA provides that non-producing marginal fields declared as such prior to 1 January 2021 shall be converted to a PPL and shall benefit from the fiscal terms for new acreage under the Act. This impacts the relationship between the Farmee and the Farmor under the Farm-out Agreement.[162] Generally, the relationship between the Farmor as the licence holder and the Farmee as the awardee of a marginal field is established by an FOA. Typically, the FOA provides for the terms and conditions of the farm-out arrangement and the scope of the relationship between both the Farmee and Farmor.

94. The introduction of PPL also has implications for decommissioning and abandonment under the pre-existing FOA. Under the PIA, and by virtue of section 233, a lessee and licensee are required to set up, maintain and manage a decommissioning and abandonment fund held by a financial institution that is not its affiliate. The fund is held in the form of an escrow account accessible by the regulators and such funds are expected to form part of the decommissioning and abandonment fund established under the Act.[163] Pursuant to this provision, a PPL awardee may be required to, in addition to the decommissioning obligations under the FOA, comply with the above provisions of the PIA by setting up a separate decommissioning fund for the farmed-out area in accordance with the terms set out in the Act. This implies that the decommissioning obligations under the FOA must now be aligned as much as possible with statutory obligations under the PIA.

95. The sub-category of the above is Non – Producing Marginal Fields held by an OML holder not transferred to the Government within three years of the effective date of the PIA. Under this third category, the PIA provides that, for a marginal

---

162. *See* generally s. 94(2) of the PIA.

163. Section 233 of the PIA provides for Decommissioning and Abandonment fund, thus:

> 233. (1) Each lessee and licensee shall set up, maintain and manage a decommissioning and abandonment fund held by a financial institution that is not an affiliate of the lessee or licensee, in the form of an escrow account accessible by the Commission or the Authority, as the case may be, under the provisions of the escrow agreement and where funds have been accrued prior to the effective date, such funds shall form part of the decommissioning and abandonment fund established under this Act.

field that has not been transferred to the Government within three years of the Effective Date, the holder of the OML shall provide a field development plan for the marginal field to the Commission; farm-out the field with the consent of the Commission; or relinquish the field in accordance with the provisions of the Act.[164] However, where none of the conditions above is fulfilled within the specified time-frame set out by the Commission, such fields will automatically be relinquished to the Government.[165] It is important to note that under the second condition above, the PIA envisages the creation of a Farmor-Farmee relationship between the holder of an OML and the Farmee thus, providing for a continuation of the leasehold relationship between the parties under this category.[166]

XV. Assignments Mergers, Transfers and Acquisitions

96. The PIA restricts the assignment of petroleum licence or lease. The holder of a PPL or PML cannot assign, novate or transfer his licence or lease or any right, power or interest.[167] A shareholder of an incorporated joint venture shall not sell or transfer its shares[168] without prior written consent of the Minister who shall only grant consent upon the recommendation of the Commission.[169] Where a licensee or lessee wishes to assign, novate or otherwise transfer its interest or a shareholder of

164. Section 94 (a–c) of the PIA provides:

> Within three years of the effective date, any marginal field that has not been transferred to Government, shall be subject to the following process and the holder of the oil mining lease:
>
> (a) present a field development plan for the marginal field;
> (b) with the consent of the Commission and on terms and conditions as the Commission may approve under regulations, farm out the discovery; or
> (c) relinquish the field in accordance with the provisions of this Act.

165. Section 94(6) and (7) confirms this position and states the consequence, thus:

> (6) The failure to present a field development plan under section 94 (4) (a) of this Act or within the time frame specified under section 94 (5) of this Act shall require the relinquishment of the marginal field.
> (7) A marginal field relinquished under subsection (4) (c) or (6) shall be vested in the Government and be administered by the Commission.

166. Section 94(5) states that the consent of the Commission to the farm-out of a marginal field under subs. (4) (b) shall, amongst others, be subject to the farmee presenting a field development plan over a period of time agreed with the Commission and a regulation made under this Act.
167. *See also* subs. (15) restricts a holder of Petroleum Exploration Licence (PEL) from assigning, novating, or transferring his licence or any right or interest without prior written consent of the Commission.
168. Subsection (14) generally describes 'change of control' for the purpose of s. 94 to means 'any person or persons acting jointly or in concert, to acquire direct or indirect beneficial ownership of a percentage of the voting power of the outstanding voting securities of the holder, by contract or otherwise, that exceeds 50% at any time'.
169. Section 95(1–2) of the PIA. For the purpose of this section, the Act states in subs. (3) that:

an incorporated joint venture desirous of selling or transferring its shares under subsection (1), it shall make an application for approval of the transfer to the Commission in the prescribed format and accompanied with any other information deemed relevant pursuant to any regulations published by the Commission.[170]

97. The restriction on assignment of licence or lease is qualified. A holder of a licence or lease may by way of security, wholly or partly assign, pledge, mortgage, charge or hypothecate its interests under the applicable licence, lease or grant a security interest in respect of the interest, subject to the consent of the Commission. The Commission shall not unreasonably withhold consent but shall act on same within sixty days of the receipt of the application and recommend to the Minister who shall not unreasonably withhold approval. However, where approval is declined, the Minister shall state the reasons for his decision. But where no response is given by the Minister within sixty days after the recommendation of the Commission, approval shall be deemed granted.[171]

98. Any grant of approval shall be promptly recorded in the designated register. Approval or refusal shall likewise be communicated to the applicant, and in case of refusal, reasons for the decline shall be stated and communicated.[172] In granting or declining approval, the Minister shall take into consideration if the proposed transferee is a company incorporated in Nigeria; of good reputation and standing; and has sufficient technical knowledge, experience and financial resources to enable it effectively carry out all responsibilities of a licensee or lessee under the licence or lease and the implications of the application in view of relevant provisions of the *Federal Competition and Consumer Protection Act.*[173]

---

for the purpose of subsection (1), a change of control in the holder of a licence or lease under subsection (1) shall be deemed to be an assignment.

170. *Ibid.*, subs. (4).
171. *Ibid.*, subs. (7)(a–b). *See* and compare similar arguments made by the Author in respect of 'deemed grant or deemed approval' under several sections of the PIA.
172. *Ibid.* subs. 8–10).
173. *Ibid.*, subs. (11). *See also* the *Federal Competition and Consumer Protection Act*, 2019 (the 'FCCP Act') signed into law on 30 Jan. 2019. It is a comprehensive legal framework for the regulation of competition and anti-trust issues in Nigeria. The FCCP Act introduces significant changes to Nigerian law including the repeal of the merger provisions in the ISA 2007 and the Consumer Protection Act, 2003. It also establishes the Federal Competition and Consumer Protection Commission (the 'Commission'), which has the responsibility of initiating broad-based policies, advising the Federal Government on national policies relating to competition and consumer protection, performing adjudicatory roles, eliminating anti-competition agreements, enforcing provisions of the FCCP Act and rules and regulations made pursuant to the FCCP Act. In addition, a Competition and Consumer Protection Tribunal (the 'Tribunal'), is established and is conferred with the jurisdiction to: (i) hear appeals from or review any decision of the Commission taken in the course of the implementation of any provisions of the FCCP Act; (ii) hear appeals from or review any decision from the exercise of powers of any sector-specific regulatory authority in a regulated industry with respect to competition and consumer protection matters; and (iii) issue orders and make rulings as may be necessary for the performance of its functions under the FCCP Act. *See* O Fayokun, et. al, 'A Review of the Federal Competition and Consumer Protection Act 2019', on-line at *Aluko*

XVI. Revocation of Licence and Lease

99. The PIA provides a long list of basis and grounds for revocation of a licence or lease.[174] Minister may revoke PPL or PML upon receipt of the written recommendation of the Commission where the applicable licensee or lessee fails to conduct petroleum operations in accordance with good international petroleum industry practices, the provisions of the PIA and any other relevant legislation. It may also be revoked if the licensee or lessee interrupts production for a period of over 180 consecutive days without justification or as provided for in the applicable licence, lease or approved field development plan. For this ground, an event of force majeure shall be an acceptable justification for such interruption.[175]

100. Failure to fulfil the terms and conditions of the applicable licence or lease or the approved field development plan; failure to pay to the Government, as they become due, rents, royalties, taxes or other payments or production shares under the Act or to furnish any reports or data on operations as required by law after having been advised in writing by the Commission of such failure, shall each constitute a ground for revocation of licence or lease.[176] A licensee or lessee who assigns, novates or otherwise transfers any interest in the applicable licence or lease other than in accordance with section 95 of the Act or has obtained an interest in the applicable licence or lease based on false representation or contrary to corrupt practices and money laundering laws is liable to have such licence or lease revoked.[177]

101. The Act provides further that a licence or lease may be revoked where the beneficiary is declared by a court of competent jurisdiction to be insolvent, bankrupt or liquidated unless such is part of a solvent plan or scheme of re-organization, amalgamation or arrangement.[178] Other grounds are failure to comply with environmental obligations required by applicable law or by the provisions of the applicable licence or lease or the grantee is owned wholly or in part, directly or indirectly or is controlled by a former or serving public official or member of the Government, who obtained his interest in the applicable licence or lease other than as permitted by applicable law.[179] Failure to submit and advance a field development plan and work commitment under sections 78 and 79 of this Act; refusal to abide by any expert determination, arbitration award or judgment arising from the dispute resolution provisions set forth in a licence, lease or the Act, or non-compliance with

---

& Oyebode: https://www.aluko-oyebode.com/insights/review-of-the-federal-competition-and-consumer-protection-act-2019/, accessed 22 Jan. 2023.

174. *See* generally s. 96(1)(a–n) and (2) of the PIA.
175. *Ibid.*, subs. (1)(a–b).
176. *Ibid.*, subs. (1)(c–e).
177. *Ibid.*, paras (f–g).
178. *Ibid.*, para. (h).
179. *Ibid.*, paras (i–j). Subsection (2) further provides that:

> (2) subsection (1) (j) shall apply to a former public official or member of Government only where the applicable interest was acquired while the public official was in office or was a member of the Government. This is a firm bid to curtain public corruption by public officials.

domestic crude oil supply or domestic gas delivery obligations under the Act and any subsidiary regulation; or with the host communities obligations under the Act shall likewise form basis of revocation of erring licence or lease.[180]

102. The Act provides that notice of revocation shall be served on the applicable licensee or lessee.[181] Prior to revocation, a default notice is served showing the grounds upon which the Commission may recommend revocation of the licence or lease to the Minister with an option to remediate within sixty days.[182] Revocation shall abate if the Commission is satisfied with the remedy provided but if infractions persist, the licence or lease may, subject to the provisions of section 99 of the Act, be revoked in accordance with section 96 of the PIA.[183]

103. Upon revocation, notice of default is sent by the Commission to the last known address of the licensee or lessee or its legal representative in Nigeria, or published in the Federal Government Gazette or on the website of the Commission. Each mode of service of notice of revocation shall constitute notice to the licensee or lessee of the notice of default. Revocation of a PPL or PML is without prejudice to any liability or obligation which the licensee or lessee may have incurred in favour of the Commission, the Government or any third party; or claim which the Commission, the Federal Government or any third party may make against the licensee or lessee. Once revocation decision is made, the Commission shall cause the same to be published in the Federal Government Gazette and shall accordingly amend relevant registers maintained by it to reflect the revocation.[184]

104. A revoked producing lease is managed by way of interim operations or management. The PIA prescribes that, within thirty days of the revocation of a PML or participating or shareholder interest in a PML which is active and in operation, the Minister may, on the recommendation of the Commission, appoint an interim operator to ensure petroleum operations continue from the areas and zones subject to the terms of the PML, based on good international petroleum industry practices. The interim operator shall be for a duration as may from time to time be determined by the Commission, which contract shall be on a service fee basis. The Commission may conduct a fair, transparent and competitive bidding process for the grant of a new PML to replace the revoked lease during the tenure of an interim operator.[185]

XVII. Revocation of Participating or Shareholders Interest

105. Revocation of participating or shareholders interest takes a different approach under the PIA. The Act provides for selective revocation where interest is

180. *Ibid.*, paras (k–n).
181. *See* s. 97(1–6) of the PIA.
182. *Ibid.*, subs. (1)(a–b).
183. *Ibid.*, subs. (3).
184. *See* generally subs. (4)(a–b), (5)(a–b) and (6) of the PIA.
185. *See* generally s. 98(1–3).

conjoined. The Minister may revoke the participating or shareholders interest of the holder or holders to which the grounds apply and shall not revoke the interests of the other holder or holders to which the grounds do not apply.[186] The right of a defaulting holder shall cease upon revocation but without prejudice to any obligation or liability incurred or imposed on the defaulting holder under the terms and conditions of the licence or lease prior to the time of the revocation.[187] By virtue of subsection (4), the interests of each non-defaulting holder shall not be affected by a revocation of the interest under subsection (1)(b). The Act prescribes that the non-defaulting holders shall take such measures as provided for under the Joint Operating Agreement (JOA) or shareholder agreement to redistribute the revoked participating or shareholder interest to the non-defaulting holders or third parties.[188] Failure of the non-defaulting party to take responsibility for rents, royalties, taxes, profit share or comply with an obligation under the licence or lease may form a basis for revocations.[189]

XVIII. Fees, Royalties, Rents and other Payments to the Government

106. Payment of fees, royalties and others to the Nigerian Government in the amount and time prescribed in the licence or lease is a statutory obligation under the PIA and regulations made by the Commission.[190] Failure to make payment within thirty days is considered a debt to the Commission with interest accruing at a prevailing Central Bank of Nigeria (CBN) rate.[191] Payment to the Government cannot be waived under any circumstance,[192] and the Commission may task steps in the recovery of the debt after the expiration of the thirty-day period.[193]

---

186. Section 99(1)(a–b). Subsection (2) describes a holder to which the grounds apply under subs. (1)(a) as a 'defaulting holder' and a holder to which the grounds do not apply under subs. (1)(b) is referred to as a 'non-defaulting holder'.
187. *Ibid.*, subs. (3).
188. *Ibid.*, subs. (4).
189. Subsection (6) states that 'the Minister may revoke a licence or lease, where a non-defaulting holder under subs. (1) (b), fails to (a) take responsibility for the payment of rents, royalties, taxes, production shares, profit shares or other contractual payments to Government of the defaulting holder under the licence or lease; or (b) comply with any other obligation under the licence or lease in a manner that may result in the revocation of the licence or lease under section 96 of this Act'.
190. *See* s. 100(1) of the PIA.
191. *Ibid.*, subs. (2).
192. *Ibid.*, subs. (4).
193. Subsection (3) provides that:

> The Commission may, after the 30 days period referred to under subsection (2) and until the debt is repaid, together with accrued and unpaid interest:
>
> (a) enter into and upon any land, property or premises owned, possessed or occupied by the holder of the licence or lease;
>
> (b) seize, distrain and sell any petroleum, petroleum products, engines, machinery, tools, implements or other effects belonging to the holder of the licence or lease, and the costs incurred by the Commission in connection with the seizure, distress and sale shall be added to the debt; and

XIX. Environmental Management and Remediation Damage

107. Petroleum operator or licensee or lessee who engages in upstream and midstream petroleum operations shall within one year of the effective date or six months after the grant of the applicable licence or lease, submit for approval an Environmental Management Plan (EMP) in respect of projects which require environmental impact assessment to the Commission or Authority, as the case may be.[194] The EMP is required to be in accordance with applicable legislations[195] and the Commission or Authority, as the ease may be, shall approve the EMP where same is in compliance with relevant environmental Acts. The applicant must have demonstrated capacity or provided for the capacity to rehabilitate and manage (any) negative impacts on the environment taking into account the policy thrust of the Government regarding environment al protection and management practices.[196]

108. Before an EMP is approved for a petroleum operator by the Commission or Authority, the licensee or lessee shall make a financial contribution to an *Environmental Remediation Fund* (ERF) for the rehabilitation or management of negative environmental impacts with respect to the licence or lease. The amount of such financial contributions shall take into consideration the size of the operations and the level of environmental risk they entail. Contributions to ERF shall be subject to audit by the licensee or lessee, in accordance with guidelines of the Commission or Authority.

XX. Gas Flaring Penalties and Gas Domestic Delivery Obligations

109. Gas flaring is generally prohibited for all licensees, lessees or marginal field operators except in the case of an emergency, pursuant to an exemption granted by the Commission, or as an acceptable safety practice under established regulations.[197] Violation of this provision amounts to an offence under the Act. A violator is liable to a fine as prescribed by the Commission under applicable regulations, which shall be payable in the same procedure as payment of royalties to the Government, but it shall not be recoverable as part of costs or tax-deductible expenses by the violating licensees, lessees or marginal field operators. Such penalties shall

---

(c) out of money arising from the sale of any item referred to in paragraph (b), pay off the debt and any surplus shall be paid by the Commission to the holder of the licence or lease.

194. *See* s. 102(1)(a–b) of the PIA.
195. *Ibid.*, subs. (2).
196. *Ibid.*, subs. (3)(a–b), (4). By virtue of subs. (5–7), the PIA imposes other conditions for approval of EMP by petroleum operators. The Commission or Authority may request for additional from the licensee or lessee or may direct that the EMP to be adjusted or amended before or after approval by the Commission or Authority provided no operator shall be allowed or granted approval to use chemical of petroleum operations without the Commission's prior approval.
197. Section 104(1) of the PIA.

be applied for the purpose of environmental remediation and relief of the host communities of the settlors on which the penalties are levied.[198]

110. The Act prohibits flaring or venting of natural gas. It subjects violators to payment of penalties prescribed pursuant to the Flare Gas (Prevention of Waste and Pollution) Regulations. The Commission shall have the right of access, free of charge, to such natural gas that is destined for flaring at the flare stack. The Act provides that a licensee shall, prior to the commencement of petroleum production, install metering equipment conforming to the specifications prescribed on every facility from which natural gas may be flared or vented as the Commission or the Authority may prescribe in a regulation.

111. Like the above provisions, failure or refusal to install metering equipment may result in penalties by way of fines as may be imposed by the Commission or the Authority,[199] except in cases where exemption is granted to allow the flaring or venting of natural gas for a specific period where it is required for facility start-up or for strategic operational reasons, including testing.[200] To curtail incidents of gas flaring and venting of natural gas, the Act imposes *Natural Gas Flare Elimination and Monetisation Plan* (NGF&MEP) on all licence or lessee producing natural gas.[201]

XXI. Domestic Crude Oil and Gas Obligations

112. The PIA imposes domestic crude oil supply and gas delivery obligations to curtail scarcity and hardship often encountered by local or domestic consumers of petroleum and gas resources.[202] Although the supply of crude oil and condensates for the domestic market shall be on a willing supplier and willing buyer basis, the

198. *Ibid.*, subs. (2–4).
199. *Ibid.*, s. 106(1–2).
200. Section 107(a–b) grants some exceptions to the provisions of the PIA on gas flaring and natural gas venting.
201. Section 108 of the PIA provides that:

> Notwithstanding any provision to the contrary under this Act, a licensee or lessee producing natural gas shall, within 12 months of the effective date, submit a natural gas flare elimination and monetisation plan to the Commission, which shall be prepared in accordance with regulations made by the Commission under this Act.

202. *See* generally ss 109 and 110 of the PIA. By virtue of subs. (12), upon being allocated the volumes to be supplied under the domestic gas supply obligation under subs. (1), the lessee shall submit a marketable natural gas production and supply plan consistent with these obligations to the Authority.
Subsection (13) also provides that a producer-customer of the domestic gas aggregator shall pay compensation to customer-client for any loss suffered as a result of default to supply marketable natural gas in accordance with a gas purchase order issued by the domestic gas aggregator. By virtue of subsection (14), a lessee who does not comply with the domestic gas delivery obligation as directed by the Commission shall in addition to the penalties provided under subsection (8), not be

Commission may nonetheless impose a domestic crude oil supply obligation on lessees of upstream petroleum operations, including applicable penalties.[203] The Act also gives the Commission power to specify details to be contained in domestic crude oil supply obligations to holders of crude oil refining licences.[204]

113. The Act also imposes domestic gas delivery obligations on all lessees. The Commission issues guidelines for this purpose to prescribe and allocate the domestic gas delivery obligation among all lessees before 1 March of each year based on the domestic gas demand requirements determined or updated under section 173 of the Act[205] and ensures compliance by every lessee.[206]

114. The Act encourages voluntary contracting between a lessee and wholesale customers of the strategic sectors or with wholesale gas suppliers supplying the strategic sectors for delivery of marketable natural gas on a free market basis and notifies the Commission. For the purpose of meeting domestic gas delivery obligations, the Commission may further require a lessee producing natural gas to carry out works and operations which may be required to increase production and to dedicate a specific volume of the natural gas produced towards the requirements of the domestic market.

115. The obligation to domestic gas delivery may be suspended or discontinued by the Commission where the Authority has determined under section 167 (3)[207] of

---

entitled to supply natural gas to any new midstream gas export operations, provided that this provision shall not apply to gas sales agreements already entered into; and where the lessee is supplying natural gas to midstream gas export operations, the Commission may impose other sanctions as are prescribed in a regulation made under this Act.

203. *Ibid.*, s. 109(1–2).

204. *See* generally subs. 4(a–c).

205. Section 173 of the PIA provides for domestic gas demand requirement, thus:

> (1) The Authority shall, prior to the 1st of March of each calendar year, determine the domestic gas demand requirement and inform the Commission of this requirement.
> (2) Subject to subsection (3), the domestic gas demand requirement shall be the total amount of marketable natural gas required for all wholesale customers of the strategic sectors.
> (3) Each wholesale customer of the strategic sectors shall have the right to negotiate its own supply contracts directly with lessees or suppliers and where the wholesale customer is of the view that the contracts are satisfactory for its requirements, it shall inform the:
> (a) Authority that there is no need to be a customer client of the domestic gas aggregator; and
> (b) Commission of the lessees from which the required marketable natural gas has been obtained.

206. Section 110(1)(a–b).

207. *See* s. 167 (3) of the PIA which provides for Natural gas prices for the strategic sectors and gas distributors, thus:

> (3) The price control and the corresponding role of the domestic gas aggregator shall not be required, where the:
> (a) entire domestic gas demand requirement under section 173 (2) is covered by contracts under sections 110 (2) and 173 (3) of this Act; or

the Act that the natural gas market has attained full market status.[208] Generally, however, the Act imposes a rigid condition that approval for the supply of natural gas for export projects shall, from the effective date, be subject to prior compliance by the lessee with its domestic gas delivery obligation. To encourage self or voluntary compliance, domestic gas delivery contracts entered into by lessees or licensees prior to the effective date and continuing after the date shall be counted towards their domestic gas delivery obligation.[209]

§8. General Administration of Midstream and Downstream Petroleum Operations

116. Chapter 3 of the PIA generally provides for the administration of midstream and downstream petroleum operations. This complements extensive provisions of the PIA on the establishment of the *Nigerian Midstream and Downstream Petroleum Regulatory Authority* (the 'Authority').[210] In the exercise of its statutory powers, the Authority may grant, renew, modify or extend individual licences or permits. However, where it relates to the establishment of refineries, the licence shall be issued by the Minister on the recommendation of the Authority.[211] The PIA gives the Authority power to grant a licence for midstream or downstream petroleum operations, where such an application meets the technical standards required for petroleum operations based on good international petroleum industry practices; the location and size of the area occupied by the facilities. It grants such licences where the right of way is acceptable to the Authority; meets the health, safety and environmental standards, as determined by the Authority as well as where it provides for the efficient and economic use of facilities and pipelines.[212]

117. The Authority shall grant a licence for midstream petroleum operations subject to a number of considerations.[213] Such an application must also include a detailed programme for the recruitment and training of Nigerians in all phases of petroleum operations handled directly by the licensee or through agents and contractors of the licensee, and provision for scholarship schemes, internships, continuous professional development and other training requirements.[214]

(b) domestic market for natural gas is largely characterized by free market based contracting for natural gas between willing buyers and willing sellers, based on criteria established by the Authority in consultation with the stakeholders and at such time the provisions of subsections (4), (5), (6) and (7) and section 168 shall no longer be applicable and the criteria under this subsection may include that certain classes of wholesale customers, but not all, of the strategic sectors will no longer be subject to price controls as part of an ongoing process towards full free market conditions.

208. *Ibid.*, s. 110(12) of the PIA.
209. *Ibid.*, subs. (15–16).
210. *See* Part IV, s. 29 of the PIA.
211. *See* s. 111(1) of the PIA.
212. *Ibid.*, subs. (2)(a–d).
213. *Ibid.*, subs. (3)(a–e).
214. *Ibid.*, subs. (3)(f)(i–ii).

118. Applications for renewal or extension of licence or permit are also made to the Authority in the form and manner prescribed by the regulation and accompanied by the payment of a prescribed fee, where applicable, together with prescribed information as well as a decommissioning and abandonment plan, where the licence contemplates the construction of pipelines, storage tanks, processing or other facilities.[215] Where an applicant is an affiliate of a body corporate that has applied for or holds any other licence or permit, such status or relationship shall be disclosed to the Authority in its application.[216]

119. A decision granting the extension or renewal of the licence or permit shall be made by the Authority within ninety days of the application. If the application is refused, it shall likewise communicate the applicant and state reasons for refusal with a view to giving the applicant a deadline within which to make further representation on the application.[217] A representation is only considered if it furnishes new information not previously considered, as no application or representation in respect to refusal shall be considered, save for the right of a dissatisfied applicant to apply to the Federal High Court for a judicial review.[218]

I. Assignment or Transfer of Licence and Permit

120. Assignment or transfer of licence or permit is possible under the PIA but with strict conditions. Written consent of the Authority is required by way of an application to the Authority, which may require the applicant to publish a notice of the application in the form, manner and time prescribed by regulation.[219] The Authority shall follow the same procedure with appropriate modification in the determination of whether a licence or permit is to be assigned or transferred. It shall apply the same rules or criteria and consider relevant issues as those considered in fresh applications, including any representations made by third parties in respect of the application for assignment or transfer of licence or permit.[220]

121. Notice of grant or refusal shall be accordingly communicated, including an opportunity for making a re-presentation upon initial refusal.[221] However, subsection (5) also provides for the contentious and seemingly problematic 'deemed grant'. Where the Authority does not approve or refuse an application and fails to communicate its decision to an applicant for the assignment or transfer of a licence

215. *Ibid.*, subs. (4)(a–c).
216. *Ibid.*, subs. (6).
217. *See* generally s. 111(7–9), *ibid.*
218. *Ibid.*, subs. (10–12).
219. *See* s. 117(1) and (2) of the PIA, *supra* note 4.
220. *Ibid.*, subs. (3)(a–d).
221. Subsection (4) provides that the Authority shall, subject to subs. (3), communicate in writing, its approval or refusal of an application for assignment or transfer of a licence or permit within the time prescribed by regulation under this Act. By virtue of subs. (6), Where the Authority refuses the grant of an application for an assignment or a transfer of a licence or permit, it shall communicate to the applicant the reason for the refusal and shall give reasonable time within which further representation may be made by the applicant or by a third party in respect of the application.

or permit within the prescribed time, the application shall be deemed to be approved. This notwithstanding, where the Authority grants its consent to an assignment or transfer of a licence or permit, it shall notify the applicant in writing, subject to any condition it may consider appropriate.[222]

II. Suspension, Amendment or Surrender of Licence and Permit

122. The PIA confers the Authority with powers to suspend or amend the conditions applicable to a licence or permit or include additional conditions after giving the holder a written notice of its intention, accompanied by a draft copy of the proposed suspension or amendment. It shall also give the holder an opportunity to make a written submission to it within the time specified by regulation subject to the right of a dissatisfied holder to seek appropriate redress at the Federal High Court against the decision of the Authority on suspension of amendment, as the case may be.[223]

123. Without suspension or amendment, a holder may of its volition, surrender a licence or permit. The Act states that the holder of a licence or permit may, upon an application in the prescribed form, and upon fulfilling any conditions prescribed by the Authority in a regulation surrender the licence or permit, where the licenced or permitted activity is no longer required. It may also be surrendered where the licenced or permitted activity is not economically justifiable or in a situation where another qualified person is willing and able to assume the rights and obligations in accordance with the requirements and objectives of the Act. A licence or permit may also be surrendered where the holder has compiled with the requirements of the law in respect of relinquishment, decommissioning and abandonment of installations and reclamation of land.[224]

III. Grounds for the Revocation of Licence or Permit

124. The PIA provides detailed grounds and instances in which a licence or permit may be justifiably revoked by the Authority. A licence or permit may be revoked where the holder becomes insolvent, bankrupt, enters into an agreement or composition with its creditors or takes advantage of any enactment for the benefit of the debtors or goes into liquidation, except as part of a scheme for an arrangement or amalgamation. It may also be revoked upon the transformation or dissolution of the company or corporation, except it is for the purpose of amalgamation or reconstruction, provided that prior written consent of the Authority has been obtained. A

222. *Ibid.*, subs. (7).
223. *Ibid.*, s. 118(1–4).
224. *See* generally s. 119(1)(a–d). However, it needs to be noted that by subs. (2) and (3), a holder of the licence or permit who has commenced activities and has ongoing operations shall, except a shorter period is stipulated in the licence or permit, give the Authority a minimum of 1.2 months' notice in writing of its intention to cease its activities. The form and procedure to be followed in surrendering a licence or permit under subs. (2) shall be as prescribed by regulation.

licence or permit may be revoked where the holder fails to commence activity within the timeframe prescribed or where he fails to comply with applicable laws and regulations on the terms and conditions of such licence or permit.[225]

125. The holder of a licence or permit issued by the Authority may have its benefits and privileges revoked where it interrupts midstream or downstream petroleum operations for a period of more than 180 consecutive days without justification, unless by an event of force majeure or where it assigns or transfers any interest in the licence or permit without obtaining the prior written consent of the Authority.[226] Revocation of licence or permit may be triggered where the holder acquired the licence or permit based on false representation or contrary to corrupt practices and money laundering laws.[227] Failure to comply with environmental obligations[228] or where the holder is owned wholly or in part, directly or indirectly or is controlled by a former or serving public official or member of the Government, who obtained his interest in the applicable licence or lease other than as permitted by applicable law may also constitute basis for revocation.[229] A holder that fails to abide by any expert determination, arbitration award or judgment arising from the dispute resolution provisions set forth in a licence or the Act may also have its licence or permit revoked.[230]

§9. Administration of Midstream and Downstream Petroleum Liquids Operations

126. The introduction of a distinct regulatory structure for petroleum liquids under the *PIA*[231] is one of the innovative frameworks of the new petroleum regime in Nigeria. Prior to the PIA, petroleum liquids[232] were regulated as component parts of oil and gas ('mineral oil'). Part V of the PIA provides for the administration of midstream and downstream petroleum operations in Nigeria.[233] The PIA saddles the Authority with statutory responsibilities to issue licences in respect of all activities for midstream and downstream petroleum liquids operations. Such licences are issued to establish, construct or operate a terminal or other facility for the export or importation of crude oil or petroleum products; for crude oil refinery; to establish,

225. *See* s. 120(1)(a–d) of the PIA.
226. *Ibid.*, subs. (1)(e–f).
227. *Ibid.*, subs. (1)(g).
228. *Ibid.*, subs. (1)(h).
229. *Ibid.*, subs. (i). It needs to be noted that by virtue of subs. (2), the ground of revocations contained in para. (i) shall apply to a former public official or member of Government where the applicable interest was acquired while in office or was a member of the Government.
230. *Ibid.*, subs. (1)(j).
231. *See* the *Petroleum Industry Act, (PIA) No. 6 of 2021.* According to the Long Title to the PIA, it is 'An Act to Provide Legal, Governance, Regulatory and Fiscal Framework for the Nigerian Petroleum Industry, the Development of Host Communities; and For Related Matters'. The PIA commenced on the 16 Aug. 2021.
232. Petroleum liquids means crude oil, condensate, and any finished or intermediate products manufactured or extracted in a petroleum refinery.
233. *See* generally Part V, ss 174–208 of the PIA, *supra* note 4.

construct or operate a pipeline for the bulk transportation of petroleum liquids or engage in bulk transportation of petroleum liquids by rail, barge or other means within Nigeria.[234] Licences for midstream and downstream petroleum liquids may also be issued by the Authority to establish, construct or operate a facility for the bulk storage of petroleum liquids, to operate a petroleum liquids transportation network; engage in the bulk sale of petroleum liquids; or to undertake construction or operation of any facility for the production of lubricants or petrochemicals based on petroleum products.[235]

127. The PIA outlaws undertaking midstream and downstream petroleum liquids operations without a licence issued by the Authority.[236] The above is not a closed list of restricted or licensed activities. The Authority may, by regulation, prescribe additional activities to be undertaken only on the basis of a licence or permit and shall have the power to issue licences or permits for the activities in accordance with this Act. Where a person engages in any of the activities set out in subsection (1), (2) or (3) without a licence or permit, the Authority shall seal the premises where the activity is undertaken without a permit. It may dismantle and seize the facilities by which the activities were undertaken; confiscate equipment or materials employed by the person in such activity; or impose penalties as prescribed by regulations under this Act.[237]

128. The Act criminalizes carrying out midstream and downstream petroleum liquids operations without a licence issued by the Authority. A person who engages in any petroleum liquids activities without a licence or permit commits an offence and is liable on conviction to imprisonment for a term of one year or to a fine prescribed by regulation, in the case of an activity requiring a licence; or six months or to a fine prescribed by regulation, in the case of an activity requiring a permit.[238] The Act allows a window of eighteen months for a holder of a subsisting lease, licence or permit who is engaged in activities in midstream or downstream petroleum liquids operations to apply to the Authority to issue the appropriate licence or permit, where applicable.[239]

129. The Act confers powers in the Authority to make special regulations for midstream and downstream petroleum liquids operations in addition to any matter provided under section 113 of the Act. Such special regulations may include the establishment and operation of a wholesale market, to ensure the continuity of supply of petroleum products to customers. This applies to the owners and operators of crude oil refineries, transportation pipelines and other facilities or vessels for the

234. *See* s. 174(a–d), of the PIA.
235. *Ibid.*, subs. (e–f).
236. *Ibid.*, subs. (2)(a–c).
237. *Ibid.*, subs. (3–4)(a–d).
238. *Ibid.*, subs. (5)(a–b).
239. *Ibid.*, subs. (6).

bulk transportation of petroleum liquids, bulk storage facilities for petroleum liquids and terminals and outlets for retail trading of petroleum products. The Authority also has powers to make regulations on matters ancillary to or consequential to the above-listed activities.[240]

I. Grant of a Crude Oil Refining Licence

130. The objective of petroleum industry liberalization and decentralization is further amplified in the requirement of the PIA on the grant of a crude refining licence which is made subject to the procedural steps ad requirements of sections 111 and 174 of the Act. It requires an application to be made to the Authority by a qualified person in a prescribed form and upon payment of a prescribed fee. The Authority recommends to the Minister the grant of a crude oil refining licence which shall permit the licensee to procure, construct, install and operate facilities to process crude oil on its own account into derivative chemicals and petroleum products as well as sell such chemicals and petroleum products at the exit of the refinery.[241]

131. In considering and recommending an application for a crude oil refining licence, the Authority shall take into account the economic case for a refinery, including the potential demand for its use.[242] Once a crude oil refining licence is granted, the licensee shall be under statutory obligations to: (a) procure, construct, install, operate and maintain its refinery and associated facilities in an economical, safe, reliable and environmentally friendly manner; (b) shut down its facilities in emergencies and in order to carry out maintenance or in accordance with curtailment directives issued by the Authority; and (c) manage its facilities as a reasonable and prudent operator.[243]

132. The crude oil refiner is also under an obligation to avoid any act or omission that may affect the compatibility of the refinery with any facility or network that is likely to prejudice the public interest or the integrity of network operations; and produce petroleum products of a quality suitable for the transportation system as specified in the licence. It shall also produce petroleum products to a quality suitable for use in accordance with the specifications approved by the Authority; treat

240. *See* s. 175 (a–b) of the PIA.

241. *See* s. 183(1)(a–b). The grant of a crude oil refining licence entitles the refiner to access rights. Section 185 states that:

> A crude oil refiner shall have the right of access to facilities, including harbours, jetties, petroleum bulk storage, transportation facilities and pumping installations in accordance with the open access or third party access requirements and the tariff methodology approved by the Authority.

242. *Ibid.*, subs. (c).

243. *See* s. 184(a–c) of the PIA.

all customers in a non-discriminatory manner under section 116 of the PIA Act as well as abstain from activities, which in the opinion of the Authority may prevent, restrict or distort competition.[244]

II. Bulk Petroleum Liquids Storage Licence

133. The grant of a bulk Petroleum liquids storage licence under the PIA is subject to similar provisions and conditions for the grant of crude oil refining licence. Subject to sections 111 and 174 of the Act, the Authority may upon approval of an application and payment of prescribed fees, grant and issue bulk petroleum liquids storage licence to a qualified person authorizing the holder to undertake the bulk storage of petroleum liquids whether for its own account or on behalf of customers as provided for in the licence.[245] The Authority takes into consideration the economic case for a bulk storage facility, including the potential demand for its use in considering and granting an application for a bulk petroleum liquids storage licence.[246]

134. The general duties of a bulk storage licensee include to establish and make available to the public at its offices, the (i) procedure for obtaining third-party access or open access, as provided for in the licence, throughput and terminating its services, and (ii) method of response to the request for its service. Other obligations of the licensee include to procure, construct, install, operate and maintain its facilities in a safe, economical, reliable and environmentally friendly manner taking into account any strategic plans formulated by the Authority.[247] It is also under an obligation to shut down its facilities in emergencies and in order to carry out maintenance or in response to curtailment directives issued by the Authority.

135. The licensee is under a statutory obligation to grant third-party access to use or have access to spare capacity within its facilities for the purpose of ensuring competitive supply of crude oil and petroleum products, where the licensee operates on its own account.[248] It shall consult with the Authority and obtain written permission prior to any modification of technical and operational rules of practice concerning the operation of its facilities. It shall also conduct its licensed activities in a non-discriminatory manner between all classes of customers under section 116 of the Act, where the licence is for bulk storage for customers and is operated on an open-access basis as well as manage its facilities as a reasonable and prudent operator and abstain from activities, which in the opinion of the Authority may prevent, restrict or distort competition.[249]

244. *Ibid.*, subs. (d–h).
245. Section 187(1) of the PIA.
246. *Ibid.*, subs. (2).
247. Section 188(a)(i–ii),(b–c) of the PIA.
248. *Ibid.*, subs. (d–e).
249. *Ibid.*, subs. (f–h).

136. Like the crude refiner, a bulk petroleum liquids storage licence is also subject to certain statutory conditions. For example, where the licence is operated for licensee purposes only, it may own the petroleum liquids contained in the storage and where the licence is operated on an open-access basis, the licensee shall not own the petroleum liquids. The licensee shall conduct its licensed activities safely and reliably in compliance with any law in force and prescribed health and safety-related regulations issued under the Act. It shall likewise have regard to the effect of its licensed activities on the environment and comply with the requirements for environmental protection, management and restoration as well as mark, maintain and secure the boundaries of its facilities and associated infrastructure constructed under the terms of its licence and any law in force.[250]

III. Petroleum Liquids Transportation Pipeline Licence

137. Petroleum liquids transportation pipeline licence is another category of licence issued by the Authority under its powers under the PIA. The licence is granted to a qualified person upon an application to the Authority and payment of the fee prescribed for such applications. The licence confers exclusive right to own, construct, operate and maintain a transportation pipeline for the bulk transportation of petroleum liquids within a route as defined in the licence for its own account with third-party access provisions or as a common carrier as stipulated in the licence.[251] It is granted based on the economic case for a petroleum liquids transportation pipeline including the potential demand for its use.[252]

138. As part of the general duties statutorily imposed on a Petroleum liquids transportation pipeline owner, the licensee shall establish and make available to the public at its offices, the procedure for obtaining and terminating transmission and interconnection services, and the method of response to the request for its service.[253] It shall construct, operate and maintain its petroleum liquids transportation pipeline in a safe, economical, and reliable manner taking into account any strategic plans formulated by the Authority. The licensee shall also manage supply shortfalls as well as meet on a reasonable basis request for transportation above contractual volumes. It must shut down its petroleum liquids transportation pipeline in emergencies and in order to carry out maintenance or in response to curtailment directives issued by the Authority.[254]

139. The licensee shall provide access on a non-discriminatory basis under section 116 of the PIA. It must also consult and obtain written permission from the Authority prior to any modification of technical and operational rules of practice

250. *See* s. 189(a–d).
251. *See* s. 190(1). Of the PIA.
252. *Ibid.*, subs. (2).
253. Section 191(a)(i–ii).
254. *Ibid.*, paras (b–d).

concerning the operation of its pipeline as well as manage its transportation pipeline as a reasonable and prudent operator and abstain from activities, which in the opinion of the Authority may prevent, restrict or distort competition.[255]

IV. Petroleum Liquids Transportation Network Operator Licence

140. The grant of a petroleum liquids transportation network operator licence is similar to the terms and conditions under which other categories of midstream and downstream petroleum liquids licences are granted.[256] General duties of a petroleum liquids transportation network operator include to establish and make available to the public at its offices, the procedure, terms and conditions for obtaining and terminating access and interconnection services to the transportation network, and method of response to the request for its service.[257] The licensee must operate an efficient and economical transportation network for the safe and reliable conveyance of specified petroleum liquids in a manner that is designed to meet all reasonable demands for the specified petroleum liquids. The holder also ensures the development and operation of a network code and terms for access to the transportation network in collaboration with the Authority, shippers, licensees and permit holders operating essential infrastructure.[258]

141. Like other licensees, the holder also has a duty to ensure equitable and transparent open access, subject to the provisions of section 116, to the transportation network in accordance with the network code. It must manage the transportation network as a reasonable and prudent operator and abstain from activities, which in the opinion of the Authority may prevent, restrict or distort competition, and may enter into agreements with transportation pipeline owners, distributors and wholesale customers for connection to, and operation of, the transportation network.[259]

---

255. *Ibid.*, paras (e–h).
256. *See* generally s. 193(1)(a–d) and (2) of the PIA. It states that:

> Subject to sections 111 and 174 of this Act, the Authority may upon approval of an application and payment of prescribed fees, grant and issue a qualified person a petroleum liquids transportation network operator licence authorising the conduct of activities specified in the licence, which shall include:
>
> (a) conveyance of petroleum liquids through the transportation network;
> (b) balancing the inputs and off takes from the transportation network;
> (c) providing open access to the transportation network; and
> (d) charging for the use of the transportation network.
>
> (2) The Authority shall grant only one petroleum liquids transportation network operator licence for specified petroleum liquids within a geographically defined area to a single network operator, provided that the Authority may, at its discretion, issue licences to other parties for the operation of isolated or dedicated pipelines.

257. Section 194(a)(i–ii).
258. *Ibid.*, paras (b–e).
259. *Ibid.*, paras (f–i).

142. A petroleum liquids transportation network operator may exercise a number of powers and rights to facilitate the conduct of its licensed activities. The list of such privileges includes the power to request and obtain from shippers information required to operate the nominations and balancing mechanism to operate the network or to facilitate competition. It has the right to recover, on the basis of an invoice, expenses reasonably incurred in undertaking its licensed activities, subject to any conditions imposed by the Authority with respect to the level and structure of its charges and right to purchase petroleum liquids for its own operations for purposes such as testing and commissioning of facilities, compression purposes and line fill.[260]

143. A number of statutory conditions are attached to a petroleum liquids transportation network operator licence. These may include an obligation to develop market rules in accordance with the provisions of the Act. A petroleum liquids transportation network operator may be the owner of any or all of the petroleum liquids transportation pipelines in the petroleum liquids transportation network. Where third parties are owners of certain petroleum liquids transportation pipelines in the petroleum liquids transportation network, the owners shall be paid by the petroleum liquids transportation network operator the tariffs determined for non-operating owners of the pipelines.[261] The operator shall avoid creating a monopoly position in the geographical area to charge franchise or other access charges for providing access to the petroleum liquids transport network other than the charges specifically permitted under the PIA and regulations made pursuant thereto.[262]

V. Wholesale Petroleum Liquids Supply Licence

144. A wholesale petroleum liquids supply licence may be granted to a qualified person by the Authority upon an application and payment of prescribed fees.[263] For this purpose, 'a qualified person' shall include a company that is a lessee producing crude oil or condensates or both or is a holder of a crude oil refining licence and shall be entitled to apply for and be issued a wholesale petroleum liquids supply licence by the Authority.[264] A wholesale petroleum liquids supply licence entitles and authorizes the supplier to sell and deliver petroleum liquids to bulk customers in Nigeria or for export.[265]

145. A wholesale petroleum liquids supplier shall undertake the activities contemplated by the licence in addition to providing a reliable supply of petroleum liquids to purchasers on request, provided that it is economically feasible. It shall also abstain from activities, which in the opinion of the Authority may prevent, restrict

260. *See* s. 195(a–c) of the PIA.
261. *See* s. 196(1–3) of the PIA.
262. *Ibid.*, subs. (4).
263. Section 197(1) of the PIA.
264. *Ibid.*, subs. (2).
265. *Ibid.*, subs. (3).

or distort competition.[266] A wholesale petroleum liquids supplier has a right to terminate wholesale supply to a customer in the event of non-payment, recover from a customer on the basis of an invoice as well as right to enter a premises for the purpose of reading the meters, testing, maintaining metering equipment, disconnecting customers and to remove meters.[267]

146. A number of statutory obligations are imposed on a wholesale petroleum liquids supplier and include ensuring a reliable and efficient supply of petroleum liquids to customers on request, provided that it is economically feasible. It must ensure the supply of petroleum liquids on request to a customer who is willing and able to pay for connection to the transportation network or transportation pipeline, subject to safety and network capacity constraints as well as conduct licensed activities safely, reliably and in an environmentally friendly manner in compliance with any law in force and any health and safety related regulations issued by the Authority.[268] The licensee or petroleum liquids supplier shall undertake its licensed activities in a manner that best complies with the covenants and conditions of the licence and with due regard to customer protection measures approved by the Authority.[269]

VI. Licence for Distribution of Petroleum Products

147. A licence may be granted to a qualified person by the Authority for distribution of Petroleum products upon an application and payment of statutory fees, and subject to general conditions for licences under sections 111 and 174 of the PIA.[270] General duties of petroleum product distributor include developing and maintaining a safe, efficient, reliable and economical service for the distribution of petroleum products to individual customers and petroleum product retailers. It must carry on its business in a manner that will promote competition and avoid monopoly in the retail supply of petroleum products in Nigeria and conduct its licensed activities safely and reliably in compliance with any law in force and prescribed environmental, health and safety regulations. It must also publish the prices to be charged and to be paid by a person to whom the distributor sells petroleum products in a manner to ensure adequate publicity unless the Authority prescribes otherwise. The licensee must also avoid undue preference or discriminate between persons or any class of persons in establishing prices as well as comply with customer protection measures approved by the Authority.[271]

---

266. *See* s. 198(a–b) of the PIA.
267. *See* s. 199(a–c).
268. Section 200(1) (a–c) of the PIA.
269. *Ibid.*, subs. (2).
270. Section 201 of the PIA.
271. Section 202 (a–f).

VII. Licence to Construct and Operate a Facility for Retail Supply and Distribution

148. The Authority is also empowered by the PIA to grant a licence to construct and operate a facility for retail supply and distribution of petroleum products, as in the case of others, subject to sections 111 and 174 of the PIA. The licence is issued to a qualified person to establish, construct and operate a facility to be employed for retail sale of petroleum products.[272] The Authority issues guidelines in respect of the process for the establishment, construction and operation of facilities to be employed by petroleum product retailers for the retail sale of petroleum products.[273]

VIII. Licence to Construct and Operate a Facility for the Production of Petrochemicals

149. Petrochemicals are one of the essential midstream and downstream petroleum liquids under the regulatory preview of the Authority. Therefore, subject to sections 111 and 174 of the PIA, and upon an application and payment of prescribed fees, the Authority may grant and issue to a qualified person a petrochemicals production licence which will authorize the holder to establish, construct and operate a facility for the production of petrochemicals as well as to sell the petrochemicals produced.[274] The activities and operations of a licensee shall be subject to guidelines issued by the Authority in respect of petrochemical production licences.[275]

IX. Contravention and Enforcement of Conditions of Leases, Licences or Permits

150. The Commission or Authority may issue contravention notice where it appears that the holder of a lease, licence or permit is contravening, has contravened or is likely to contravene any of the conditions of the lease, licence or permit to draw the attention of other persons affected or likely to be affected by the contravention or threatened contravention of the lease, licence or permit. The notice shall specify the actual or potential contravention. It shall also direct the holder to do or not to do, the things specified in the notice as well as stipulate the remedy and the timeframe for compliance. It may, where the situation requires, notify the holder of the lease, licence or permit of its intention to issue an enforcement order.[276]

---

272. Section 203 (1) of the PIA.
273. *Ibid.*, subs. (2).
274. Section 204(1) of the PIA.
275. *Ibid.*, subs. (2).
276. *See* s. 217(1)(a–c) of the PIA.

151. Contravention notice provides room for a fair hearing. The holder of the lease, licence or permit and any other interested party shall be entitled to make representations against or in support of a notice published on a date.[277] Failure to comply with the notice of contravention by a holder of the lease, licence or permit may leave the Commission or Authority with no alternative than to issue an enforcement order.[278] Enforcement order may not be issued if the holder of the lease, licence or permit is able to demonstrate to its satisfaction that it is not contravening or about to contravene a condition of a lease, licence or permit. The Commission or Authority may be persuaded against issuing a contravention order where the holder has ceased to contravene a condition of the lease, licence or permit. If the earlier contravention was deliberate, the Commission or Authority may impose a penalty as prescribed by regulation, at its discretion.[279] The Act provides for grave consequences for failure to comply with enforcement order. It states that:

> A holder of a lease, licence or permit who fails to comply with the enforcement order under this section, contravenes the provisions of this Act and is liable as follows, the:
>
> (a) Commission shall revoke the permit or recommend to the Minister to suspend or revoke the licence or lease.
> (b) Authority shall revoke the permit or recommend to the Minister to suspend or revoke the lease, licence.
> (c) Commission or Authority, as the case may be, shall impose any other penalty prescribed by regulations.[280]

152. The above penalties are not static and may be reviewed by a regulation in reflection of inflationary trends or for any other justifiable reason or reasons.[281] The Commission or Authority may order the sealing up of any premises, including any facility or plant engaged in petroleum operations, where there has been a contravention of the PIA or any regulation made pursuant to it.[282] In case of dispute between a lessee, licensee or permit holder and the Commission or the Authority, the Act provides that the Federal High Court 'shall settle' it.[283]

X. Jurisdiction of the Federal High Court to 'Settle'

153. It is very important to amplify that the above provisions are nebulous. It provides that 'any dispute between a lessee, licensee, or permit holder and the

277. *Ibid.*, subs. (2).
278. *Ibid.*, subs. (3).
279. *Ibid.*, subs. (4).
280. *Ibid.*, subs. (5)(a–c).
281. *Ibid.*, subs. (6).
282. *Ibid.*, subs. (7).
283. *See* s. 217(8) of the PIA *Ibid.*

Commission or Authority shall be settled by the Federal High Court'.[284] It fails to indicate whether the word 'settle' in the context of this provision means 'decide', 'mediate', 'adjudicate' or 'resolve'. The jurisdiction vested in the Federal High Court is to 'settle'. The word 'shall' is used in this provision to connote peremptory compliance. The simplest interpretation would appear to mean that the Federal High Court has a statutory duty of getting the parties to 'settle'. Adjudication may not necessarily 'settle' a dispute but impose a judgment that parties must comply with. Settlement may be achieved by mediation or other forms of alternative dispute resolution mechanisms. In this context, the emphasis is to 'settle', which connotes that the Federal High Court shall guide the parties to amicably resolve their dispute. It provides in clear terms that:

> 217. (8) Subject to any other provisions in this Act, any dispute between a lessee, licensee or permit holder and the Commission or the Authority shall be settled by the Federal High Court.

154. Potentially, the above provisions may rob the Federal High Court of jurisdiction to impose a judgement on the parties, as the court's role in this scenario is to, by law, 'settle' the disputes for parties (amicably) without imposing or giving judgement. This connotes that the Court 'SHALL' only exercise its settlement jurisdiction and may not have jurisdiction as to adjudication or any other forms of judicial determination or resolution including giving judgement in this situation.

155. The issue of jurisdiction of the Federal High Court could be contentious given the fact that exclusive jurisdiction of the Court is purely a Constitutional matter.[285] The reality of the provisions of section 217(8) analysed above is that, without contravening the above constitutional provisions, the Federal High Court would have jurisdiction to the extent and for the purpose specifically conferred by a particular statute. This further reinforces the above argument that the jurisdiction of the Federal High Court in this regard is limited to 'settling' the dispute among the parties, and nothing more as argued and illustrated above. It appears the Federal High Court cannot adjudicate or give a binding judgement on the dispute save for aiding 'settlement'. This is one of the most problematic provisions of the PIA that may subsequently become hotly litigated.

XI. Abandonment, Decommissioning and Disposal

156. In Nigeria, decommissioning and abandonment provisions of the PIA is similar, but structured differently. Decommissioning is now very strictly regulated under the PIA in line with international standards and global best practices. The decommissioning and abandonment of petroleum wells, installations, structures, utilities, plants and pipelines for petroleum operations on land and offshore shall be

284. *Ibid.* This provision is contentious as to the nature and extent of the jurisdiction vested in the Commission or Authority.

285. *See* s. 251(1) CFRN on exclusive jurisdiction of the Federal High Court.

conducted in accordance with good international petroleum industry practices and guidelines issued by the Commission or Authority in line with standards prescribed by the International Maritime Organisation (IMO) on offshore petroleum installations and structures.[286]

157. Decommissioning and abandonment shall not take place without the written approval of the Commission or Authority, which shall require a lessee, licensee or permit holder to commence the decommissioning and abandonment of a well, installation, structure, utility and pipeline, where such decommissioning and abandonment is required under good international petroleum industry practices or the guidelines.[287] Notice of intention to decommission or abandon by a licensee or lessee shall be in writing to the Commission or Authority.[288]

158. Installations and structures on land shall be completely removed and the environment restored to its original condition, except for buried transportation pipelines and gathering lines. The decommissioning and abandonment programme shall not be approved by the Commission or Authority unless relevant environmental, technical and commercial regulations or standards are complied with. Before approval, the Commission or Authority's considerations and recommendations shall be taken in light of individual circumstances. It shall also reflect the potential for reuse of a transportation pipeline together with other existing facilities in connection with further hydrocarbon developments before decommissioning. It must ensure that all feasible decommissioning options have been considered and a comparative assessment made and that any removal or

---

286. Section 232(1)(a–b) of the PIA.
287. *Ibid.*, subs. (2) and (3).
288. *Ibid.*, subs. (5). The Act further provides in subs. (6)(a–e) that:

> upon a notice in subsection (5), the lessee or licensee, shall prior to any decommissioning and abandonment, submit to the Commission or Authority, as the case may be, a programme setting out:
>
> (a) estimate of the cost of the proposed measures;
> (b) details of measures proposed to be taken in connection with the shutdown of operations and decommissioning and abandonment of disused installations, structures or other assets used in petroleum operations as the case may be;
> (c) clear descriptions of the methods to be employed to undertake the work programme, which shall be in line with good international petroleum industry practices and environmental development;
> (d) steps to be taken to ensure maintenance and safeguard, where any installation, structure or pipeline remained disused and in position or are to be partly removed with respect to deep and ultra-deep water environment and where the installation, structure or pipeline is partly removed, the licensee or lessee shall remain liable for any residual liability arising from the installation, structure or pipeline not removed; and
> (e) assessment of the environmental and social impact of the decommissioning and abandonment measures.

partial removal of an installation, structure or transportation pipeline is to be performed in a manner that guarantees sustainable environmental development.[289]

159. Pending obligations on decommissioning and abandonment plan shall be enforced by the Commission or Authority against any holder of a current licence or lease or a holder of an expired licence or lease who was responsible for the applicable decommissioning and abandonment plan with respect to a licence or lease that has expired to carry out its remaining or unfulfilled decommissioning and abandonment obligations.[290]

160. The Commission or Authority may recall a licensee or lessee responsible for a decommissioning and abandonment programme with respect to a licence or lease that has expired or is surrendered or a licensee or lessee that has transferred or divested its interest or equity, to carry out an obligation under the Act. Where a new company has assumed all respective obligations, upon prior approval of the Commission or Authority consequent to the transfer or divestiture, the licensee or lessee shall have no further responsibilities. The PIA imposes a duty on the Commission or Authority to keep a register or list of the installations, structures and pipelines on land and offshore in Nigeria being used for petroleum operations including their current status which shall be made available or accessible to the public annually.[291]

XII. Decommissioning and Abandonment Fund

161. This is a designated fund set up by the lessee and licensee to maintain and manage a decommissioning and abandonment plan held by a financial institution that is not an affiliate of the lessee or licensee, in the form of an escrow account. The fund shall exclusively be used to pay for decommissioning and abandonment costs and shall be accessible by the Commission or the Authority, under the provisions of the escrow agreement. Where funds have been accrued prior to the effective date, such funds shall form part of the decommissioning and abandonment fund established under the Act.[292] Where a lessee or licensee fails to comply with the decommissioning and abandonment plan, the fund shall be accessed by the Commission or Authority to pay for the performance by a third party of such lessee's or licensee's obligations under section 232 of the Act.

---

289. *Ibid.*, subs. (10)(a–d) of the PIA. By virtue of para. (e), the PIA further clarifies that any recommendation to leave an installation, structure or gathering line in place is made with regard to its likely deterioration and to the present, possible and future effects on the environment and in the case of offshore installations and structures, consistent with the applicable good international petroleum industry practices.

290. *Ibid.*, subs. (11).

291. *Ibid.*, subs. (13) and (14). However, subs. (12) provides that in archiving and maintaining the database of installations, structures and assets set out in subsection (14) the Commission or Authority, as the case may be, shall prescribe the manner and method in which the data shall be submitted by operators.

292. Section 233 (1) and (2) of the PIA.

162. The decommissioning and abandonment plan shall be designed in a way to establish the yearly amount to be contributed to the respective decommissioning and abandonment fund. The yearly amount shall be based on a reasonable estimate by the licensee or lessee of the applicable decommissioning and abandonment costs, projected to span the estimated life of the facilities cost estimates of which shall be approved by the Commission or Authority. The estimated life of the facilities shall be based on the estimated life of the field, in case of facilities used for upstream petroleum operations; and the period of time for which the safe operations of the facilities were designed, in case of facilities used for midstream petroleum operations.[293]

163. The estimated yearly contribution to the abandonment and decommissioning plan shall be reviewed every ten years and funded by the applicable licensee or lessee from the yearly amount contributed. For effective monitoring, the PIA provides that a licensee or lessee shall inform the Commission or Authority of the establishment of its decommissioning and abandonment fund not more than three months from the date of commencement of production for upstream petroleum operations or the commissioning of the facilities for midstream petroleum operations. It shall also furnish the Commission or Authority, on an annual basis with statements of accounts with respect to its decommissioning and abandonment fund.[294]

164. In respect of a farm-out agreement with one or more third parties, a decommissioning and abandonment plan funded in whole or in part by the applicable third parties shall be provided for in the applicable farm-out agreement. Contributions to the decommissioning and abandonment fund shall be eligible for, and as part of, cost recovery and also be tax deductible. This does not apply if it is disbursed from the decommissioning and abandonment fund.[295] This means it is recovery as costs and tax deductible is applicable only when paid into the fund by the lessee or licensee, but where it is a disbursement from the fund, it shall not be recoverable as costs and not tax deductible. This is to avoid the incidence of double tax benefits in respect of the same pool of funds. Excess of the decommissioning and abandonment fund shall be considered an income for production sharing or tax purposes and the amount after withholding profit oil and any tax shall be returned to the licensee or lessee.[296]

§10. Administration of Midstream and Downstream Gas Operations

165. The *PIA* makes extensive provisions for regulating the administration of midstream and downstream gas operations in Nigeria.[297] Chapter 4 of the PIA

293. *Ibid.*, subs. (6) of the PIA.
294. *Ibid.*, subs. (9)(a–b).
295. *Ibid.*, subs. (10) and (11).
296. *Ibid.*, subs. (12).
297. *See* generally part IV of the *Petroleum Industry Act*, 2021, ss 125–173.

generally provides for the administration of midstream and downstream gas operations and vests the *Nigerian Midstream and Downstream Petroleum Regulatory Authority* (the 'Authority')[298] with administrative and regulatory functions. The PIA provides a list of activities that must not be undertaken in the midstream and downstream gas operation unless with a licence issued by the Authority.[299] The Act restricts certain downstream gas activities and related operations without a licence from the Authority.[300]

I. Licences Requirement for Midstream and Downstream Gas Operations

166. The midstream and downstream gas operations or activities requiring licences from the Authority are contained in section 125 of the PIA. It includes activities to establish, construct or operate a facility for the processing of natural gas; establish, construct or operate a facility for the storage of natural gas; establish, construct or operate a gas transportation pipeline; engage in bulk transportation of natural gas by rail, barge or other means of transportation including to operate a gas transportation network. The PIA also listed activities for the purpose of establishing, constructing or operating a terminal, jetty, or other facility for the export or

298. *See* Part IV, s. 29 of the PIA. It provides thus:

29.

(1) There is established the *Nigerian Midstream and Downstream Petroleum Regulatory Authority* (in this Act referred to as 'the Authority'), which shall be a body corporate with perpetual succession and a common seal.
(2) The Authority shall have the power to acquire, hold and dispose of property, sue and be sued in its own name.
(3) The Authority shall be responsible for the technical and commercial regulation of midstream and downstream petroleum operations in the petroleum industry.

299. Section 125(1) of the PIA provides that except in accordance with an appropriate licence issued by the Authority, a person shall not undertake the following activities with respect to midstream and downstream gas operations:

(a) establish, construct or operate a facility for the processing of natural gas;
(b) establish, construct or operate a facility for the storage of natural gas;
(c) establish, construct or operate a gas transportation pipeline;
(d) engage in bulk transportation of natural gas by rail, barge or other means of transportation;
(e) operate a gas transportation network;
(f) establish, construct or operate a terminal, jetty, or other facility for the export or importation of natural gas;
(g) engage in wholesale gas supply; or
(h) engage in the construction or operation of petrochemical or fertiliser plants.

300. Subsection (2)(a–c) similarly provides that except in accordance with an appropriate licence issued by the Authority, a person shall not undertake the following activities with respect to downstream gas operations:

(a) retail trading, distribution or supplies of natural gas;
(b) establishment, construction or operation of a gas distribution network; or
(c) establishment, construction or operation of a facility for the supply or trading of natural gas.

importation of natural gas including engaging in wholesale gas supply or the construction or operation of petrochemical or fertiliser plants.[301]

167. The Authority may prescribe additional activities to be undertaken on the basis of a licence or permit and shall have the power to issue licences or permits for the activities in accordance with the Act.[302] It may seal the premises of a person who engages in any of the activities set out in subsection (1), (2) or (3) without a licence or permit. It may also seize the facilities by which the activities were undertaken; confiscate and dispose of equipment or materials employed by the person in the activity in a manner prescribed by regulations under the Act and may impose penalties as prescribed by regulations or any combination of penalties.[303]

II. Grant of a Gas Processing Licence

168. The PIA provides for the grant of a Gas Processing Licence (GPL) by the Authority subject to an application, approval and payment of prescribed fees. GPL is granted or issued to a qualified person to install and operate facilities on its own account or on the basis of open access for customers as stipulated in the licence. GPL may be granted for gas-related activities including gas conditioning plants, to condition natural gas removing $C0_2$, H_2S or other impurities; or for purposes of gas processing plants, to produce ethane, propane, butane, other natural gas liquids and marketable natural gas. It may also be issued for the purpose of gas to liquids plants; liquefied natural gas (LNG) plants; ethane extraction plants; and other plants, which in the opinion of the Authority, require a GPL.[304]

169. The PIA imposes a number of statutory duties and obligations on the holder of a GPL to construct, operate and maintain its gas processing equipment and facilities in an economical, safe, reliable and environment ally sustainable manner.[305] The licensee shall also avoid any act or omission that may affect the compatibility of the processing facility with any natural gas facility or network that is likely to prejudice public interest or the integrity of network operations and shall operate the facilities in a manner that results in output of products with specifications as determined by the Authority.[306]

301. *See* s. 125(1)(a–h) of the PIA, *supra* note 4.
302. *Ibid.*, subs. (3).
303. *Ibid.*, subs. (4)(a–e).
304. *See* generally s. 129(1)(a–f) of the PIA for a list of activities that may be issued Gas Processing Licences (GPLs) by the Authority. By subs. (28), the PIA provides that in considering an application for a gas processing licence, the Authority shall take into account the economic case for the specific facility, including the potential demand for its use.
305. *See* s. 130(a–c) of the PIA.
306. *Ibid.*, subs. (d–e).

III. Bulk Gas Storage Licence (B-GSL)

170. The PIA provides for the grant of B-GSL. It gives the Authority power to grant a Bulk Gas Storage Licence (B-GSL) subject to section 111 on licence application and a list of activities contained in section 125 of the Act. A B-GSL may be granted by the Authority upon an application and approval of the same and payment of prescribed fees. A B-GSL is granted to authorize the holder to undertake the bulk storage of natural gas either for its own account or on behalf of customers as stipulated in the licence.[307]

IV. General Duties of a Bulk Gas Storage Licensee

171. The holder of a bulk gas storage licence (B-GSL) shall undertake the activities contemplated by the licence in a manner that complies with listed statutory obligations, which include establishing and making available to the public at its offices, the procedure and terms for obtaining third-party access or through services on an open access basis.[308] B-GSL licensee also has an obligation to construct, operate and maintain its facilities in a safe, commercial, reliable, and environmentally sustainable manner taking into account any strategic plans formulated by the Authority or shut down its facilities in emergencies and in order to carry out maintenance or in response to curtailment directives issued by the Authority.[309]

172. The above-listed obligations also extend to where the B-GSL licensee operates for its own account, grant to third parties the right to use.[310] The statutory obligations of a licensee of B-GSL also cover conducting its licensed activities in a non-discriminatory manner under section 116 of the Act (General non-discrimination provisions),[311] where the licence is issued on an open access basis, as well as an obligation to manage its facilities as a reasonable and prudent operator and abstain from activities, which in the opinion of the Authority may prevent, restrict or distort competition.[312] The PIA allows the Authority to impose further peculiar conditions to a bulk gas storage licence in addition to those under section 114 of the Act.

---

307. *See* s. 132(1) of the PIA. Subsection (2) further provides that the Authority shall, in considering an application for a bulk gas storage licence, take into account the economic case for a bulk gas storage facility, including the potential demand for its use.
308. *See* s. 133(a)(i–ii).
309. *Ibid.*, subs. (b–c).
310. *Ibid.*, subs. (d–e).
311. Section of 116 of the PIA on 'General non- discrimination provisions' states that:

> A holder of a licence or permit shall not discriminate against customers, classes of customers or their related undertakings in respect of access, tariffs, prices, conditions or standards of service, except for justifiable and identifiable differences regarding matters such as quantity, transmission distance, length of contract, load profile, interruptible supply or other distinguishing features approved by the Authority.

312. *See* s. 133(f–j).

V. Grant of Gas Transportation Pipeline Licence

173. The grant of a Gas Transportation Pipeline Licence (G-TPL) is made subject to the provisions of section 111 on licence applications and section 125 of the Act on listed activities requiring a licence for midstream and downstream gas operations. The Authority is the statutory body vested with powers to grant a G-TPL upon an application and payment of prescribed fees.[313] A G-TPL is issued with the exclusive right to own, construct, operate and maintain a gas transportation pipeline within a route as defined in the licence for its own account with third-party access provisions or as common carrier as stipulated in the licence.[314]

174. General duty of a holder of G-TPL is to undertake the activities contemplated by the licence in a manner that complies with general obligations under the licence. The holder must establish and make available to the public at its offices, the procedure for obtaining and terminating transmission and interconnection services for natural gas, on a third-party access or open-access basis as determined in the licence and publish the tariffs established by the Authority and state the method of response to the request for its service.[315]

175. The G-TPL holder is to construct, operate and maintain its gas transportation pipeline in a safe, economical, and reliable manner taking into account any strategic plans formulated by the Authority. It is also expected to shut down its gas transportation pipeline in emergencies and in order to carry out maintenance or in response to curtailment directives issued by the Authority.[316] Holder of G-TPL must provide access on a non-discriminatory basis under section 116 of the PIA, where the licence is granted on a common carrier basis, as well as consult with and obtain from the Authority written permission prior to any modification of the technical and operational rule of practice concerning the operation of its pipeline.[317]

176. The holder also has a general duty to manage its gas transportation pipeline as a reasonable and prudent operator; and where the pipeline is operated on a common carrier basis, ensure the development and operation of terms for access to the gas transportation pipeline in conjunction with the natural gas shipping community in compliance with the relevant network code. The conditions applicable to a gas transportation pipeline licence are similar to those applicable to the bulk gas storage licence.[318]

313. *See* s. 135(1).
314. *Ibid.* Subsection (2) states that the Authority shall, in considering an application for a gas transportation pipeline licence, take into account the economic case for a gas transportation pipeline, including the potential demand for its use.
315. *See* s. 136(a)(i–ii).
316. *Ibid.*, subs. (b–d).
317. *Ibid.*, subs. (e–f).
318. *See* generally s. 133 of the PIA, *supra* note 4.

VI. Grant of Gas Transportation Network Operator Licence

177. The Gas Transportation Network Operator Licence (GT-NOP) also comes within the categories of midstream and downstream gas operation licences for which the PIA vests the Authority with statutory powers. Like other categories of licences, the GT-NOP is granted on similar terms and conditions for the conveyance of natural gas through the gas transportation network on an open-access basis; balancing the inputs and off takes from the gas transportation network; providing access to shippers based on the gas network code under section 160 of the Act[319] to the gas transportation network; and charging for the use of the gas transportation network based on tariffs established by the Authority.[320]

178. The general duties, rights and obligations of a gas transportation network operator are similar to other categories of operators. This includes establishing and making available to the public at its offices, the procedure, terms and conditions for obtaining and terminating access and interconnection services to the transportation network, and method of response to the request for its service and a long list of duties similar to other categories of operators.[321]

179. The Act vests the Authority with powers to grant the operator of GT-NOP statutory privileges for the purpose of its operations and activities. The operator has the right to recover on the basis of an invoice expenses reasonably incurred in undertaking its licensed activities, subject to any restrictions or conditions imposed by the Authority with respect to both the level and structure of its charges. It may also purchase natural gas for its own operations.[322]

VII. Wholesale Gas Supply Licence

180. The grant of a Wholesale Gas Supply Licence (WGSL) to a qualified person is based on an application and payment of prescribed fees.[323] Preference is

319. Section 160 of the PIA provides for Gas network code, that:

(1) The operation of a gas transportation network shall be in accordance with the existing network code issued by the Government.
(2) The Authority may in consultation with stakeholders in midstream and downstream gas operations modify the network code or create other network codes for common carrier operations.
(3) The Authority shall make copies of the gas network code available to interested parties upon payment of prescribed fees.

320. *See* s. 138(1) of the PIA. Subsection (2) states that the Authority shall grant only one gas transportation network operator licence within a geographically defined area to a single network operator, provided that the Authority may at its discretion, issue licences to other parties for the operation of isolated or dedicated gas transportation pipelines and for connecting to the gas transportation network.
321. *See* s. 139(a)(i–ii).
322. *See* s. 140(a–c) of the PIA.
323. Section 142(1–3).

given to a company that is a lessee producing natural gas. The Act uses the word 'shall be entitled to apply for and be issued' with a wholesale gas supply licence by the Authority. This ordinarily connotes that any qualified lessee of a natural gas-producing licence is automatically qualified to be granted a WGSL.[324]

181. A wholesale gas supply licence authorizes the supplier to: (a) purchase natural gas directly from any lessee or third party; and (b) sell and deliver wholesale gas to wholesale customers and gas distributors at any location in Nigeria.[325] General duties of a wholesale gas supplier as listed in the PIA include that the holder shall undertake the activities contemplated by the WGSL in a manner that complies with the general obligations to provide a reliable supply of wholesale gas to wholesale customers who have entered into a gas purchase and sale agreement with the supplier as well as abstain from activities, which in the opinion of the Authority may prevent, restrict or distort competition.[326]

182. The rights granted to a wholesale gas supplier are balanced against certain conditions imposed by the Act under section 114 dealing with general conditions of licences or permits, as well as those the Authority may impose.[327] For this purpose, a WGSL shall be deemed to be granted subject to the supplier requesting security or applying a credit scoring methodology approved by the Authority in deciding whether supply is economical.[328] The WGSL is further deemed granted subject to conducting its licensed activities safely and reliably in compliance with any law in force and prescribed health and safety regulations issued under the PIA or any other Act. The licensee is also to comply with customer protection measures in accordance with sections 164, 165 and 166 of the Act as well as conduct or undertake its licensed activities in a manner that complies with the conditions of the licence.[329]

VIII. Retail Gas Supply Licence

183. The Authority may, in a similar vein, grant a retail gas supply licence (RGSL) authorizing the holder to sell or retail compressed or liquefied marketable natural gas to customers based on being a wholesale customer or third-party access to gas distribution systems of gas distributors.[330] The licence authorizes the holder to establish, construct and operate facilities to deliver compressed natural gas and small-scale facilities for LNG not requiring a gas processing licence, for transportation by truck, railcar or marine vessel to customers in compressed or liquefied form, including customers using LNG as marine bunker fuel.[331] An RGSL entitles

324. *Ibid.*, subs. (1).
325. *Ibid.*, subs. (3).
326. *See* s. 143 (a–b) of the PIA.
327. *See* generally s. 145 of the Act.
328. *Ibid.*, subs. 1(a).
329. *Ibid.*, subs. 1(c). *See also* subs. (2) which imposes general obligation to comply with conditions of the licence.
330. *See* s. 146(1)(a–b).
331. *Ibid.*, subs. (2) of the PIA.

the retailer to purchase marketable natural gas directly from a lessee, wholesale gas supplier or third party on a free market basis and sell as well as deliver compressed or LNG to customers at any location in Nigeria on a free market basis.[332]

IX. Gas Distribution Licence

184. Gas distribution licence (GDL) may be granted by the Authority on terms similar to other categories of licences with rights to establish, construct, and operate a gas distribution system and to distribute and sell its natural gas without discrimination to consumers in a local distribution zone. A holder of a GDL is entitled to sell natural gas to customers that are not wholesale customers.[333] Once a GDL is granted, the rights and duties under the licence shall be exclusive to the gas distributor for the validity period of the distribution licence.[334] A GDL may be granted to include provisions for providing third-party access to the gas distribution network to a gas retailer or gas distributor on its own initiative and to permit access to a gas retailer to the gas distribution network under terms and conditions agreed to by the parties.[335]

185. Upon a grant by the Authority, a GDL shall undertake a number of statutory duties as provided by the PIA to develop, operate and maintain an economical gas distribution network for the safe and reliable conveyance of natural gas as well as ensure reliable and efficient distribution of natural gas to customers on request, provided that it is economical to do so.[336] It also includes a duty to distribute and sell natural gas on request to a customer who is willing and able to pay for connection to the gas distribution network, subject to safety and network capacity constraints. By law, it must conduct licensed activities safely and reliably in compliance with any law in force and any health and safety-related regulations issued by the Authority under the PIA or any other Act.[337]

186. The statutory duties imposed on the gas distributor include to connect all customers within its local distribution zone in accordance with regulations if economically practicable to do so as well to offer and publish terms and conditions of access to its gas distribution network as required including gas prices applicable to different classes of customers, which have been approved by the Authority.[338] The gas distributor shall also prepare a distribution development plan (DDP),[339] within

332. *Ibid.*, subs. (3)(a–b).
333. *See* s. 148(1–2) of the PIA. However, by subs. (3–4), the Authority shall, in considering an application for a gas distribution licence, take into account the economic case for the licence, including the potential demand for its use, and the geographical limit of a local distribution zone shall be defined in the relevant gas distribution licence.
334. *Ibid.*, subs. (5).
335. *Ibid.*, subs. (6)(a–b).
336. Section 149(a–b).
337. *Ibid.*, subs. (c–d).
338. *Ibid.*, subs. (e–f).
339. This is also subject to arrangement for gas distribution under s. 152 of the PIA. It states that:

one year after the effective date or after having been granted the licence, for connecting customers within its local distribution zone. Any amendments to DDP must be based on economic or social developments in the zone which must be considered and approved by the Authority.[340]

X. Domestic Gas Aggregation Licence

187. Domestic gas aggregation licence (DGAL) is granted by the Authority subject to sections 111 and 125, for a period of two years effective from the date of the grant of the licence. It is renewable for a further period of two years in each instance until the attainment of liquidity in the domestic gas market pursuant to the criteria of section 167 (3) of the Act, after which gas aggregation shall cease and the domestic gas aggregation licence shall be terminated by the Authority. The board of domestic gas aggregators shall determine the fees for the services which shall be paid by the producer clients and customer clients in order to ensure self- financing of the domestic gas aggregator.[341]

188. Functions of a domestic gas aggregator shall include supporting the implementation of the domestic gas delivery obligation as well as implementing a natural gas management model through which the demand and supply of natural gas for use in the strategic sectors shall be monitored.

189. The aggregator is also tasked with the responsibility of conducting its operations in a business-like and transparent manner. This also includes a restriction that it shall not engage in any anti-competitive behaviour and practices, and abstain from activities that may restrict or distort competition. It shall also establish an escrow account into which customer clients shall contribute their payments for the marketable natural gas received and from which the domestic gas aggregator shall pay the producer clients for their supplies. It shall likewise undertake all things necessary or incidental to the carrying out of its functions and duties under the Act.[342]

190. The domestic gas aggregator shall be a not-for-profit company limited by guarantee established under the CAMA. This means an entity that performs the function of domestic gas aggregator shall not be a company that is controlled by licensees or lessees of upstream petroleum operations or by wholesale customers or is an affiliate of such entities. A permissible exception is where the ownership of the

---

A gas distributor shall consult stakeholders on the proposed distribution development plan and any amendments within its local distribution zone and consider all representations received.

340. *Ibid.*, subs. (g–i).
341. Section 153(1–4) of the PIA.
342. *Ibid.*, subs. (e–h).

company is by a combination of licensees or lessees, wholesale customers and other interested parties, such as licensees of gas transportation pipelines and gas transportation networks.[343]

XI. Wholesale Customers

191. The PIA recognizes customers as crucial stakeholders in the gas sector. The Authority shall consult with interested stakeholders in issuing regulations for defining the class or classes of customers that shall constitute eligible wholesale customers under the Act. The classification shall specify the qualifying criteria which may be amended from time to time to facilitate the introduction of competition in supply. The Authority shall develop arrangements for the safe and efficient trading of wholesale gas where it determines that there is a need for formal arrangements for the trading of wholesale gas. It may also issue appropriate regulations for the trading and settlement of wholesale gas in consultation with industry participants and interested stakeholders.[344]

§11. Technology Transfer and Energy Regulation in Nigeria

192. In the municipal petroleum industry, technology transfer is usually governed by national legislation, and by contractual clauses. At the time oil was discovered in Nigeria, there was little or no indigenous manpower to explore petroleum and its allied resources in the country.[345] The country also lacked the technical ability or skills to negotiate technology transfer agreements that would be favourable in the long term for rapid development. Unwittingly, Nigeria and its agencies signed and/or executed technology agreements that proved directly or indirectly inimical to the national interest. Such agreements contained monopoly pricing and restrictive business practices, ranging from export restrictions, discriminatory royalty rates, coercive packaging, and tie-in-clause, dealing with capital equipment, raw materials and components, most of which were tied to the strings of the technology suppliers.[346] In most contracts, provisions on Research and Development were non-existent while little or no attention was paid to the training of Nigerian staff. In several instances multinational oil companies often take undue advantage of Nigeria by insisting on the 'stabilization' effects of such contracts, showing utter unwillingness to 'renegotiate'.[347]

343. *See* s. 155(1–2) of the PIA.
344. Section 159(1–2).
345. Yinka Omorogbe, *Oil and Gas Law in Nigeria* (Malthouse Press Limited, 2001) at p. 16.
346. *Ibid.*
347. The issue of 'stabilization' and 'renegotiation' clauses in energy contracts often become needlessly contentious. *See* for example, S.K.B. Asante, 'The Stability of Contractual Relations in the Transnational Investment Process' (1979) 28 *International and Comparative Law Quarterly*, 406; and F.A. Mann, 'The Proper Law of Contracts Concluded by International Persons' (1959) 35 *Brit. Y.B.*

193. The above and other challenges created the ineluctable need for regime change. The Petroleum Decree No. 51 of 1969 (now Petroleum Act) was promulgated[348] by the Nigerian government to bridge the gap and to impose regulatory provisions making it 'a matter of law' for the oil companies to employ Nigerian personnel rather than expatriate staff. The regulation specified that at least 60% of managerial, professional and supervisory categories and 75% of the total senior staff be Nigerians by January 1970 at the earliest and by December 1978 at the latest.[349] This is what in some quarters is termed the 'Nigerianization' policy.[350] In response to this, the foreign companies supported the establishment of departments and appropriate curricula for the training of Nigerians in oil-related technological, science and engineering disciplines in Nigerian Universities through the award of scholarships and grants.[351]

194. The era of indigenization would appear to have foisted a 'process of Nigerianization' of foreign interest covering other areas of the economy through the repealed *Nigerian Enterprises Promotion Acts* No. 4 of 1972, and the *Nigerian Enterprises Promotion Acts* No. 3 of 1977, respectively.[352] The indigenization policy impacted in such a manner that it had the effect of divesting totally or in various percentages, the ownership of foreign interest in most businesses in favour of Nigerians commencing from the dates stated in the repealed acts. However, in the case of the upstream petroleum companies, government acquisition did not extend to ownership of shares in such enterprises, but only stakes in their operations.[353]

Int'l L. 34, 56; Virtus Chitoo Igbokwe, 'Determination, Interpretation and Application of Substantive Law in Foreign Investment Treaty Arbitrations' (2006) 23:4 *Journal of International Arbitration,* 267–299; Virtus Chitoo Igbokwe, 'Developing Countries and the Law Applicable to International Arbitration of Oil Investment Disputes' (1997) 14 *Journal of International Arbitration,* 99–124.

348. Petroleum Decree No. 51 of 1969 later became designated 'The Petroleum Act, Cap P 30, LFN 2004, with the advent of democratic regime.

349. T. Turner, 'The *Transfer of Oil Technology and the Nigerian State. Development and Change,* (1976) p. 378.

350. The Nigerian government had continued to introduce various policy and legal framework to change or reposition the country's petroleum sector. In 1972 the government issued an indigenization decree, which barred aliens from investing in specified enterprises and reserved participation in certain trades to Nigerians. At the time, about 70% of commercial firms operating in Nigeria were foreign-owned. In 1975 the Federal Government bought 60% equity in the marketing operations of the major oil companies in Nigeria, as full nationalization was rejected as a means of achieving the objective of indigenization. The indigenization policy of the government attempted to strengthen the Nigerian economy through one or a combination of the following objectives: (a) the transfer of ownership and control to Nigerians in respect of those enterprises formally wholly or mainly owned and controlled by foreigners; (b) fostering widespread ownership of enterprises among Nigerian citizens; (c) the creation of opportunities for Nigerian indigenous businessmen; and (d) the encouragement of foreign businessmen and investors to move from the unsophisticated area of the economy where large investments are more needed.

351. *Ibid.*

352. *Ibid.*, at 19.

353. *Ibid.*

195. A sharp policy reversal was noticed with the repeal of the two acts and the enactment of the *Nigerian Enterprises Promotion (Repeal) Act*, No. 7 1995.[354] For instance, total decentralization, deregulation and de-indigenization of the oil and gas sector of Nigeria were brought to bear under the new investment promotion law, unlike the old indigenization regime.[355] Prior to the local content regime, the interest of the Nigerian government in the oil and gas sector was limited to enforcing a few petroleum regulations that existed including collection of taxes from the oil companies particularly with the passing of the *Petroleum Profits Tax* in 1959.[356] The absence of the Nigerian Government's participation in the petroleum sector before 1971 arose from Nigeria's underdeveloped colonial economy.[357]

196. Nigeria's interests in the oil and gas sector were limited to nominal ownership of the petroleum *in situ*, and collection of taxes, royalties and lease rentals, the rates of which were usually either influenced or dictated by transnational companies.[358] The local content policy is also embedded with the objective of 'technology transfer'. One of the policy measures put in place for achieving these includes designated funds for petroleum technology.

197. On 4 June 1973, the Petroleum Technology Development Fund (PTDF) was established as a fund for the purpose of training and educating Nigerians in the petroleum industry.[359] By virtue of the provisions of section 1, the establishment of the fund is for the purpose of paying moneys comprising the balance of monetary assets outstanding in the accounts of the Gulf Oil Company Training Fund at the commencement of this act. It also pays all further sums payable to or received by the minister charged with responsibilities for matters relating to petroleum development in terms of any agreement made by the government and any company in relation to petroleum oil prospecting or mining concessions. The funds also pay any other sums, from time to time, freely donated or accruing to the government or the fund for the training and education of Nigerians in the petroleum industry as the said minister may direct, and moneys in the said fund together with interest (if any) payable in respect thereof shall be applied for the purposes specified in section 2 of this act.[360]

198. In 1975, the Petroleum Training Institute (PTI) was established towards the development of technological capabilities in the oil industry.[361] The purpose of its establishment was to provide course instruction, training and research in petroleum

354. *Ibid.*, at 16–17.
355. *See* ss. 20 and 27, *Nigerian Investment Promotion Act,* Cap N117 Laws of the Federation of Nigeria 2004 which states the requirements of foreign investment in Nigeria.
356. *Ibid.*
357. *See* G. Etikerentse, *Nigerian Petroleum Law* (2nd ed.) (Dredew Publishers, 2004) at 17.
358. *Ibid.*
359. Established by *The Petroleum Technology Development Fund Act* 1973; now Cap P15, Laws of the Federation of Nigeria, 2004.
360. *Ibid.*
361. Established by the *Petroleum Training Institute Decree* No. 37 of 1972 (now Act, 1972, Cap. P16 LFN 2004).

technology and to produce technicians and skilled personnel required for oil production.[362] In further pursuit of the objective of enhancing local manpower and technology, a merger between the MPR and the Nigerian National Oil Corporation (NNOC), led to the establishment of the Nigerian National Petroleum Corporation (NNPC) in 1977.[363] Part of its aim was the regulation of foreign and local producing firms, advancing technology transfer and the development of local content and indigenous participation in the industry. In a bid to further these aims, three upstream subsidiary companies were established in 1988; the Nigerian Engineering and Technical Company (NETCO), the Nigerian Petroleum Development Company (NPDC) and the Integrated Data Services Limited (IDSL). However, despite these seemingly positive steps towards the gradual achievement of a successful technology transfer and indigenous participation in the oil and gas industry, not much success was recorded.

§12. Overview of Statutory Provisions on Technology Transfer

199. To breathe life, meaning and purpose into the policy of the Nigerian Government in the area of technology development and transfer, particularly in the energy sector of the country, a number of enactments and other statutory provisions have been made and/or inserted into sector instruments by way or acts, laws, policies, regulations among others. Notable ones among such statutory instruments are briefly examined below with particular emphasis on provisions for the transfer of technology in the energy sector.

I. The Repealed Petroleum Act 1969

200. There are no specific provisions hinging on technology transfer in the Petroleum Act 1969.[364] However, paragraph 38 of Schedule 1 stipulates that:

> The holder of an oil mining lease shall ensure that:
>
> (a) within ten years from the grant of his lease:
>   (i) the number of citizens of Nigeria employed by him in connection with the lease in managerial, professional and supervisory grades (or any corresponding grades designated by him in a manner approved by the minister) shall reach at least 75% of the total number of persons employed by him in those grades; and
>   (ii) the number of citizens of Nigeria in any one such grade shall not be less than 60% of the total; and
>
> (b) all skilled, semi-skilled and unskilled workers are citizens of Nigeria.

362. Section 1(2)(a) of the *Petroleum Training Institute Act.*
363. Established by Decree No. 33 of 1977 (now Act), Cap N123 LFN 2004.
364. Petroleum Act 1969, Cap. P10 Laws of Federation of Nigeria (LFN) 2004.

201. In addition, the Petroleum (Drilling and Production) Regulations 1969 made pursuant to the powers conferred upon the Minister by the Petroleum Act,[365] imposes specific obligations on the holders of oil mining leases and Oil Prospecting Licences (OPL) to train and employ Nigerians.[366] The regulations also require oil prospecting licensees to prepare and submit (to the minister for approval) a detailed programme for the recruitment and training of Nigerians in all phases of petroleum operations.[367] The petroleum operator has an obligation to report on the training programme and the process of 'Nigerianization' at or about the end of June or December each year.[368] These provisions are aimed at ensuring that companies utilize local manpower in their exploration and production activities and therefore increase indigenous participation. Failure to comply with these provisions is a ground for the revocation of a lease at the instance of the minister.[369]

II. The Nigerian Oil and Gas Industry Content Development Act 2010

202. The *Nigerian Oil and Gas Industry Content Development Act* 2010[370] aims essentially at enhancing indigenous participation in the Nigerian energy sector.[371] The act is the first legislative enactment that has specific provisions on technology transfer in the oil and gas industry. Sections 43–46 contain requirements on technology transfer which oil and gas operators must comply with. Under this act, each operator shall carry out a programme in accordance with the country's own plans and priorities, to the satisfaction of the board,[372] for the promotion of technology transfer to Nigeria in relation to its oil and gas activities.[373] The operator is to submit an annual plan to the board, setting out a programme of planned initiatives aimed at promoting the effective transfer of technologies from the operator and alliance partners to Nigerian individuals and companies.[374]

203. The act also imposes a duty on the operator to give full and effective support to technology transfer by encouraging and facilitating the formation of joint

365. Section 9.
366. Part IV of the regulations, para. 26(1).
367. *Ibid.*, para. 26(2).
368. *Ibid.*, para. 29.
369. Schedule 1, para. 26(1) (b) of the Petroleum Act states that where the holder of a lease has failed to comply with any provision of the Act or any other regulation or direction given under it or is not fulfilling his obligations under the special conditions of his licence or lease the minster can revoke his licence.
370. *See* the *Nigerian Oil & Gas (Industry and Content Development) Act*, 2010 (Hereinafter referred to as 'Local Content Act'.
371. The effect of the local content act on technological transfer in Nigeria (Nigeria oil & gas) online at: http://www.nigeria-oil-gas.com/nigerian local content -26-10-2-art.html, accessed 19 May 2013.
372. The Nigerian Content Monitoring Board responsible for monitoring, coordinating and implementing the provisions of the Act.
373. Section 43.
374. Section 44.

ventures, partnering and the development of licensing agreements between Nigerians and foreign contractors and service or supplier companies. To this extent, agreements for all such joint ventures or alliances shall meet the requirements of Nigerian content development to the satisfaction of the board.[375] The operator or project promoter shall submit a report to the board annually describing its technology transfer initiatives and their results. It also requires the minister to make regulations setting targets on the number and type of such joint ventures or alliances to be achieved for each project.[376]

204. In addition to the foregoing, there are provisions contained in the act which can be linked to the achievement of technology transfer in the petroleum industry. First consideration is to be given to Nigerians in terms of consideration for employment and training in any project executed by any operator or project promoter in the Nigerian oil and gas industry.[377] In furtherance of this, every operator or project promoter is required to submit an Employment and Training Plan (E and T Plan) to the board and report to the board quarterly on the same.[378] Where Nigerians are not employed because of their lack of training, the operator shall ensure, to the satisfaction of the board that every reasonable effort is made within a reasonable time to supply such training locally or elsewhere and such effort and the procedure for its execution shall be contained in the operator's E and T plan.[379]

205. To improve local technological capability, detailed provisions on Research and Development (R&D) are also contained in the act. One such is that the minister shall make regulations on the requirements and targets for the growth of research and development in the Nigerian oil and gas industry.[380] For every project for which a plan is submitted, an operator shall carry out a programme and make expenditures, to the satisfaction of the board, for the promotion of education, attachments, training, research and development in Nigeria in relation to its work programme and activities.[381]

206. The Act also provides that the operator is to submit to the board and update every six months, the Research and Development Plan (R&D);[382] which would outline a three-to five-year plan for oil and gas-related research and development initiatives to be undertaken in Nigeria, together with a breakdown of the expected expenditure that will be made in implementing their R&D Plan.[383] The plan is to include calls for proposals for R&D initiatives associated with the operators'

375. Section 45.
376. Section 46.
377. Section 28.
378. Section 29.
379. Section 30.
380. Section 36.
381. Section 37.
382. Section 38(1).
383. Section 38(2)(a).

activities.[384] The operator is mandated to give a quarterly report of its activities in respect of its R&D Plan and the board will compare its activities to its R&D Plan.[385]

384. Section 38(2)(b).
385. Section 39.

Chapter 2. Electricity Law in Nigeria

§1. Introduction

207. The Nigerian Government enacted the *Electric Power Sector Reform (EPSR) Act* 2005 (the Act),[386] in keeping pace with the global trends in electricity governance. Under the new regime, the Nigerian Electricity Regulatory Commission (NERC) is to serve as the main regulatory body of the electric power sector. The responsibilities of NERC include licensing of successor power companies establishment of electricity tariffs, enforcement of performance standards and the protection of consumer rights. The existence of NERC is brought about by the *Act*,[387] which repeals and replaces the old NEPA and *Electricity Act*.[388] It also removes the operational and regulatory responsibilities of the electric power sector from the Federal Government of Nigeria and provides the legal basis for the restructuring of NEPA by establishing new regulatory structures.

208. The Act establishes three institutions, namely the National Electricity Regulatory Commission (NERC), which is the main regulatory body; the Rural Electrification Agency (REA), and the Power Consumer Assistance Fund (PCAF). By these reforms, the monopoly hitherto enjoyed by the erstwhile National Electric Power Authority (NEPA) for several decades has been abrogated, as the new regime aims to liberalize the sector. However, despite the nomenclature shift from NEPA to Power Holding Company of Nigeria (PHCN), the problem of declining electricity generation from domestic power plants still persists. While the Nigerian electricity sector is agreeably liberalized, the sector has witnessed some divestments from private sector players and the collapse of deal talks with some potential private/ Independent Power Producers (IPPs). For example, initial investors of the Yola Distribution Company pulled back due to unfavourable terrain due to the Boko-Haram insurgency[389] and funding challenges.[390]

386. *See Electric Power Sector Reform* (EPSR) Act 2005, Cap E7, (Revised) Laws of the Federation of Nigeria (LFN), 2004.
387. *Ibid.*, s. 31.
388. *See National Electric Power Authority (NEPA) Act*, Cap N 33, Laws of the Federation (LFN) 2004.
389. For details on the nature, extent, cause and effect of the Boko-Haram insurgency *see* Yemi Oke, *International Criminal Court, Crimes Against Humanity And The Nigerian Boko Haram Islamist Group: Can Two Wrongs Make a Right? (2012–2013) Vol. XII–XIII, Indian Journal of International Law (The Indian Society of International Law (ISIL),* Yearbook of International Humanitarian and Refuge Law, New Delhi, India, 2014, at 156–188.
390. For example, Officials of Nigeria's Bureau of Public Enterprises and former investors in two electricity companies – Yola Electricity Distribution Company and Afam Power Plc – have recently on the funding and other challenges arising from the sale of Yola Distribution company met for the refund of USD 211.81 million which the investors had paid for the two companies. Integrated Energy Distribution and Marketing Company had acquired 60% equity in YEDC after paying USD 146.8 million. The Yola Disco was successfully privatized and handed over to the core investor in 2013. However, a force majeure was declared in 2015 by the core investor citing insecurity in the North-East region of the country where the company covers. Following this, the company was repossessed by the Federal Government. *See* 'The BPE, investors meet on USD 211 million refund for Afam, Yola Disco' Punch Newspaper, 17 Jan. 2019, Online at: https://punchng.com/bpe-investors-meet-on-211m-refund-for-afam-yola-disco/, accessed 28 Feb. 2019.

§2. History of Electricity Governance in Nigeria

209. The history of electricity in Nigeria dates back to 1896 under colonial rule when electricity was first produced in Ijora, Lagos by the British Colonial Government.[391] The country subsequently witnessed significant development in electricity generation with the establishment of the Nigerian Electricity Supply Company (NESCO), which commenced operations as an electric utility company with the construction of a hydroelectric power station at Kuru, near Jos.[392] NESCO commenced operations in 1929, pursuant to the Electricity Ordinance Act of 1929.[393] NESCO was a hydroelectric power station, as the major source of energy generation at the time was water, through dams. The station's output served some locations, mainly in the Northern part of the country.

210. In 1946, the colonial government took over electricity governance to ensure national spread for the benefit of the whole country by establishing the Public Works Department (PWD), to take over the responsibility of electricity supply in Lagos. Four years later, precisely in the year 1950, a central body was established by the Legislative Council under the colonial government, which transferred electricity supply and development to a central body known as the Electricity Corporation of Nigeria (ECN). The ECN was created pursuant to the Electricity Corporation Ordinance 1950.[394]

211. The Niger Dams Authority (NDA) was established by an Act of Parliament. The authority was responsible for the construction and maintenance of dams and other works on the River Niger and elsewhere. The NDA was statutorily responsible for generating hydro-based electricity as well as improving navigation and promoting fish brines and irrigation, among others.[395] The energy produced by the NDA was sold to ECN for distribution to end users as utility voltages. This represents a classical regime of electricity governance in which power generation was separated from distribution. Reversion to this model of regulation is being promoted under the new reforms.

212. Fusion of generation and transmission began formally in Nigeria on 1 April 1962 when the amalgamation of the two existing organizations, namely the ECN and the NDA, was effected by a military decree, the *National Electric Power Authority Decree No. 4*,[396] to form a new organization known as the National Electric Power Authority (NEPA). NEPA replaced both the ECN and the NDA and was

391. Niger Power Review: 'Development of Electricity Industry in Nigeria' (1960–1985), 1985, pp. 1–6.
392. Nkiruka, C.M., *Unbundling and Privatisation of the Nigerian Electricity Sector: Reality of Myth?* (LL.M paper, CEPMLP, University of Dundee), 2010 at p. 2.
393. *See Electricity Ordinance Act of 1929.*
394. *See Electricity Corporation Ordinance* No. 15 of 1950.
395. Manafa, N., *Electricity Development in Nigeria*, Rasheen Publisher, Lagos, 1995, pp. 37–51.
396. *See* the *National Electric Power Authority Decree No. 4*, Signed on 7 Jun. 1972.

mainly and exclusively responsible for the generation and distribution of electricity in Nigeria.[397] The rationale offered for the merger was that:

> It would result in the vesting of the production and the distribution of electricity power supply throughout the country in one organization which will assume responsibility for the financial obligations. The integration of the ECN and NDA should result in a more effective utilization of the human, financial and other resources available to the electricity supply industry throughout the country.[398]

213. Generally, hydroelectricity held sway simultaneously with coal as the main source of power generation in Nigeria. But coal production and consumption were targeted at supplementing a particular sector, as most of the country's coal production was consumed locally, mainly for railway transportation. The electricity sector was the second largest user of coal resource in the country, and a huge amount of coal production in Nigeria was utilized from 1992–2002.[399]

214. After about four decades, NEPA was unable to successfully manage electricity generation, transmission and distribution in Nigeria. Consumer apathy was at its peak. The organization also got itself enmeshed in institutional corruption, administrative ineptitude and needless bureaucratic inconsistencies.[400] The organization went through a series of transformations and reforms, all without meaningful, positive outcomes, resulting in the emergence of the Power Holding Company of Nigeria (PHCN), the initial holding company prior to the privatization of the sector. NEPA was unbundled and divided into eighteen new companies and semi-autonomous business units. The moribund NEPA was divested of its wholly government interests, with a view to ensuring adequate generation, distribution and utilization of efficient and stable electricity nationwide.

§3. Electricity Regulation under NEPA

215. The merger of ECN and NDA gave rise to the National Electric Power Authority on 11 April 1972. NEPA was established as a vertically integrated monopoly responsible for the generation, transmission and distribution of power in

397. Power Sector Reforms in Nigeria: Opportunities and Challenges by O.I. Okoro, P. Govender and E. Chikuni.
398. Niger Power Review: 'Development of Electricity Industry in Nigeria (1960–1989)', 1989, pp. 10–15.
399. O.I. Okoro et al., *supra* note 397.
400. *See* Yemi Oke:

    - (2018) 'Beyond Power Sector Reforms: The Real Business of technology-driven power generation, transmission and distribution in Nigeria' an industry-wide research sponsored by Good Governance Africa (GGA).
    - (2017) Corruption in the Nigerian Power Sector: 1999 to 2015 sponsored by *Socio-Economic Rights and Accountability Project (SERAP)*.

Nigeria. By virtue of the NEPA Decree,[401] all commercial electric supply shall be the exclusive preserve of NEPA. This monopoly continued until the regime of privatization and commercialization began in 1988.

216. The commercialization and privatization regime[402] listed NEPA as one of the state enterprises to be commercialized. The activities of the Technical Committee on Privatization and Commercialization (TCPC), otherwise called the Committee on Privatization, led to the enactment of the *NEPA Act*[403] to replace the old *NEPA Decree of 1972*. The new *NEPA Act* re-established NEPA as a commercial and self-accounting authority with powers to develop and maintain an efficient, coordinated and economically viable electricity supply in every part of Nigeria.[404] NEPA was also vested with powers over all assets of existing institutions and bodies.[405] Pursuant to the old act, licence may be obtained by an independent body to supply electricity in accordance with the terms of the licensing authority.[406]

217. The repealed Electricity Act 1990 regulates and controls all aspects of electricity in Nigeria, which include electrical installations, generation, supply, consumption and others. The legal framework of electricity in the NEPA era included the repealed NEPA Act and regulations made pursuant to the Act. The *Electricity Act* comprised of four regulations.[407] The *Electricity Supply Regulations* comprised of three parts. Part I deals with regulations prescribing the conditions on which licences may be issued and the fees payable for such licences. Part II deals with controlling the use and management of any works or lines erected after the coming into operation of the regulations, and which works are used for generating, transferring, converting or conveying electrical supply so as to secure the safety of consumers and members of the public from injurious harms. Part III deals with penalties for breaches of terms of licences and regulations.

218. Subsequent to the above, the Nigerian regime of electricity governance witnessed a major shift towards liberalization of NEPA's monopolistic status in the sector. The Electricity Act of 1990 was amended in 1998 by virtue of a military decree (now Act).[408] The amendment stripped NEPA of its monopoly, in terms of power generation, to pave the way for IPP in the country. This gave rise to full-blown

---

401. *Supra* note 107.
402. *See* the *Commercialization and Privatization Decree No. 25*, 1988, now an Act of the National Assembly of Nigeria.
403. *See* the repealed *NEPA Act Cap* 106, Laws of the Federation of Nigeria (LFN) 1990.
404. *Ibid.*, s. 1.
405. *Ibid.*, s. 5.
406. *Ibid.*, s. 3.
407. These regulations are:

    (i) Electricity Supply Regulations.
    (ii) Electricity Wiring Regulations.
    (iii) Electricity (Private licenses) Regulations.
    (iv) Electricity (Annual Returns) Regulations.

408. *See* the *Electricity (Amendment) Act,* No. 28 of 1998.

reforms that eventually led to the repeal of the *NEPA (Amendment) Act* and regulations made pursuant thereto, as well as the dissolution of NEPA and its replacement with the Power Holding Company of Nigeria (PHCN) as part of the large-scale reform in the Nigerian electricity sector, under the EPSR Act of 2005.

§4. The Power Sector Reforms in Nigeria

219. The Nigerian state is characterized by a confluence of factors. On the one hand, economic interests, political forces, capitalists' entities and other bureaucratic institutions determine the kind of laws or policies suitable or adoptable by the Nigerian state per time. The same situation manifests vividly in the electricity sector of Nigeria, which led to the current power sector reform.[409] The reform is not peculiar to Nigeria, as the nature of the electricity industry led to a wave of new regulatory regimes across the globe.[410] The current regime of power sector reform began in the year 2000 with the implementation of the *Electric Power Implementation Committee* (EPIC). The committee drafted the *National Electric Power Policy* (NEPP) in 2001 leading to the 2005 Act. The reform consists essentially of two main components: restructuring and privatization. The objective was to stimulate competition and promote financial accountability by unbundling the old structure under NEPA into three constituents segment, namely generation, distribution and transmission. The general aim and objectives of the reform include:

(i) improvement in the performance and operation of the utility through increased private sector participation;
(ii) private sector investments;
(iii) meeting current and future demand for electricity;
(iv) establishing new market structure/rules and trading arrangement;
(v) setting up an independent regulator to oversee the affairs of the sector; and
(vi) promoting competition, transparency and efficiency.[411]

---

409. A writer also opined that, propelled by insufficient electricity supply, persistent power outages, low generating capacity, high technical losses and non-technical loses characterizing the electric sector, the Nigerian government embarked on a number of reforms to reverse the ugly trends. This followed the objective of commercialization and privatization of certain public enterprises, including NEPA, under the Commercialization and Privatization Decree (now Act) of 1988. Nkiruka, C.M., *supra* note 392. *See also* Sanyaolu, H.A. *Electricity Power Sector Reform in Nigeria: Utilizing Restructuring and Regulatory Reform as a Means of Achieving a More Efficient and Competitive Sector* (Thesis, CEPMLP, University of Dundee, 2008).

410. A good number of developed countries have unbundled their electricity industries by separating generation from transmission. The private sector now dominates generation as in the case of England and Wales. These models have also been implemented in a number of countries across the globe like Chile, Argentina, Bolivia, Ecuador, Thailand, China and lately Senegal, Uganda and Nigeria. *See* E. Gnansonuou, 'Boosting the Electricity Sector in West Africa: An Integrative Vision' (2008) *International Association of Energy Economies, Third Quarter*, at 23.

411. Chigbue, I.N., 'Electric Power Sector Reform: Privatization, Regulation and Other Challenges' a presentation at the National Workshop on Electric Power Sector Liberalization, Abujam 30 Mar. 2006, online at: http://worldstagegroup.com/truecolour/media/11152404.ppt, accessed 28 Apr. 2010.

220. Under the new regime, the Nigerian Electricity Regulatory Commission (NERC) is to serve as the main regulatory body of the reformed electric power sector.[412] The existence of NERC is brought about by the EPSR *Act.*[413] The Act repeals and replaces the NEPA and *Electricity Act.*[414] It also removes the regulatory powers for the electric power sector hitherto vested in NEPA by the Federal Government of Nigeria, thus creating the legal basis for restructuring NEPA and the subsequent establishment of new regulatory structures and institutions.[415] The monopoly hitherto enjoyed by the erstwhile National Electric Power Authority (NEPA) for several decades was abrogated, as the new regime aims to liberalize the sector.

§5. Overview of the Electric Power Sector Reform Act

221. The aim of the Act is multifaceted. It seeks to provide legal frameworks for the formation of several legal entities (corporations) to take over the assets and liabilities of the old electricity regulatory body and to establish the NERC as the new regulatory agency for the generation, transmission and distribution of electricity in Nigeria. According to the EPSR Act, the law:

> seeks to provide for the formation of companies to take over the functions, assets, liabilities, and staff of the National Electric Power Authority; develop competitive electricity markets; establish the Nigerian Electricity Regulatory Commission; provide for the licensing and regulation of the generation, transmission, distribution and supply of electricity; enforce such matters as performance standards, consumer rights and obligation; and to provide for the determination of tariffs; and to provide for matters connected with or incidental to the foregoing.[416]

222. The Act brought about the existence of a regulatory agency known as the Nigerian Electricity Regulatory Commission (NERC) as a body corporate with perpetual succession and power to sue or be sued in its corporate name and to as well perform all acts that bodies corporate may by law perform.[417] The objectives of NERC include: (a) to create, promote and preserve efficient industry and market structures, and to ensure the optimal utilization of resources for the provision of electricity services; (b) to maximize access to electricity services, by promoting and facilitating consumer connections to distribution systems in both rural and urban areas; (c) to ensure that an adequate supply of electricity is available to consumers;

412. The responsibilities of NERC include licensing of successor power companies, establishment of electricity tariffs, enforcement of performance standards and the protection of consumer rights.
413. *See Electric Power Sector Reform* (EPSR) Act 2005, s. 31.
414. *See* National Electric Power Authority (NEPA) Act, Cap N 33, Laws of the Federation (LFN) 2004.
415. The Act establishes three institutions, namely the *National Electricity Regulatory Commission* (NERC) which serves as the main regulatory body; the *Rural Electrification Agency* (REA), and the *Power Consumer Assistance Fund.*
416. *See* the 'Explanatory Memorandum' to the EPSR Act, *ibid.*
417. *Ibid.,* s. 13.

(d) to ensure that the prices charged by licensees are fair to consumers and are sufficient to allow the licensees to finance their activities and to allow for reasonable earnings for efficient operation; (e) to ensure the safety, security, reliability and quality of service in the production and delivery of electricity to consumers; (f) to ensure that regulation is fair and balanced for licensees, consumers, investors and other stakeholders; and (g) to present quarterly reports to the president and National Assembly on its activities.[418]

223. In carrying out its objectives, the NERC also performs the following statutory functions: (a) promote competition and private sector participation, when and where feasible; (b) establish or, as the case may be, approve appropriate operating codes and safety, security, reliability, and quality standards; (c) establish appropriate consumer rights and obligations regarding the provision and use of electric services; (d) licence and regulate persons engaged in the generation, transmission, system operation, distribution and trading of electricity; (e) approve amendments to the market rules; (f) monitor the operation of the electricity market; and (g) undertake such other activities which are necessary to carry out or give effect to the objects of the NERC.[419]

224. Despite these challenges, the current electricity governance model under NEPA is radically different from the regime of the ESPR Act, 2005. A major difference in the conceptual and ideological basis of the NEPA regime and the EPSR era is that the NEPA Act intended a wholly state-owned sector and government-controlled regulatory institution for the electricity sector. NEPA served as a statutory body to effectuate state monopoly in the sector.[420] Compared to the NEPA era, the EPSR Act expressly provides for a liberalized regime of electricity by promoting competition and a level playing field in the power sector – a sharp departure from the old regime of state monopoly in the sector.[421]

225. Sections 80 and 81 of the EPSR Act provide for consumer protection and require high-performance standards by the operators to engender maximum utility and safety to consumers of electricity. Regrettably, section 27 of the repealed NEPA Act declares that NEPA is not responsible for safety either of the consumers or for the efficiency or safety of their cables, appliances or consumers. Section 35 of the NEPA Act forbids any other person or state government agency from obtaining licences to operate power plants or generate electricity in contradiction to the level-playing, competitive structure under the EPSR Act of 2005.

§6. Structure and Challenges of Electricity Governance in Nigeria

226. In terms of structure and operations, electricity governance in Nigeria under the *National Electric Power Authority* (NEPA) is radically different from the

418. *Ibid.*, s. 32(1).
419. *Ibid.*, s. 32(2).
420. *See* for example, ss. 1 and 3 of the NEPA Act.
421. *See* ss. 25, 26, 28, 29, and 82 of the EPSR Act.

regime of the EPSR Act.[422] A major difference is that the *NEPA Act* intended a wholly state-owned and government-controlled electricity sector in Nigeria.[423] NEPA merely served as a statutory body to effectuate state monopoly in the sector.[424] The *EPSR Act* expressly provides for a liberalized regime of electricity and promotes competition and a level playing field in the power sector. It embraces radical, private sector involvement by way of direct and indirect investments, including technical partnerships with the Nigerian government.[425] The new regime makes a sharp departure from the old paradigm of state monopoly in electricity governance in Nigeria.[426] Despite this policy direction, Nigeria's power sector still faces social challenges in addition to a number of logistical, technical, legal and constitutional constraints as illustrated below.

I. Host Community Concerns

227. Host community issue is a threat to power generation and energy access in Nigeria. This factor is capable of undermining the activities of both local and foreign electricity companies operating in Nigeria and other countries in the Western Africa subregion. Host community hostility is a new generation of foreign investment risk.[427] Matters affecting the host populations rarely receive much attention.[428] Most legislative and contractual documents on the exploitation of energy resources, including electricity generation, transmission and distribution tend to be

422. *See* the *National Electric Power Authority* (NEPA) Act, Cap N 33, Laws of the Federation of Nigeria (LFN) 2004.
423. *See* Yemi Oke, 'Beyond Power Sector Reforms: The Need for Decentralized Energy Options (DEOPs)', *supra* note 414 . *See also* Yemi Oke, 'National Grid or National Greed', The Punch Newspaper (7 Dec. 2011) 14 and (8 Dec. 2011) 16. *See also* Chigbue, I.N., 'Electric Power Sector Reform: Privatization, Regulation and Other Challenges' a presentation at the National Workshop on Electric Power Sector Liberalization, 30 Mar. 2006, online at: http://worldstagegroup.com/truecolour/media/11152404144.ppt, accessed 18 Apr. 2013.
424. *See* for example, ss. 1 and 3 of the NEPA Act, *supra* note 414.
425. *See* Yemi Oke, 'Manitoba Hydro and Electricity Undertakings in Developing Countries: The Case of Nigeria' (2012) 36: 1 *Manitoba Law Journal*, at 37–65.
426. *See* ss. 25, 26, 28, 29, and 82 of the EPSR Act, *supra* note 414 . For example, ss. 80 and 81 of the *EPSR Act* provide for consumer protection, and require high performance standards by the operators to engender maximum utility and safety to consumers of electricity. Regrettably, s. 27 of the repealed NEPA Act declares that NEPA is not responsible for safety either of the consumers or for the efficiency or safety of their cables and appliances of consumers. Section 35 of the NEPA Act forbade any other person or state government agency from obtaining licences to operate power plants or generate electricity, in contradistinction with the level-playing, competitive structure under the EPSR Act of 2005.
427. According to Akpan, concerns in energy resource exploitation has traditionally concentrated on the relationship between the host State and the foreign investor. *See* George S. Akpan, 'Host Community Hostility to Mining Projects: A New Generation of Risk?' in Bastiba, E. & Walde, T., and Warden-Fernandez, J., (Eds) *International and Comparative Mineral Law and Policy: Trends and Prospects* (The Hague: Kluwer Law International, 2005) at 311.
428. *Ibid.,* at 312.

silent on devising institutional means to protect the host populations against sometimes devastating environmental, health and social impacts of the activities of energy companies.[429]

228. The Nigerian electricity regime ostensibly provides for an institutional framework to protect the host community[430] located around hydro-based power generation installations under the *Hydro-Electric Power Producing Areas Development Commission (HEPADC) Act.*[431] The experience of Nigeria in the series of agitations by the resource-bearing communities led to the enactment of the *HEPADC Act,*[432] in which the Commission is charged with responsibility for managing the environmental or ecological distortions brought about as a result of operation of dams, and related matters.[433] The *HEPADC Act* takes a cue from similar regulatory frameworks in the area of communities' agitations ranging from the *Oil Mineral Producing Areas Development Commission* (OMPADEC),[434] the *Niger Delta Development Commission* (NDDC)[435] and the Ministry of Niger Delta, among others. The model of regulatory frameworks for placating the oil-producing communities is replicated with the enactment of the *HEPADC Act.*[436] A major inadequacy of the *HEPADC Act* is that it focuses on communities within hydroelectric power generation.

II. Constitutional Challenges

229. Nigeria's power sector also faces likely constitutional hiccups. In a number of ways, the provisions of the EPSR *Act* 2005 (the Act) would appear to contradict the *Constitution of the Federal Republic of Nigeria (CFRN)* (as amended). The Nigerian constitution provides for electricity regulation under items 13 and 14 of the Second Schedule, Part II, Concurrent Legislative List to the extent that: *The National Assembly may make laws for the Federation or any part thereof with respect to: (a) electricity and the establishment of electric power stations; (b) the generation and transmission of electricity in or to any part of the Federation and from one State to another State.*

---

429. *Ibid.*, Akpan argues that inability of members of the host communities to have recourse to effective remedies in both the host and the home State and in international law, against activities of players in the energy sector that have deleterious effects on them has potential of creating a new source of risk to foreign investment in the sector.
430. For detailed discussion on hydroelectric power producing states and communities, *see* Yemi Oke, *Nigerian Electricity Law and Regulation* (LawLords Publications., Abuja/Lagos: March 2013), Ch. 7 at pp. 118 and 126–132.
431. *See Hydro-Electric Power Producing Areas Development Commission*, Cap H5A, Laws of Federation of Nigeria (LFN), 2004.
432. *Ibid.*
433. *See* the long title to the *HEPADC Act, ibid.*
434. *See* the *Oil Minerals Producing Areas Development Commission (OMPADEC)* Decree No 23 of 1992.
435. *See* the Niger Delta Development Commission (establishment) Act, Cap N86 Laws of the Federation of Nigeria (LFN), 2004.
436. *See HEPADC Act supra* note 431.

230. A potential challenge in the sector is that, by virtue of paragraph 14, State governments in Nigeria are at liberty to engage in licensing and regulation of electricity subjects as provided by the constitution. Item *14 states that: A House of Assembly may make laws for the State with respect to: (a) electricity and the establishment in that State of electric power stations; (b) the generation, transmission and distribution of electricity to areas not covered by a national grid system within that State; and (c) the establishment within that State of any authority for the promotion and management of electric power stations established by the State.*

231. Apparent from the above section is that the Nigerian Constitution provides for decentralized electricity governance. It is therefore curious why State governments in Nigeria are yet to avert their attention to this gap.[437] While the Constitution provides for a decentralized regulatory framework, the EPSR Act provides for a centralized regime, which is outside the contemplation of the Constitution, thus making it null and void to the extent of its inconsistency.[438] The act also established an agency, to be known as the Rural Electrification Agency (REA).[439] The REA administers the Rural Electrification Fund (REF), a designated fund to provide, promote and support rural electrification programmes which also ordinarily comes within the ambit of off-grid electricity structure for State regulation.

III. Rural Electricity

232. Rural electricity is off-grid and comes squarely within the ambit of regulatory purviews of the State Governments in Nigeria[440] bearing in mind that the Constitution vests local government administration in the State governments.[441] The objective and purpose of Rural Electrification Fund (REF), Rural Electrification Project (REP) and Rural Electrification Agency (REA) are noble, at least on paper.[442] However, REF has generated more ripples than intended in its short history largely due to corruption and mismanagement of the REF.[443] It is the considered view of the author that vesting Rural Electrification Agency (REA), Rural Electrification Fund (REF) and Rural Electrification Project (REP) in the hands of

437. *See* items 13 and 14 on Electric Power (F), in the Second Schedule, *Part II, Concurrent Legislative List, Constitution of the Federal Republic of Nigeria* (CFRN) 1999 (as amended).
438. *Ibid.*, s. 1 (1) and (3) of the CFRN, 1999 (as amended).
439. Section 88 (1) of the EPSR Act, *supra* note 415.
440. *See* Item 14, of the Sch. II to the CFRN, *supra* note 12.
441. Section 6(7) CFRN 1999 (as amended).
442. *See* s. 88(13)(a–d) of the EPSR Act, *supra* note 127.
443. *See* Yemi Oke, 'Corruption in the Nigerian Electricity Sector' (a Report Commissioned by Socio-Economic Rights and Accountability Project (*SERAP*), 2017, 1–163 at pp. 10–42. The arrest of some principal officers of the National Assembly over the *Rural Electricity Project* by the *Economic and Financial Crimes Commission* (EFCC) has further reinforced the argument on the current structure of the electricity governance in Nigeria. *See* 'The Raging Scandal over Government's Rural Power Projects' Guardian online at: http://www.ngrguardiannews.com/weekend/Article01//indexn2_html?pdate=150509&ptitle=The%20raging%20scandal%20over%20govt's%20rural%20power%20projects accessed 17 Jun. 2016.

the Federal Government runs counter to the intendment of the Nigerian Constitution. An attempt to bring an 'off-grid' subject within 'National-Grid' is tantamount to what the writer had referred to in another piece as 'National Greed'.[444]

IV. Captive Power Generation

233. Power to regulate captive electricity generation should ordinarily vest in the State Governments. Therefore, the *NERC Regulations for the Granting of Permits for Captive Power Generation,* 2008[445] is, *ipso facto*, unconstitutional. Under this regulation, the *Nigerian Electricity Regulatory Commission* (NERC) grants captive electricity permits to an individual, a company, a partnership or any association of individuals whether incorporated or not.[446] The word *Captive Power Generation means generation of electricity in excess of one (1) MW for the purpose of consumption by the generator, which is consumed by the generator itself, and not sold to a third-party.*[447] The underlining objective of the regulation is to streamline the procedure for power generation by interested person(s), groups or corporate organizations in excess of 1 MW, but without the intention of trading or engaging in the sale of electricity to a third party.

234. There is no direct or specific provision under the Act authorizing the NERC to regulate the captive generation of electricity. Section 62 of the EPSR Act expressly excludes captive generation. It only provides that no person shall construct, own or operate an undertaking for the purpose of electricity generation, transmission, distribution, systems operation or electricity trading in excess of 1 megawatt without a licence from the Commission.[448] Thus, even under sections 32(1)(a), 32(1)(e), and 32(2)(d) of the Act, the NERC has a general but not specific statutory duty to regulate the operation of captive generating plant, among others.[449] Like the REA, REF and REP, captive generation of electricity is also off-grid, and comes within the ambit of legislative competence and regulatory purviews of the State governments in Nigeria, in line with the intendment of the Constitution.[450]

---

444. *See* Yemi Oke 'National Grid' or 'National Geed'? *supra* note 423.
445. The *Nigerian Electricity Regulatory Commission (NERC) Regulations for the Granting of Permits for Captive Power Generation,* 2008 is made pursuant to s. 96(1) of the Electric Power sector Reform Act, 2005 which gives the Commission power to make regulations for the granting of permits for captive power generation.
446. *See* s. 2 of the regulations. The section defines 'person' to include an individual, a company, partnership or any association of individuals whether incorporated or not.
447. *See* s. 2(1) of the *Captive Power Generation Regulations, supra* note 445.
448. *See* generally s. 62(1)(a–e), (2) and (3) of the Electric Power Sector Reform Act, *supra* note 386.
449. A careful reading of the provisions of s. 32(1)(a), 32(1)(e), and 32(2)(d) of the Act shows that the NERC is vested with no specific but general powers to create, promote and preserve efficient electricity industry including ensuring the safety, security, reliability and quality of service in the production and delivery of electricity to consumers as well as licence and regulate persons engaged in the generation of electricity, transmission, system operation, distribution and trading of electricity.
450. Yemi Oke, 'Rural Electrification and Captive Power Generation' (2013) 3 *Nigerian Lawyers' Journal, Law Digest* (UK), summer 2013, at 51–52.

V. Revocation of Land for Electricity Purposes

235. Revocation of land for electricity purposes is another potentially sensitive issue capable of undermining private sector-led electricity sector in Nigeria. The issue of land ownership and management is capable of generating tension between electricity companies and local communities.[451] Land ownership is a sensitive subject under Nigerian law. The EPSR Act provides that for the purpose of electricity, a generation licensee, transmission or distribution licences, or a proposed licensee for generation, transmission and distribution services may apply to the NERC in a manner as may be prescribed, for a declaration that the land is required for purposes of generation, transmission or distribution of electricity.[452]

236. The Act provides that when the president issues a notice requiring the land for public purpose pursuant to section 28(4) of the Land Use Act,[453] the Governor of a State shall revoke the existing right of occupancy in respect of the land and grant a certificate of occupancy in favour of the licensee.[454] Revocation of land for 'overriding public interest' may not ordinarily justify revocation of existing rights of occupancy or allocation of same to a business enterprise simply because such entities trade in electricity or related activities. Companies holding either generation, transmission or distribution licences are business enterprises trading with the ultimate objective of profit maximization in electricity.

237. Revocation of right of occupancy to land for purposes of electricity undertakings is a negation of total deregulation and commercialization of electricity in Nigeria.[455] As argued elsewhere,[456] the principle of compulsory purchase, compared to revocation of right of occupancy, enables the acquiring authority to assume the obligation of paying for the full value of the land to be purchased or taken.[457] Compulsory purchase of land is particularly suitable where private-commercial motives intermingle with public interest[458] as it makes for the payment of actual market value for the land purchased or acquired. Compared to revocation of right of occupancy where land is required for the purpose of electricity undertakings either

451. For detailed analyses on land and electricity in Nigeria, *see* Yemi Oke, *Nigerian Electricity Law and Regulation*, (Lawlords, Abuja/Lagos, 2013) Ch. 5, at pp. 83–95.
452. *See* s. 77(1) of the EPSR Act, *supra* note 127.
453. *See Land Use Act*, Cap L5, Laws of the Federation of Nigeria 2004.
454. *See* s. 77(9) of the EPSR Act.
455. *See* Public Enterprises (Privatization and Commercialization) Act, *supra* note 402.
456. *See* Yemi Oke, 'Compulsory Purchase as an Alternative to Revocation of Title to Land for Electricity Purpose in Nigeria' (2013) *Journal of Private and Property Law*, University of Lagos, at pp. 36–59.
457. *See* s. 63 of the *Lands Clauses (Consolidated) Act* 1845. The provisions of the Act formed the basis of the decision of the Privy Council in *Director of Buildings and Lands v. Shun Flung Ironworks* [1995] 2 AC, 111; [1995] 1 All ER 846; [1995] 19 EG 147. *See* Barry Denyer-Green, *Compulsory Acquisition and Compensation* (8th ed.) (EG Books, London: 2005), at 168.
458. *Ibid.*

for generation, transmission or distribution; a fair and just end is attained that makes for a win-win situation, unlike the acrimonious relationship between land owners or resource-bearing communities and oil companies in Nigeria.[459]

459. Yemi Oke 'Compulsory Purchase as an Alternative to Revocation of Title to Land for Electricity Purpose in Nigeria', *supra* note 456.

Chapter 3. Electricity Generation, Transmission and Distribution in Nigeria: Law, Practice and Institutions

§1. INTRODUCTION

238. In Nigeria, the burden of ensuring a competitive electric power sector through the enforcement of laid down regulations and law vests in the Nigerian Electricity Regulatory Commission (NERC),[460] as sector regulator. The NERC as a regulator is the engine room for effective operationalization of sector law, regulations, rules and objectives. The electric power sector regulator manages and oversees the affairs and activities of the sector as the official watch dog of the industry. It carries out activities ranging from the issuance and renewal of licences and permits, electric company's operations, interaction with customers and compliance with sector or industry regulations. It also collects appropriate/statutory fees from sector operators and ensures that companies operate in line with established rules, regulations and procedures. In addition to the above, the NERC carries out oversight duties of reviewing service quality to meet or exceed established standards and ensures that electrical rates are appropriate for the quality of service without taking undue advantage of electricity consumers.

239. The NERC was established under Part III of the Act[461] as a body corporate with perpetual succession which can sue or be sued in its corporate name, and pursuant to the provisions of the act, performs all acts that bodies corporate may by law perform.[462] The minister may issue general policy directions to the Commission on matters of electricity in undertakings. Though the NERC as a sector regulator is expected to act with independence, especially where such directive(s) conflict(s) with the Act or the Nigerian Constitution, in practice, once ministerial directives are issued, they must be complied with by the regulatory agency.[463]

§2. ELECTRICITY LICENCES

240. Generally, no one ventures into the electricity business in Nigeria by way of constructing, owing, or operating an undertaking or engaging in the business of electricity transmission, system operation, electricity distribution or trading in electricity except in accordance with a licence issued pursuant to the Act or deemed to have been issued under section 98(2) of the Act.[464] The Act permits the construction, owning or operation of an undertaking for generating electricity not exceeding

460. *See* s. 31 of the *See Electric Power Sector Reform* (EPSR) Act 2005.

461. *See* generally ss. 31–61.

462. *Ibid.*, s. 30(1).

463. By virtue of s. 33(1), 'The Minister may issue general policy directions to the Commission on matters concerning electricity, including directions on overall system planning and coordination, which the Commission shall take into consideration in discharging its functions under s. 32(2), provided that such directions are not in conflict with this Act or the Constitution of the Federal Republic of Nigeria'.

464. Section 62(1)(a–e).

1 megawatt (MW) in aggregate at a site or an undertaking for distribution of electricity with a capacity not exceeding 100 kilowatts (KW) in aggregate at a site, or such other capacity as the Commission may determine from time to time, without a licence.[465]

241. By virtue of the above proviso, permissible generation or transmission of electricity or related undertaking without a licence exists under the act to the extent that generation of 1 megawatt (MW) in aggregate or undertaking for distribution of 100 kilowatts (KW) in aggregate without a licence is statutorily permissible under the act. Though the Commission reserves the right to extend the magnitude of exempted electricity undertakings without a licence, the rationale behind the statutory cover for fragmentations of 1 MW generations and 100 KW distributions across the country with the implied health, social and environmental implications is not explained in the act. By virtue of the Act, a maximum of an eighteen-month interim licence may be granted for any or all the activities in section 62(1) relating to electricity transmission, system operation, electricity distribution and trading in electricity.[466]

242. Legal and related issues or dispute as to whether or not a person engaging or is about to be engaged in a business for which a licence is required under section 62(1) shall be referred to the Commission. In case of violation of the requirement of issuance of electricity licence, the act stipulates a fine of NGN 500,000 or imprisonment for a period not exceeding two years or both fine and imprisonment. The Commission may also order any person who contravenes the above provisions to cease operations and may make further orders including an order to another licensee to disconnect facilities to prevent the continuation or reoccurrence of the contravention.[467]

§3. Types and Duties of Licensees

243. The Act imposes general duties on the licensees to comply with the provisions of their licence, regulations, codes and other requirements issued by the Commission from time to time.[468] Mindful of the legal rights of the licensees, the Act qualifies compliance to the effect that, unless stayed by a court of competent jurisdiction, they (the licensees) shall have a duty to implement or follow, as the case may be, the order or written notices of the Commission notwithstanding that the licensee has or may intend to take legal action challenging any such order or notice.[469]

465. Subsection (2).
466. *Ibid.*, subs. (3).
467. Section 62(6).
468. Section 63(1).
469. *Ibid.*, subs. (2).

I. Generation Licences

244. The Act recognizes certain categories of licences. For instance, subject to such terms as the Commission may fix in the licence, a generation licence may be granted to authorize the licensee to construct, own, operate and maintain a generation station for purposes of generation and supply of electricity.[470] A generation licensee may sell power or ancillary services to any of the classes of persons specified in the licence.[471] The Act gives the Commission power to issue generation licences to one or more of the successor companies formed under section 8 of the Act, or to entities that are not successor companies formed as IPP[472] as part of interim measures to give effect to the reforms in the Nigerian electricity sector.

II. Transmission Licences

245. Transmission licences are issued by the Commission to a licensee to authorize the carrying on of grid construction, operation and maintenance of a transmission system within Nigeria, or to set up a transmission system that connects Nigeria with a neighbouring country.[473] This is without prejudice to the right and obligation of a transmission licensee that is a successor company formed under section 8 of the Act to carry out system operation, including procurement of ancillary services, pursuant to the terms of a system operation licence issued by the Commission. This means in addition to exercising the right of a generation licensee, a successor transmission company shall additionally perform the duties of a system operation. The above right is restricted to a successor transmission licensee as, going by the above provisions a transmission licensee under section 65(1) of the Act has no obligations to carry out system operation and related or ancillary services.

III. System Operation Licence

246. A system licence is one that authorizes a licensee (system operation licensee) to carry out systems operation activities as specified in the licence such as generating scheduling, commitment and dispatch; transmission scheduling and generation outage coordination; transmission congestion management; international transmission coordination; procurement and scheduling of ancillary services and system planning for long-term capacity.[474]

247. A system operation licensee is also empowered to carry out the administration of the wholesale electricity market, including administration of settlement payments in line with the market rules as well as other activities as may be required

470. Section 64(1).
471. *Ibid.*, subs. (2).
472. Subsection (3)(a–b).
473. Section 65(1).
474. Section 66(1)(a–e).

for a reliable and efficient system operation.[475] However, procurement of ancillary activities of a system operation licensee shall be awarded in accordance with an open, transparent and competitive procedure pursuant to a procedure established by the Commission unless the circumstances otherwise require, or the Commission does otherwise directs an alternative method.[476]

IV. Distribution Licences

248. A distribution licence authorizes a licensee to construct, operate and maintain a distribution system and facilities including connection of customers for the purpose of receiving a supply of electricity, the installation, maintenance and reading of meters, billing collection and other distribution activities or services as may be prescribed.[477] A distribution licensee shall also have a specific obligation to ensure electricity distribution to its distribution customers pursuant to the terms of the trading licence issued to it by the Commission.[478]

249. The Act recognizes the right to purchase and resell electricity with prior consent of the Commission. Thus, a distribution licensee issued with a trading licence under section 67(2) may purchase power for resale from another trading licensee and may, with prior approval of the Commission, purchase power from other sources.[479] This is subject to the condition that the contract for bulk purchase of electricity by a distribution licensee shall be awarded according to an open, transparent and competitive process established by the Commission unless otherwise directed, or the Commission requires an alternative method.

V. Trading Licences

250. A trading licence is one that permits the licensee to engage in the purchasing, reselling and trading of electricity.[480] Notwithstanding the issuance of a trading licence, the Commission retains authority to determine the terms and conditions under which electricity trading will take place. In doing so, the Commission shall take into account the circumstances, nature and activities for which the licensee is authorized to engage.[481]

251. Where the Commission is of the opinion that the circumstances so demand, it may issue a temporary bulk purchase and resale licence to give a licensee right to purchase electrical power and ancillary services from IPP and successor companies

475. *Ibid.*, subs. (1)(f–g).
476. Section 66(2).
477. Section 67(1)(a–c).
478. Section 67(2).
479. Section 67(3).
480. Section 68(1).
481. *Ibid.*

for the purpose of resale to other licensees or eligible customers.[482] The Act also provides that all contracts for the purchase of electrical power and ancillary services by the holder of a temporary licence be awarded in an open, transparent and competitive manner. It also provides for omnibus power to vary open and competitive bids in a manner that had been queried above.[483]

§4. Restriction on Licences

252. Licences are issued on terms and such terms must be strictly adhered to by the licensees. Transferability of a licence is expressly prohibited unless in the manner excluded or exempted by the Act. The Act provides:

> A licensee shall not, except as provided in section 26(7), assign or cede his licence or transfer his undertaking, or any part thereof, by way of sale, mortgage, lease, exchange or otherwise without the prior consent of the Commission. Provided that, should the Commission determine that in any instance the circumstances so require, it may establish licence terms and conditions providing specific or general consent for any or all of the foregoing.[484]

253. Acquisition of right by a licensee is prohibited by the Act. A licensee shall not acquire by purchase or otherwise, or affiliate with, the licence or undertaking of any other licensee or person that is in the business of electricity generation, transmission and distribution, including system operation or trading save for prior written consent to the Commission.[485] Acquisition of right in existing licensee or undertaking is limited to sections 65(2) on transmission licensee that is a successor company,[486] section 67(2) on distribution licensee[487] and section 68 of the Act which generally provides for electricity trading licences. The Commission may impose conditions such as adherence to its codes as part of the requirements for consent.[488]

§5. Application for Electricity Licences

254. To apply for any of the above categories of electricity licences, an application shall be made to the Commission in the form and manner prescribed and

482. *Ibid.*, subs. (2).
483. *Ibid.*, subs. (3).
484. Section 69 (1).
485. *Ibid.*, subs. (2).
486. Section 65(2) provides that 'The transmission licensee that is a successor company formed under s. 8 may also have obligation to carry out system operation, including the procurement of ancillary services, pursuant to the terms of a system operation licence issued by the Commission to such licensee'.
487. Section 67(2) states that: 'A distribution licensee may also have the obligation to provide electricity to its distribution customers, pursuant to the terms of a trading licence issued by the Commission to the distribution licensee'.
488. Section 69(2).

accompanied by the appropriate fee and such information or document as may be prescribed or required by the Commission.[489] The procedure and requirements for applying for an electricity licence are:

(1) An application made to the NERC in the required format supported by necessary documents and statutory or administrative fees.[490]
(2) The applicant sponsors an advert within thirty days of giving notice of the application in a newspaper circulating in the area in which he intends to operate as a licensee.[491]
(3) The notice shall be in the form prescribed by the Commission and shall state the period stipulated by the Commission within which objections or representation may be made in respect of the application.[492]
(4) The Commission shall not issue any licence until all objections or representations received by it have been considered and determined.
(5) An applicant holding more than 10% or such percentage as prescribed of shares in a corporate body which has applied for or holds another licence issued by the Commission shall disclose such interest to the Commission.[493]
(6) An applicant shall only be issued with a licence if: (a) upon compliance with all requirements for issuance of an electricity licence, the Commission finds that an applicant is likely to comply with the provisions of the Act including all codes of conduct, standards, regulations and licence terms and conditions as applicable to the nature of service or system it intends to provide or operate; and (b) that the grant of the licence is in the interest of the public.
(7) Subject to the above, the Commission shall issue the appropriate licence, as the case may be to the applicant.[494]
(8) If on consideration of an application that satisfies the requirements of subsection (1) the Commission is not satisfied as to the additional matters in section 70(4)(a-b), it shall refuse to issue a licence to an applicant.[495]
(9) Before refusing to issue a licence on the ground that an applicant has not satisfied the grounds in section 70(4), the Commission shall notify the applicant in writing that it proposes to refuse the application and state its reasons for doing so.
(10) Before final refusal, the Commission shall afford the applicant adequate opportunity to make representations in the matter.[496]
(11) The Commission has one month upon receipt of an application and all documents and information submitted in respect of the application and notification of adequacy of the documents submitted by an applicant shall not exceed one month.[497]

489. Section 70.
490. Section 70(1).
491. *Ibid.*, subs. (2).
492. *Ibid.*
493. *Ibid.*
494. *See* generally s. 70(4)(a–b).
495. Section 70(5).
496. *Ibid.*
497. Section 70(6).

(12) The Commission shall within six months of receipt of documents and adequacy of the same notify the applicant of its decisions or proposed decision pursuant to subsections (4) and (5).
(13) Irrespective of the above procedures, the Commission may establish simplified procedures for undertakings and businesses that are limited in size and scope to expedite the application and licensing process.

§6. TERMS AND CONDITIONS OF LICENCES

255. Electricity licences are issued on terms and conditions prescribed in the licence or on such terms and conditions as may be reasonably imposed by the Commission on the use of a tariff methodology.[498] The terms and conditions of an electricity licence may require the licensee to enter into agreements on specified terms with other persons for the provision of or use of electric lines and associated equipment operated by the licensee, purchase of power and other resources in an economical and transparent manner and to refer dispute for arbitration, mediation or determination by the Commission.[499]

256. Specific terms and conditions may also be imposed in the case of a licensee who has more than 10% shares in another licensee,[500] to divest itself within a specified period of time of any holding of shares in another licensee, including adherence to codes of conduct issued by the Commission.[501] To renew a distribution licence, the Commission may also impose a condition requiring the licensee to make such reasonable provision as may be specified in the licence to facilitate rural electrification.[502] A licensee may also be under an additional obligation to provide the Commission with periodic information in such details and form as the Commission may require.[503]

257. The Act specifically incorporates antitrust provisions to avoid market monopoly. It provides that the grant of a licence by the Commission shall not be the basis for restricting or hindering the grant of another licence for a similar purpose. Unless where expressly limited by the terms and conditions of the licence or the Commission, a licensee shall not claim exclusivity of licensed activity though the Commission may restrict competition and allow a licensee exclusive activity for all or part of the period of the licence or for a specific period of time, geographical location or a combination of the factors or considerations as deemed expedient by the Commission.[504] For control of activity and viability, the Commission also requires as a condition for its licence, that every licensee shall, save for those

498. Section 71(1).
499. *Ibid.*, subs. (2)(a–c).
500. *See* s. 70(3).
501. Section 71(3).
502. *Ibid.*, subs. (4).
503. Subsection (5).
504. Subsection (6).

exempted by nature of licence, prepare and submit to it each year accounting information as may be required.[505] Further measures are also provided in the Act by way of a requirement that a licence shall contain details as to the rights and obligations of the licensee, including procedures to be followed at the expiration of the licence term or period.[506]

§7. RENEWAL AND AMENDMENT OF LICENCES

258. The validity of a licence is ten years from the date of issue. This is subject to the power of the Commission to extend the licence period for an additional period not exceeding five years at a time if taking into account the nature of the undertaking or business of the licensee it is in the interest of the public to so extend the licence period.[507] Every licence and renewal shall be deemed to have incorporated in it a provision that the licences shall comply with the market rules to the extent applicable to the licensee.[508] A licensee desiring renewal of his licence shall apply to have the licence renewed before the expiration of the current term.[509] Application for renewal of electricity licence shall be made to the Commission in the form and manner prescribed within the stipulated period and must be accompanied by appropriate fees and payments of other administrative charges (if any).[510] All the terms and conditions stipulated under section 71(1–11) shall apply *mutatis mutandis* to renewal of electricity licences.[511]

259. Electricity licences may be amended in Nigeria by the Commission on terms and conditions deemed appropriate on the following grounds:

(i) where the licensee requests an amendment;
(ii) pursuant to the conditions stipulated in section 71(7) of the Act on modification of terms or conditions;
(iii) upon receiving a complaint from any consumer, eligible consumer, consumer association, association of eligible consumers, customers or other licensee; or
(iv) on Commission's own initiative.[512]

260. The conditions for amendment of an electricity licence are similar to that of application for a licence, as follows: (a) the applicant/licensee makes an application; (b) the licensee causes a notice to be published of the proposed amendment

505. Subsection (8).
506. Subsection (9).
507. Section 71 (10).
508. Subsection (11).
509. Section 72 (1).
510. Subsection (2).
511. Subsection (3).
512. *See* generally s. 73(1)(a–d).

to the licence in accordance with such directions as may be given by the Commission; (c) the publication must state the period within which objections and representations could be made in respect of the amendment; (d) the Commission shall not amend until all objections or representations received have been considered and determined.[513]

261. Where the application for amendment of electricity licence relates to a licensee who provides services to an area covering a building or place occupied by the Federal Ministry of Defence for defence purposes, the Commission shall obtain the consent of the Federal Ministry of Defence before making the amendment to the licence.[514] However, before making amendments in a licence otherwise than on direct application of licensee, the Commission shall publish the proposed amendments, stating the period within which objection or presentation may be made to the Commission, and it shall not amend until such objections or representations received have been considered and determined.[515]

§8. Cancellation of Licences

262. The Act provides for grounds upon which electricity licences may be cancelled by the Commission. An electricity licence may be cancelled if upon receiving a complaint from any consumer, eligible consumer, consumer association, association of eligible consumers or other licensee or the Commission on its own initiative inquires into the conduct or functioning of any licensee in carrying out the licensee's obligations under the Act, rules or regulations, codes of conduct, or terms and conditions of the licence.[516]

263. If cancellation of an electricity licence is done pursuant to an inquiry by the Commission the licensee shall be invited to show cause as to why the licence should not be cancelled. The Commission may then proceed to cancel the licence if: (i) the licence was issued by fraud or the misrepresentation or non-disclosure of a material fact by the licensee; (ii) the licensee has wilfully or unreasonably contravened any provision of the Act as applicable to the licensee; (iii) the licensee has failed to comply with any term or condition of the licence, the breach of which is expressly declared by such licence to render it liable to cancellation; or (iv) the financial position of the licensee is such that he is unable to fully and efficiently discharge the duties and obligations imposed by the licence.[517] The Commission shall notify the licensee in writing of its intention to cancel the electricity licence and the reason for doing so shall be served on the licensee. Upon service of the notice, the Commission shall allow the licensee sixty days to demonstrate that the circumstances warranting such cancellation have ceased such that doing so is no longer

513. Section 73(2).
514. *Ibid.*, subs. (3).
515. Subsection (4).
516. Section 74(1).
517. *Ibid.*, subs. (2)(a–d).

necessary.[518] If the Commission is satisfied upon all inquiries that it is in public interest that the affected licence be cancelled, it shall proceed to issue a notice in writing to cancel the licence or take such other actions or steps it considers appropriate in the circumstance.[519]

264. The Commission may elect to allow the licence remains in force on such terms and conditions as deemed necessary to impose on the licensee, as against cancellation. If this option is exercised, the terms and conditions imposed shall form part of the licence.[520] However, where cancellation becomes inevitable, the Commission shall serve on the licensee a notice of cancellation and may make orders in respect of existing undertaking of the licensee including order for sale of such undertaking to another party where necessary, in order to maintain continuity in the provision of electricity services.[521]

§9. Enforcement of Licences

265. Enforcement of licence is tantamount to notice of contravention.[522] If satisfied that a licensee is contravening, has contravened or is likely to contravene any of the conditions of the licence, the Commission may serve the licensee an order requiring it to do or refrain from doing specified acts or things listed in the order for the purpose of rectifying or avoiding any contravention or threatened contravention of any condition of the licence.[523] The order may also state the period within which the rectification action stipulated in subsection (1)(a) may be commenced and completed.[524] Notice of the order may be published by the Commission in any manner as it deems fit to draw the attention of other persons affected or likely to be affected by the contravention or threatened contravention of the licence.[525]

266. Prior to serving the order of contravention or threatened contravention on the licence, the Commission shall serve a notice upon the licensee concerned specifying the grounds upon which the order is to be issued and what steps the Commission considers reasonably necessary for the purpose of rectification or avoiding contravention or threatened contravention of any condition of licence. The notice shall state the maximum period of time for implementing the required rectification actions. The Commission may also allow the licensee to make representation within the stipulated period from the date of service of the notice.[526]

518. Subsection (3).
519. Subsection (4).
520. Subsection (5).
521. Subsection (6).
522. Notice of contravention is the procedural steps required to be taken by the Commission under the act before the issuance and service of the order of contravention preparatory to cancellation or suspension of electricity licences.
523. Section 75(1)(a).
524. *Ibid.*, subs. (1)(b).
525. *Ibid.*
526. Section 75(2)(a–c).

267. Upon considering the representation made by the licensee, the Commission may serve or refrain from serving or defer issuance or service of the order of contravention of the condition of the licence as the case may be.[527] Where order of contravention or threatened contravention of licence is issued, it shall specify a penalty for each day that the licensee is subjected to the order or remains in violation or threatened of the said condition of licence or default, and the amount shall not exceed NGN 10,000.00 for each day.[528]

§10. Regulation on Application for Licences

268. The Nigerian Electricity Regulatory Commission Application for Licences, (Generation Transmission, System Operations, Distribution & Trading) Regulations, 2010 provides for the procedure for making application to the NERC for all kinds of electricity licences. Under the regulations, interested parties or entities could make application(s) to the Commission for various categories of electricity licences including generation, transmission, system operations, distribution and trading licences. It specifically repeals the 2006 regulations[529] on the same subject,[530] as well as the Electricity (Private Licences) Regulations of 1965.[531] Prior to the 2010 Regulations, the 2006 Regulations and the Private Licences Regulations of 1965 were the instruments guiding applications for electricity licences in Nigeria.[532]

§11. Application for Licence

269. Under the regulations, an application for a licence shall be in writing and addressed to the Chairman of the Commission. It shall be signed and dated by the applicant or their authorized representative and submitted in three paper copies plus an electronic version in Microsoft office software contained in a CD-ROM.[533] The format of the application shall be as specified in Schedule 2 of the Regulation[534] and must contain all the documents and information specified in the schedule relating to the specific licence applied for.[535] The applicant shall upon submission of the application pay the necessary processing fee as provided for in the *Regulations for License and Operating Fees, 2010* or as amended.[536]

527. *Ibid.*, subs. (3).
528. *Ibid.*, subs. (4).
529. *See* Regulation 1 (4) of the *Nigerian Electricity Regulatory Commission Application for Licences (Generation, Transmission, System Operations, Distribution & Trading) Regulations, 2010.*
530. The 2010 Regulations substantially make similar provisions as the 2006 version.
531. *See* Regulation 1(5) of the 2010 Regulations, *supra* note 1. This provision specifically repeals the *Electricity (Private Licences) Regulations of 1965.*
532. *See* the *Nigerian Electricity Regulatory Commission Application for Licences (Generation, Transmission, System Operations, Distribution & Trading) Regulations, 2006.*
533. Regulation 3 (a), (b), and (c), *supra* note 532.
534. *Ibid.*, Regulation 4.
535. Regulation 5.
536. Regulation 6.

270. Upon submission and acknowledgement of receipt of the application package, the Commission may, upon review, require the applicant to furnish, within a specified period, any additional information within one month from the date of receipt of the application package from the applicant.[537] An application shall lapse if the applicant fails or neglects to submit all required documents within sixty days from the date the Commission requests additional information.[538] The implication of this provision of the regulation is that once an application lapses, it cannot be reactivated unless the same is resubmitted as a fresh or new application upon payment of prescribed processing and other fees.[539]

271. The Commission shall pass a resolution confirming that an application is complete and duly made, and notify the applicant in writing within thirty days of the resolution, that the application is duly made with a request that the applicant publishes the statutory public notice.[540] An applicant shall cause a public notice to be issued in the prescribed form and manner and shall bear the cost of the publication.[541] Statutorily, public notice in respect of the application for electricity licences shall be published in at least two daily newspapers, one of which must be a local newspaper with wide circulation in the area where the applicant intends to operate as a licensee, and the other shall be a national newspaper. The notice shall state the period within which objection or representation may be made to the Commission in connection with the application.[542] No licence shall be issued by the Commission until all objections or representations received by it regarding the applications have been considered.[543]

272. Written objections could be filed by any person to the Commission within twenty-one days of the statutory publication in two paper copies and an electronic copy contained in a CD-ROM, and a copy of the petition or objection shall be made available to the applicant for a reply.[544] The application may be placed for hearing upon evaluation and consideration of the objection within thirty days, subsequent upon service of notice of inquiry by the Commission to the applicant, the persons who filed the objection and other authority or person or body as deemed appropriate.[545] An objection may be refused if considered frivolous and vexatious, but the findings of the Commission shall be recorded in writing.[546]

273. It needs to be pointed out that an application for a licence, an amendment, a renewal or an extension of tenure of a licence may be withdrawn in writing at any

537. Regulations 7 and 8 (a).
538. *Ibid.*, 8 (b).
539. *Ibid.*, 8.
540. Regulation 9.
541. Regulation 10 (a).
542. *Ibid.*, sub-regulation (b).
543. *Ibid.*, sub-regulation (c).
544. Regulation 11 (a) and (b).
545. *Ibid.*, at 11 (c) and (d).
546. *Ibid.*, 11 (e) and (f).

stage, and once withdrawn cannot be reactivated unless it is resubmitted as a new one.[547] Withdrawal of an application is a matter of right subject to the above regulation.

§12. Approval or Refusal of Licence

274. After due consideration of the application by the Commission and after hearing the persons who filed objections if any, the Commission shall grant or refuse to grant the licence[548] and notify the applicant of its decision to approve or refuse the grant of the licence within six months of its acknowledging the receipt of the application.[549] Where the Commission intends to grant a licence it shall notify the applicant of the approval and the conditions to be fulfilled before the grant. On the contrary, if it intends to refuse the licence it shall also notify the applicant of its intention and the reasons for the decision.[550] The applicant shall be given twenty-one days after the receipt of the notice of intention to refuse a licence to make additional representation to the Commission after which the NERC may either grant or refuse the grant of the licence. Reasons given by the Commission for refusing the licence shall be clearly stated in writing and made available to the applicant.[551]

§13. Amendment and Renewal of Licence

275. The regulations list the conditions on which terms and conditions of a licence may be amended as: (i) on application by the licensee in the form specified in Schedule 3 of the Regulation; (ii) upon receipt of a complaint from any consumer, eligible customer, consumer association, association of eligible consumers and other licensees; or (iii) on the Commission's own initiative.[552] An application for amendment may be made any time after the issuance of the licence, but at least nine months before the expiration of the licence.[553] Amendments other than those initiated by the licensee may be effected by the Commission on the terms and conditions of the licence if satisfied that:

(i) any circumstance exists which renders it necessary in the public interest to amend the licence;
(ii) the licensee is unable to meet certain requirements set by the Commission in the terms and conditions;
(iii) the licensee has defaulted in complying with certain provisions of the Act, regulations of the Commission, Market Rules and Network Codes; and
(iv) there is a material change in the circumstances of the licences.

547. Regulation 20 (a) and (b).
548. Regulation 12 (a).
549. *Ibid.*, 12 (b).
550. *Ibid.*, 12 (c) and (d).
551. Regulation 12 (e), (f) and (g).
552. Regulation 13 (a) (i–iii).
553. *Ibid.*, 13 (b).

276. The applicant shall pay a non-refundable fee for processing as provided for in the *Regulations for Licence and Operating Fees 2010*, as amended.[554] However, where the application is for amendment of a licence, the applicant shall publish a notice of the proposed amendment to the licence in the manner specified by the Commission. A similar procedure shall be followed in the application for amendment of a licence as obtainable in a fresh application for an electricity licence, save that the Commission shall be responsible for the publication of statutory notice where the proposed amendment is initiated by it.[555] However, the Commission shall for defence purposes[28] obtain the consent of the Federal Ministry of Defence before making an amendment to a licence in respect of a licensee providing service to an area covering a building or place occupied by the Federal Ministry of Defence.

277. Renewal of licence is through an application made to the Commission at least nine months before the expiration of the licence, in the form specified in Schedule 4 of the Regulation.[556] Fees shall be payable to the Commission, and the procedure prescribed in Chapter 2 for the grant of a fresh licence shall apply for the purpose of application for renewal of a licence.[557]

§14. Extension of Tenure of Licence

278. Application for extension of tenure of licence must be made by an applicant within the first five years of the initial term of the licence.[558] The applicant shall pay a non-refundable processing fee and the application shall be in the form specified in Schedule 5 of the Regulation. The procedure for granting of licence shall be followed in the case of an application for extension of tenure, and the Commission shall consider the application and give its decision within three months of the submission of the licence.[559] An application for extension of tenure of a licence can only be granted once during the initial tenure of the licence being extended, subject to the same rule in case of application in respect of a building being used by the Ministry of Defence.[560]

§15. Suspension of Licence

279. The Commission may of its own initiative or upon receiving complaints or information from any consumer, eligible customer, consumer association or association of eligible customers initiate inquiry into the conduct or activities of

554. *Ibid.*, 13 (d).
555. *Ibid.*, 13 (e) and (f).
556. Regulation 14 (a).
557. *Ibid.*, 14 (b) and (c).
558. Regulation 15 (a) and (b).
559. *Ibid.*, 15 (e) and (f).
560. *Ibid.*, 15 (g) and (h).

any licensee, and may suspend the licence if satisfied that one or more grounds have been established.[561] The grounds for suspending a licence granted by the Commission are if a licensee:

(i) is unable to fully discharge the functions or perform the duties imposed on it by the terms and conditions of the licence, the Act, applicable legislations, regulations of the Commission, Market Rules, Rules and Regulations and Network codes; or
(ii) has defaulted in complying with the terms and conditions of the licence, any decisions or orders of the Commission; or
(iii) is carrying out its licensed business in a form and manner which constitutes an immediate threat to public health and safety or the health or safety of any person; or
(iv) if the licensee refuses to submit itself to investigations or inquiry by the Commission or obstructs any officer assigned to do so or fails to produce documents for inspections as directed by the Commission; or
(v) any circumstance exists which renders it necessary in the public interest to suspend the licence.[562]

280. Upon suspension, the Commission shall inform the licensee of its decision and the basis of the same in writing or give the licensee an opportunity to make representations against the proposed suspension or undertake to rectify or remedy the situation. In case of rectification, the licensee shall take steps to rectify within thirty days of receiving the Commission's letter informing it of the proposed suspension of licence.[563] The representation so made shall be taken into consideration by the Commission in its final decision, and if it decides to suspend the licence, it shall notify the licensee of the date on which the suspension shall take effect including making an order empowering another person or licensee to take over the operations of the undertaking of the suspended licensee in order to ensure continuity.[564] The Commission may further review the suspension order and either cancel the licence or lift the suspension, but it shall not impose a suspension order on a licensee in excess of six months, and for this purpose, it may review it before the expiration of the term of suspension.[565]

§16. Cancellation of Licence

281. The Commission may cancel a licence in like manner as contained in regulation 16 (a–c) above.[566] However, there are variations in the grounds for suspension and cancellation of a licence. The Commission may cancel a licence if:

561. Regulation 16 (a), (b).
562. *Ibid.*, 16 (c)(i–v).
563. *Ibid.*, 16 (d) and (e).
564. *Ibid.*, 16 (f) and (g).
565. *Ibid.*, 16 (h) and (i).
566. Regulation 19 (a). *See* and compare basis and ground of suspension and cancellation of licence under Regulation 16 (a–c).

(i) the licence was issued through fraud or misrepresentation or non-disclosure of a material fact; or
(ii) the licensee has unlawfully or unreasonably contravened any provisions of the Act, applicable legislations, regulations of the Commission, Market Rules, Network Codes, rules and Regulations; or
(iii) the licensee has failed to comply with the term or condition of the licence the breach of which is expressly declared to render it liable to cancellation; or
(iv) the licensee becomes insolvent or is adjudged bankrupt; or
(v) the financial position of the licensee is such that the licensee is unable to fully and efficiently discharge the duties and obligations imposed by the licence.[567]

282. The Commission shall give notice of proceedings for the cancellation of licence to the licensee and other interested parties upon ascertaining the existence of grounds for cancellation. The proceedings of the Commission on cancellation of licence shall ensure that the licensee is informed in writing of the intention to cancel the licence and the reason for doing so. It shall also give the licensee opportunity to demonstrate, within sixty days of receipt of the notice, that the circumstances have changed such that cancellation may no longer be warranted.[568]

283. If the Commission considers cancellation inevitable, it shall serve notice on the licensee indicating the effective date of cancellation, and it may instead of cancellation, pass any other order imposing further terms and conditions under which the licensee is permitted to operate.[569] Upon cancellation, the Commission may make an order for the sale of the undertaking of the licensee as may be necessary for maintaining continuity in the provision of electricity services.[570]

§17. Withdrawal of Licence

284. The regulations provide that the Commission may withdraw a licence for a generating station not yet in operation if the licensee:

(i) obtained the licence through fraud or misrepresentation or non-disclosure of a material fact; or
(ii) wilfully or unreasonably contravenes any provisions of the Act, applicable legislations, regulations of the Commission, Market Rules, Network codes, Rules and Regulations; or
(iii) fails to comply with the milestones upon which the licence was issued; or
(iv) contravenes any term or condition of the licence;
(v) becomes insolvent or is adjudged bankrupt; or

567. Regulation 17 (b)(i–v).
568. *Ibid.*, 17 (d)(i–ii).
569. *Ibid.*, 17 (e) and (f).
570. *Ibid.*, 17 (g).

(vi) fails to commission the licensed generating station listed in the Schedule within three years from the date of grant of licence.[571]

285. The licensee shall be informed in writing of the grounds for withdrawal of the licence, and give the licensee a reasonable opportunity to make representations against the proposed withdrawal. The licensee may choose to make representation within thirty days of receipt of the letter informing it of the ground for withdrawal of the licence, and the Commission shall take such representation into consideration in its final decision.[572] If it decides to withdraw the licence, it shall notify the licensee of its decision. A withdrawn licence cannot be reactivated, amended, renewed or have its tenure extended, save for making a fresh application for the same generating station, upon compliance with the applicable laws and payment of the prescribed fees.[573]

§18. Consumer Protection, Standards and Competition

286. Establishment of effective electricity regulatory frameworks and enforcement of such matters as performance standards, consumer rights and obligation, and matters connected with or incidental thereto is the central objective of the Act.[574] Consumer protection standards are imposed by the Act on the Commission. The Act provides that:

> The Commission shall develop, in consultation with the licensees, the following materials:
>
> (a) consumer services standards;
> (b) consumer complaint handling standards and procedures;
> (c) codes of practice for the provision of assistance to special needs customers such as the blind or disabled, the elderly or severely ill;
> (d) procedures for dealing with, and assisting where necessary, customers who have difficulty in paying bills;
> (e) procedures for applying for electricity service;
> (f) procedures for disconnecting non-paying customers or for those in breach of other terms and conditions of an applicable tariff or contract; and
> (g) the information to be provided to consumers and the manner of its dissemination.[575]

571. Regulation 18 (a) (i–vi).
572. *Ibid.*, 18 (d), (e) and (f).
573. *Ibid.*, 18 (g) and (h).
574. *See* the 'Explanatory Memorandum' to the *Electric Power Sector Reform* (EPSR) Act 2005.
575. Section 80(1)(a–g), Electric Power Sector Reform Act (ESPRA), 2005 *supra* note 386.

287. The standards and procedures developed by the Commission shall be adhered to by the licensees.[576] Standards for compensation payment to consumers shall be established for consumers who do not enjoy regular power supply.[577]

§19. Principles and Basis of Consumer Protection

288. The *Act* defines a consumer as:

> Any end-user of electricity who is a customer of a distribution licensee that is not an eligible customer and, for purposes of filing a complaint with the Commission and for any other reason that the Commission may determine, a person who is temporarily disconnected or otherwise without service, provided that a person who has applied for, but has yet to receive service shall also be deemed a consumer.[578]

289. The concept of 'Eligible customers' would appear to have re-characterized electricity consumers into two or more categories. Section 27 of the Act provides that 'the Minister may issue a directive to the Commission specifying the class or classes of end-use customers that, from time to time shall constitute eligible customers under this Act'. The phrase 'eligible customers' is defined by the Act to mean a customer that is eligible pursuant to a directive of the minister issued under section 27 of the Act.[579] Thus, if the minister designates a class of end-use customers as eligible customers they can purchase power from other licensees in addition to the distribution licences.

290. However, the word 'customer' and 'consumers' are used interchangeably though accorded different meanings under the Act and Regulations. For instance, the *NERC Regulation on Customer Complaints Handling: Standards and Procedure 2006*, defines a customer as:

> Any person or organization supplied with electricity for his own use by a distribution licensee or by any other person engaged in the business of supplying electricity to the public under the Electric Power Sector Reform Act or any other law for the time being in force and includes any person whose premises are for the time being connected for the purpose of receiving electricity from a distribution licensee or such other person as the case may be.[580]

291. The law seeks to protect electricity consumers from defects in electricity services by licensees and other electricity trading companies. Though the Act does

576. *Ibid.*, subs. (2).
577. *Ibid.*, subs. (3).
578. Section 100.
579. *Ibid.*
580. *See* Regulation *2(8), the NERC Regulation on Customer Complaints Handling: Standards and Procedure, 2006.*

not define what constitutes 'a defect' in the electric power sector, however, the definitional gaps have been filled by the *NERC Regulation on Customer Complaints Handling: Standards and Procedure 2006.*[581] It defines defect, for the purpose of consumer protection as 'a fault, imperfection or shortcoming in the quality, standards of service, equipment or material which is required to be by or under any law or regulation for the time being in force or under any contract or as claimed by the customer in relation to electricity service'.[582] The regulation also defines deficiency in relation to the electric power sector.[583]

581. *Ibid.*, para. 2(1).
582. *Ibid.*
583. It provides:

> Any fault, imperfection, shortcomings or inadequacy in the quality of service which is required to be maintained by or under any law or regulation or has been undertaken to be performed by a distribution licensee in pursuance of a contract agreement or otherwise in relation to electricity service or performance standards, viz; interruptions failure of power supply, voltage complaints, metering problems of power supply to the customer in contravention of the EPSR Act 2005.

Ibid., para. 2(12).

Chapter 4. Nigerian Gas Law and Regulation

§1. Introduction

292. A major challenge facing the petroleum industry in Nigeria is how to harness the enormous gas resources of the country. It is reported that over 386 million cubic feet of natural gas is flared every day in Nigeria.[584] In an effort to diversify its economy and also to provide natural gas for the domestic industry, the Nigerian Government in its fourth National Development Plan (1981–1986) evinced an intention to establish a multimillion-dollar liquefied natural gas project at Bonny in the Southern part of the country.[585] The project was to consist of lifting, gathering, processing and distribution of natural gas, both for export and internal use, from Nigerian oil fields. This gave birth to the Nigerian Liquefied Natural Gas Limited (NLNG), which has been adjudged to be a success story in gas utilization in Nigeria.[586]

293. The history of the development of *Natural Gas* is synonymous with the history and development of oil/petroleum in Nigeria.[587] Gas was not a popular energy source as most of the facilities currently being used for exploration in the country were built without giving any thought to putting gas-gathering infrastructure in place.[588] Gas production in Nigeria is accidental, and is mostly linked to the production of oil by way of 'associated gas'. This is separated from oil at flow stations and more than 70% of it is simply flared. Current estimates show that Nigeria produces an average of 34 billion cubic metres (bcm) of gas yearly out of which 75% is flared.[589]

§2. The Legal Regime of Gas Development in Nigeria

294. The CFRN, 1999 is the supreme law as to the origin and development of oil and gas in Nigeria.[590] The Nigerian courts have had to interpret the provision of

584. *See* Tolupe, A.O., 'Oil Exploration and Environmental Degradation: the Nigeria Experience' (2004) 4 *International Society for Environmental Information Science*. pp. 34–36. Eweje Gabriel. 'Environmental Costs and Responsibilities Resulting from Oil Exploitation in Developing Countries: The Case of the Niger Delta of Nigeria'. (2006) 69:1, *Journal of Business Ethics*, p. 30.
585. Oyewunmi, O.A. & Oyewunmi, A.E, 'Managing Gas Flaring and Allied Issues in the Oil and Gas Industry: Reflections on Nigeria' (2016) 7:4 *Mediterranean Journal of Social Sciences* (MCSER Publishing, Rome-Italy, p. 643. *See also* Amanze R. Ejiogu, 'Gas Flaring in Nigeria: Costs and Policy' (2013) 24:6 *Energy & Environment Journal* (2013), pp. 983–998 online at: http://www.jstor.org/stable/43735213 accessed 16 Jul. 2017.
586. Oyewunmi, O.A. & Oyewunmi, A.E, *ibid.*
587. *See* Amanze R. Ejiogu, *supra* note 585.
588. *Ibid.*
589. U. Udok & E.B. Akpan, 'Gas Flaring in Nigeria: Problems and Prospects', 5:1 (Global Journal of Politics and Law Research (European Centre for Research Training and Development, UK: March 2017) p. 26; M. Gidado, 'Fiscal Provisions for Gas Development and Commercialisation under the Petroleum Industry Bill (P.I.B.)' 2009 *NIALS Journal of Business Law*, p. 27.
590. *See* Attorney General Federation and Attorney General Abia State (No.2) (2002) 6 NWLR Part 764 p. 542; *NDDC v. Nigeria LNG Limited* (Unreported Suit No. FHC/PH/CS/313/2005 p. 859. Per

the constitution vis-à-vis some gas statutes and regulations. For instance in *NDDC v. Nigeria LNG Limited,*[591] *Nwodo J.* (as she then was of blessed memory) held obiter that *Schedule II of paragraph 3 of Nigerian Liquefied Natural Gas (LNG) (Fiscal Incentive, Assurance & Guarantees) Act, 1990 as Amended in 1993,* violates section 4 of the 1999 constitution in that it derogates from the constitutionally provided powers of the National Assembly to make laws for the peace, order and good governance of the Federation with respect to any matter included in the Exclusive Legislative List. *Paragraph 3 of the Schedule II Nigeria LNG* provides thus:

> without to prejudice to any other provision contained herein, neither the Company nor its shareholders in their capacity as shareholders in the Company, shall in any way be subject to new laws, regulations, taxes, duties, imports or charges of whatever nature which are not applicable generally to companies incorporated in Nigeria or to shareholders in companies incorporated in Nigeria, respectively.

295. In addition to the Constitution, there are other laws and regulations that have helped in shaping Nigeria's Gas Development. Some of these laws and regulations include *Treaty between Federal Republic of Nigeria and the Democratic Republic of Sao Tome and Principe on the Joint Development of Petroleum and other Resources* (i.e., natural gas) in areas of the Exclusive Economic Zone (EEZ) of the two states. In Attorney *General of the Federation and Attorney General, Abia* State,[592] the Supreme Court also held that the natural resources located in the EEZ and subject to the provisions of any treaty[593] or other written agreement between Nigeria and any neighbouring littoral foreign state are derived from the

---

Nwodo J. as He then was); *Abacha v. Fawehinmi* 1997 NWLR 6 NWLR Part 764 p. 124; *FAMA Oil Ltd. v. Attorney General Federation and NNPC* (Unreported Suit No. CA/A/173/2006.*See also* the following sections of the 1999 Constitution. Sections 1(1) and (3), s. 4 (1), s. 44 (3) and Second Schedule, Part II, Item 39 and s. 58 of the 1999 Constitution which provide for powers of the National Assembly to make laws for the whole country. *See also National Assembly v. President* [2003] 9 NWLR P., 130 per Oguntade JCA (as he then was); Section 6(1) which vest judicial powers of the Federation in courts for settlement of disputes arising from gas related cases and s. 251 of the Constitution which gives the Federal High Court exclusive powers/jurisdiction in mines and minerals (including oil fields, oil mining, geological surveys and *natural gas*) and from there to Court of Appeal and Supreme Court. Section 44(3) which gave control of all minerals oil and *natural gas,* in the Federal Republic of Nigeria and to be managed in such manner as prescribed by the National Assembly UNDER s. 4 of the Constitution. *See also* ss. 62, 88 and 89 of the Constitution from which standing committees of the National Assembly exercise its powers in gas related matters and monitor the Ministry of Energy, NNPC and its subsidiaries. *See* Generally Niyi Ayoola-Daniels; *Nigeria Laws, Cases and Materials on oil and Gas* Volume 1 at 34–38.

591. Unreported Suit No. FHC/PH/CS/313/2005 Pg. 859. *See also Famfa Oil Ltd. v. A.G.F. & NNPC* (Unreported Suit CA/A/173/2006) where the Court of Appeal ruled on the interpretation of para. 35 of the First Schedule to the Petroleum Act, Cap P10 LFN, 2004 and para. 2(1) of *Deep Water Allocation to Companies (Back In-Rights) Regulation, 2004.*
592. (No. 2) (2002) 6 NWLR Part 764 P. 542.
593. *See* ss. 1 and 2 of the Exclusive Economic Zone Act, Cap E 17 LFN 2004. *See also* Art. 7 of UNCLOS 1982.

Federation, and not the state.[594] The treaty has two subsidiary regulations. One is Joint Development Zone – Petroleum Regulations; and Joint Development Zone –Tax Regulations.

296. The Treaty on West African Gas Pipeline (WAGP) (Ratification and Enforcement) Act, 2004 is also part of the legal regimes of gas development in Nigeria. The Act makes provision for the treaty on the West African Gas Pipeline Project and is binding on all persons exercising legislative or judicial powers in Nigeria. The *West African Gas Pipeline Project (Special Provision) Act, 2005* provides for national legislation to implement the obligations of Nigeria under the WAGP Treaty and International project agreement of the West African Gas Project involving Nigeria, the Republic of Benin, Ghana and Togo.[595]

297. Also applicable is the West African Gas Pipeline Regulations, 2005. These Regulations were made pursuant to *section 20 of the West African Gas Pipeline Project (Special Provision) Act, 2005*. The purpose of the regulation is to provide a consistent and enforceable code, governing the design, construction, operation and maintenance of the WAGP System with a view to harmonizing the regulation of those matters in each of the states who are signatories to the WAGP Treaty. Similarly applicable in this regard is the International Convention on Civil Liability for Oil Pollution damage (Ratification and Enforcement) Act, 2006 and the International Convention on the establishment of an International Fund for Compensation for Oil Pollution Damage (Ratification and Enforcement,) Act, 2006.

298. Another local regime is the provisions of the *Associated Gas Re-injection Act No. 99 of 1979.*[596] The purpose of this Act was for every company producing oil and gas in Nigeria to submit a preliminary programme for gas reinjection and detailed plans for implementation. Section 1 of the Act placed a duty on gas companies in Nigeria to before 1 April 1980 submit to the Minister for Petroleum a preliminary programme for: (i) Scheme for the viable utilization of all associated gas produced from the oil fields; and (ii) Projects or project to reinject all gas produced in association with oil but not utilized in an industrial project. By section 2 of the Act, companies are to submit detailed programmes in respect of (i) and (ii) before 1 October 1980.

299. Section 3 of the Act deals with gas flaring and provides that gas flaring shall cease by 1 January 1984. It however contradicts itself when it states further that gas can be flared with the support of the minister in writing. Also by the provisions of section *3(2)(a) & (b)* the minister may permit gas flaring if the company pays a fee

594. *See* the Joint Ownership and Development Zone between Nigeria and Sao Tome & Principe signed in 21 Feb. 2001.
595. *See* Niyi Ayoola-Daniels, *Nigerian Law, Cases and Materials on Oil and Gas*, Volume 1, at 13.
596. Cap. A 25 LFN 2004. The Act commenced 28/9/79.

to be determined by the minister for every *28,317 standard cubic metre (SCM)* of gas flared. More worrisome is the fact that payment for gas flaring is made in the same manner as payment for royalty.[597]

300. The Associated Gas Reinjection Regulation[598] lays down conditions for the grant of ministers' licences under section 3(2) of the Associated Gas Reinjection Act No. 99 of 1979 for continued gas flaring in a particular field. The conditions include:

(a) where more than 75% of the gas produced is utilized and conserved;
(b) where the gas produced contains more than 15% impurities, such as N^2 H_2S, and CO_2 which render gas unsuitable for industrial purposes;
(c) where an ongoing utilization programme is interrupted by equipment failure;
(d) where the ratio of gas produced per day to the distance of the field from the nearest gas line or possible utilization point is less than 50,000 SCGF/KM; provided that the oil and gas ratio of the field is less than 3,500 SCF/bbl, and that it is technically advisable to reinject the gas in the field;
(e) where the minister in an appropriate case as he may deem fit orders the production of oil from a field that does not satisfy any of these conditions.

301. The *Nigeria Liquefied Natural Gas (Fiscal Incentives Guarantees and Assurance) Act No. 39 of 1990* is another crucial piece of legislation regulating gas development in Nigeria.[599] The objective of the Act was to confer a pioneer status on Nigeria LNG Limited and to exempt the company from taxes, customs duties, other levies and the provisions of the Pre-shipment Inspection of Imports Act. The Act also provides for guarantees and assurances by the Federal Government to the Company and its shareholders.[600] *Section 1(1)* gave LNG Limited a pioneer status within the provisions of the *Industrial Development (Income Tax Relief) Act.*[601] By virtue of section 1(4) of the Act, the pioneer status conferred on the company shall continue until the production of gas by the company. Production means the date of the first commercial delivery of liquefied natural gas produced by the Company to a purchaser of the liquefied natural gas upon which date the trade or business of the company shall be deemed to commence for the purposes of company income tax.

302. *Section 2* provides for a tax relief period. The section provides that notwithstanding the provision of section 10 of the Industrial Development (Income Tax

597. *See* s. 5 Deep Offshore and Inland Basin Production Sharing Contracts Act Cap D3 LFN 2004.
598. *Associated Gas Re-injection Act* Cap A25 LFN. *See also Associated Gas Re-Injection (Continued Flaring of Gas) Regulation 1984.*
599. Nigeria LNG (Fiscal Incentives, Guarantees and Assurances) Act, Cap N87 Laws of the Federation 2004.
600. This company has been enjoying all these concessions since 1990 and up till date the liquefied natural gas (LNG) projects has not come on board. *See* Institute of Geosciences and Space Technology – IGST (1991), Nigeria LNG Project Development, Report on Historical Weather Data Analysis for Port Harcourt International Airport Weather Station (1980–1989), Volumes I–IV, Rivers State University of Science & Technology.
601. Cap. I17 LFN 2004.

Relief) Act,[602] the tax relief period of the company shall commence on the production day of the company and continue for ten years but can be terminated after the first five years if the cumulative average sale price of LNG of the Company is USD 3/1 million British Thermal Units (mmbtu). Section 6 also exempts the Company from withholding Tax (WHT) while section 7 exempts the Company from customs duties. Section 9 states that the guarantees and assurances set out in the Second Schedule to the Act shall have effect with respect to the shareholders of the company.

303. There is also an incentive for the exploitation of Associated Gas (Upstream Operation) under *section 12 Petroleum Profit Tax Act.*[603] The incentives include the following:

(a) that investment required to separate crude oil and gas from the reservoir into useable products is considered part of the oil field development;
(b) that capital investment on facilities equipment to deliver associated gas in the useable form at utilization or designed custody transfer points is treated for tax purposes as part of the capital investment for oil development;
(c) that capital allowance operation expenses as the basis for tax assessment are subject to the provision of the Act and the tax incentives under the revised Memorandum of Understanding (MOU);
(d) gas transferred from the NGL facility to the Gas-to-Liquid facilities is to be at 0% PPT and 0% Royalty.

304. Likewise, the Tax Relief also includes payment of Central Bank of Nigeria charges or other bank charges imposed by the Federal Government of Nigeria on any petroleum exploration and production company in the course of the business of 'petroleum operations' which may ordinarily become deductible expenses under section 10(1) of the Petroleum Profits Tax Act.[604] However, other bank charges and Central Bank of Nigeria charges pursuant to section 10(1)(g) of the Petroleum Profits Tax Act are deductible as they are not made on behalf of the Federal Government.[605]

305. Also applicable is *Guarantees and Assurance to Nigeria LNG Limited and Its Shareholders No. 113 of 1993*, made Pursuant to section 9, Nigeria LNG (Fiscal Incentives Guarantees and Assurance) Act No. 39 of 1990. The preamble to the Act states that:

> The Federal Government of Nigeria ... , in recognition of the magnitude of and in consideration of the investments which shall have to be made in order to

602. *Ibid.*
603. Cap. P13 LFN 2004.
604. *Ibid.*
605. *See Shell Petroleum Development Company (Nigeria) Limited v. F.B.I.R* (1996) 8 NWLR Part 466 at P. 256; *Trendex Trading Corp. v. Central Bank of Nigeria* [1977] 2 W.L.R Pg. 356; *Gulf Oil Company (Nig.) v. FBIR* (1997) 7 NWLR Pt., 514 at p. 535.

prosecute the venture described in the Shareholders Contract dated 19th May, 1989 between *NNPC, Shell Gas B.V., CLEAG Limited and Agip International B.V.*, as amended, from time to time …, hereby grants to the company, it successor and to each of the shareholders, from time to time (in their capacity as such), the guarantees, assurances and undertakings following hereunder.

306. It also states that those guarantees, assurances and undertakings shall have effect from 19 May 1989, and so long as the company, or any successor thereto, is in existence and carrying on the business of liquefying and selling liquefied natural gas and natural gas liquids within and/or outside the Federal Republic of Nigeria.

307. The government also made guarantees in respect of the following: (a) the grant of licences or permits required for the importation or exportation of plant, equipment and products of the company; (b) the grant or permits, licences required for the construction, start-up and operation of the facilities; and the customs formalities in respect of imports and exports (not including personal effects) required in connection with the construction, operation and maintenance of the company facilities and products; (c) the prompt registration and certification by the National Office for Technology Acquisition and Promotion (NOTAP) of all contracts for the transfer of technology to the company by its advisers, contractors and subcontractors in accordance with the *National Office for Technology Acquisition and Promotion Act*[606] and that section 6(2) of the Act shall not apply to the company.

308. It also includes the undertaking that government shall facilitate the acquisition of lands and ensure vacant possession (for a period of not less than eighty years) of land required by the company for the venture (including a suitable residential area), together with rights of way, easement and other rights necessary for the implementation of the venture. It contains a clause that the company shall be treated as an independent autonomous commercial entity and its operations, policies, procedures and conditions of services shall be determined by the Board of Directors of the company.[607]

§3. Legal Aspects of Ownership of Natural Gas in Nigeria

309. The legal aspect of ownership of gas/natural gas in Nigeria is synonymous with the ownership of petroleum and other natural resources, as the British colonial masters vested all rights and control of minerals and mineral oils, in, under or upon any land in Nigeria and all rivers, streams and water course through Nigeria in the British Government.[608] Reference to the control of minerals is taken as reference to the control of gas even though the exploration and exploitation of gas is not

606. Cap. N62 LFN 2004.
607. *See* ss. 35 and 37 of *Companies and Allied Matter Act*, Cap C 20 LFN 2004.
608. *See* the following ordinances and statutes Mineral Ordinance of 1888; the Mining Regulation (Oil) Ordinance No. 12 of 1907; the Ordinance No.19 of 1909(contained in Cap. 130 Laws of Southern Nigeria); By 1914, Ordinance No. 19 of 1909 was replaced by the Mineral Oils Ordinance No. 17

expressly started. In 1963, three years after independence, Nigeria enacted a republican constitution which provided *inter alia* that all property which immediately before the date of the commencement of the Constitution (1 October 1963) was held by the crown or on behalf of the crown should vest in the President of the Federation on behalf of and for the benefit of the Government of the Federation.

310. Subsequent constitutions also followed the same trend. For example, section 40(3) of the 1979 and 44(3) 1999 CFRN which is *impari materia* with section 1 of the Petroleum Act also unequivocally vests in the Federal Government of Nigeria the entire property in and control of all minerals, mineral oils and natural gas in, under or upon any land in Nigeria or in, under or upon the territorial waters and the exclusive economic zone of Nigeria.[609]

311. Consistent with this, the 1979 and 1999 Constitution granted to the National Assembly exclusive legislative powers over mines, minerals and natural gas.[610] *In Attorney General of the Federation v. Attorney General of Abia and 35 ORS,*[611] the Supreme Court *per Kutigi JSC (as he then was*) held that:

> There is no dispute here in Nigeria with regard to the right of the Federal Government to the entire, property in, and control over all minerals, mineral oils

---

of 1914; *See* s. 6(1)(a) Oil Mineral (Amendment) Ordinance No. 1 of 1925, Minerals Ordinance of 1946 (Cap. 121 Laws of the Federation of Nigeria 1958; *Mineral Oils (Amendment) Ordinance, No. 5 1958.*

609. *See* ss. 1 and 2 of the Petroleum Act 1969 Cap. P10 LFN 2004; and ss. 5 and 6 NNPC Act No. 33 of 1977 Cap. N123 LFN 2004 (Cap 320 LFN 1990). *See also A.G. Federation v. A.G. Abia, supra* note 592. In this case, the Supreme Court of Nigeria held that natural resources (which is inclusive of oil and oil minerals) in s. 162(2*) of the Constitution* outside the boundary of the littoral states or states in the Southern part of Nigeria commencing from the low water mark or the seaward limit of inland waters toward the Territorial Sea of Nigeria and extending from the limits of the territorial waters to a distance of 200 hundred nautical miles (Exclusive Economic Zone belong to the Federal Government. *See also s. 1(1) and (2) of the Exclusive Economic Zone Act Cap. E17 LFN 2004 (Cap. 110 LFN 1990); ss. 1 and 2 Territorial Waters Act Cap. T5 LFN 2004 (Cap. 428 LFN 1990); s. 1 of the Sea Fisheries Act Cap. S4 LFN 2004 (Cap. 404 LFN 1990). See also United Nations Resolutions;* Resolution No. 626 (VII) of 21 Dec. 1952, providing for the right of states to exploit their natural resources *as part of their sovereignty (permanent sovereignty over natural resources). See also* Resolution No. 1803 (XVII) of 14 Dec. 1962, which limited resolution No. 626 by providing that nationalization measures could only be implemented for public purposes, security or national interest, subject to the investor receiving *'appropriate compensation' in accordance to domestic and international law*; Resolution No. 3201 (S-VI) of 1 May 1974 which saw an attempt by, developing nations to change the status quo ante bellum in the legal principles of nationalization. The resolution titled '*Declaration on the Establishment of a New International Economic Order'* stated in *Art. 4(e) that a State had the right to nationalize its resources and could not be subject to economic, political or other coercion to prevent the exercise of that right*; Resolution No. 3281 (XXIX), of 26 Jul. 1974 where the General Assembly adopted the Charter of Economic Rights and Duties of States. The resolution confirmed that the right to nationalize foreign-owned property required '*appropriate compensation, and admitted that, if compensation was not paid, the nationalizing State's international obligation would not have been fulfilled in good faith. See also* Resolution XVI. 90 of OPEC of 1968.
610. *See* s. 37 and Second Schedule, Part II, Exclusive Legislative List of the 1979 Constitution and s. 44(3), Second Schedule, Part II, Item 39 Exclusive Legislative List of the 1999 Constitution.
611. *Supra* note 320.

and natural gas in, under or upon any land in Nigeria or in, under over the territorial waters and the Exclusive Economic Zone of Nigeria.

312. The combined effect of these provisions is to vest the entire ownership and control of all natural gas, in, under or upon any lands in Nigeria (including lands under Nigeria Territorial Waters, Continental Shelf and Exclusive Economic Zone) in the Federal Government of Nigeria. The principal law concerning the ownership and administration by the government of Nigeria's petroleum and by extension of natural gas is the Nigerian Constitution. The Petroleum Act only declares the status quo when it provides in section 1(1) that the entire ownership and control of all petroleum in, under or upon any lands in Nigeria her territorial waters or continental shelf shall be vested in the state.

313. Section 14 of the 1969 Act as amended[612] defines petroleum to mean: 'mineral oil (or any related hydrocarbon) or natural gas as it exists in its natural state or strata and does not include coal or bituminous shales or other stratified deposits from which oil can be extracted by destructive distillation'. In the same section, natural gas is defined as: 'gas obtained from boreholes and wells consisting primarily of hydrocarbons'.

§4. Gas Utilization and Production in Nigeria

314. Nigeria has abundant gas resources but the gas industry has not evolved at the same pace of development as the oil industry. The reason for the neglect of the gas sector is largely due to the capital-intensive nature of the gas industry.[613] The major export-oriented gas production in Nigeria is LNG. The export of liquefied natural gas commenced in 1999 with the establishment of the Nigeria Liquefied Natural Gas Company NLNG. The company was registered under the Nigeria LNG Act[614] and designed to utilize Nigeria's enormous gas reserves. It has six trains and is building the seventh. Other major LNG projects in different stages of (abandoned) development include the USD 3.5 billion Brass LNG and the USD 7 billion OKLNG project.

315. The domestic residential market for natural gas in Nigeria is relatively small. Due to the tropical location of the region, no space heating demand exists.

612. *See* s. 15 of the Petroleum Act, Cap. P10 Laws of the Federation of Nigeria (LFN), 2004.
613. E.I Kachikwu, 'Legal Issues in Oil and Gas Industry' (1989) Gravitas, Vol 2, No 34 at 39. *See also* Tolupe, A.O., 'Oil Exploration and Environmental Degradation: the Nigeria Experience' (2004) 4 *International Society for Environmental Information Science*. pp. 34–36; Eweje Gabriel. 'Environmental Costs and Responsibilities Resulting from Oil Exploitation in Developing Countries: The Case of the Niger Delta of Nigeria'. (2006) 69:1, *Journal of Business Ethics*, p. 30. U. Udok & E.B. Akpan, 'Gas Flaring in Nigeria: Problems and Prospects', 5:1 (Global Journal of Politics and Law Research (European Centre for Research Training and Development, UK: March 2017) p. 26; M.M. Gidado, *supra* note 589.
614. Nigeria LNG (Fiscal Incentives, Guarantees and Assurances) Act, Cap. N87 Laws of the Federation 2004.

Apart from the main population centres and food refrigeration and preservation needs, the remaining cooking and water heating demands of individual consumers are relatively too small to justify the costs of a natural gas distribution and supply network for purely domestic consumers.[615]

316. Gas is central to Nigeria's power sector. Nigeria has the world's ninth largest proven gas reserves (estimated at 180,105 billion standard cubic feet a day (bscfd). However, the insufficient gas supply is the biggest constraint to available generating capacity and reduces operating capacity by an average of 2,060 megawatts daily. Although the country has abundant reserves, its gas production is low – it ranks 22 on the global production scale. The low level of gas supplied to power plants is exacerbated by insufficient gas production for the domestic market. In 2014, total gas production was ~8.9 bscfd but less than 10% was supplied to the domestic power sector for generation. This is insufficient to run the country's gas thermal power plants. As a result, only 56% of gas plants' available generating capacity is operational. An additional ~0.6 bscfd would be required to sustain the current available generating capacity.[616] The low level of gas produced for the domestic market is the result of insufficient gas-processing and pipeline infrastructure.[617] Long-term under-investment and delays in the delivery of planned gas infrastructure have resulted in a shortage of gas-processing and pipeline infrastructure. Lack of investment in gas-processing facilities and failure to complete already funded projects are key challenges. Regular vandalism of existing pipelines is another big challenge.

§5. THE NIGERIAN DOWNSTREAM GAS MARKET

317. The gas chain entails the production, transmission, distribution, supply and the end consumer. The level of interaction among the subsets determines whether or not there exists competition. Section 39 of the Companies Income Tax Act[618] (CITA) defines gas utilization as:

> The marketing and distribution of natural gas for commercial purposes and includes power plant, liquefied natural gas, gas to liquid plant, fertilizer plant, gas transmission and distribution pipelines.

---

615. Mourad Belguedj 'Strategic Gas Plan for Nigeria' Publication of Joint UNDP/World Bank Energy Sector Management Assistance Programme (ESMAP) available at: www.esmap.org/esmapsites/esmap.org/files/FR58200861713_Nigeria_strategicgasplanfornigeria.pdf, assessed on 10 Oct. 2015.
616. E.I. Kachikwu, 'Legal Issues in Oil and Gas Industry'; *supra* note 613 U. Udok & E.B. Akpan, 'Gas Flaring in Nigeria: Problems and Prospects', *supra* note 589, p. 26; M.M. Gidado, *supra* note 589.
617. M.M. Ologundudu, *'The Epileptic Nature of Electricity Supply and Its Consequences on Industrial and Economic Performance in Nigeria'*, (2014) Vol. XIV, issue IV, version 1, *Global Journal of Research in Engineering*.
618. Cap. C21 Laws of the Federation 2004.

318. The downstream gas market in Nigeria is dominated by the upstream producers, due to existing favourable regulatory structures.[619] These producers engage in limited transmission and distribution of gas to serve their needs. Despite this, Nigeria has managed to develop huge domestic gas demand centres such as four gas-fired plants with peak period gas demand of 1500 million cubic feet per day (mmcfd), cement industries at Benue and Lokoja, fertilizer companies in Lagos, iron and steel plants at Ajaokuta, petrochemical and aluminium smelting industries at various locations in the country. There is also the need for gas supply to residential users. The present import of LPG in Nigeria stands at about 20,000 Tons per year (TPY) out of a total estimated market demand of 200,000 TPY.[620] It would be wrong to assume that there is no 'solid domestic market' demand in Nigeria. What is lacking is incentivizing investment in the production and marketing of gas for the domestic market.

I. Gas Transmission

319. Transmission is concerned with the transport of natural gas through a high-pressured pipeline network other than the upstream pipeline network. The Nigerian Gas Company (NGC), the sole wholesale supplier, owns and controls the transmission lines. It operates an un-integrated 1,100 kilometres of transmission pipeline capacity of more than two bscf/day, fourteen compressor stations, thirteen metering stations and eight supply stations.[621] There are other transmission pipelines owned by the NLNG and the NNPC/SPDC/total joint venture specifically dedicated to their respective operations.[622]

II. Gas Distribution

320. The transport of gas through low-pressured pipelines to the end-users in Nigeria is done by two companies, Shell Nigeria Gas (SNG) and Gaslink Nigeria Limited (Gaslink). Gaslink has built about 100 kilometres of pipelines in Lagos State for the supply of natural gas to industrial and residential users.[623] SNG also

---

619. Banigo, I., *The Development of a Downstream (Domestic) Gas Market in Nigeria: Barriers and Reforms?* (Unpublished Dissertation submitted to CEPMLP, University of Dundee, 2005) p. 45.
620. Ukpebor, E.T.O, *Nigerian Gas Master Plan: Strengthening the Nigeria Gas Infrastructure Blueprint as a Base for Expanding Regional Gas Market*, presented at the 24th World Gas Conference, October, 2009, p. 9.
621. *See* the Nigerian National Petroleum Corporation (NNPC) Group- Gas; Nigerian Gas Company), online at: http://www.nnpcgroup.com/nnpc-group/ngc, accessed 24 Mar. 2016.
622. *Ibid.*, Kachikwu, *supra* note 613.
623. BusinessDay, 1 Dec. 2008, online at: http://www.businessdayonline.com/index.php?option=com_content&view=Article&id=1606:gaslink-completes-n7bn-pipeline-expansion&catid=85:national&Itemid=266, accessed 18 Mar. 2016.

targets the supply of gas to power plants and industrial users. Surprisingly, both distributors supply gas only to the western part of the country i.e., Lagos and the Niger delta. There are no connecting pipelines to either the south-eastern or the northern part of the country.

§6. LEGAL REGIME OF GAS FLARED DURING PRODUCTION

321. A major challenge to gas production in Nigeria is gas flaring. Gas flaring in Nigeria is as old as oil production in Nigeria. Gas flaring began in Nigeria sometime in the 1960s being the cheapest way to separate crude oil from the associated natural gas.[624] The main reason why gas flaring continues at the rate it does in Nigeria is because of the lack of political will on the part of both the government and the oil companies.[625] Nigeria has been condoning gas flaring for decades, apparently because it is blessed with many energy resources.[626] Official records indicate that the country has twelve different energy resources,[627] these include among others: oil, natural gas, tar sands, coal, nuclear, hydropower, fuelwood, solar, biomass,

624. World over, in oil production, gas is flared for the reasons below. They are:

- *During well production testing after drilling is completed:* after a shale oil/gas well is drilled and hydraulically fractured, a temporary flare is used during well production testing. Testing is important in order to determine the pressure, flow and composition of the gas or oil from the well. Flaring at the well site can last for several days or weeks, until the flow of liquids and gas from the well and pressures are stabilized.
- *For safety and during emergencies and maintenance:* a flare is an important safety device, particularly at gas-processing plants. In an emergency situation where equipment or piping becomes over-pressured, special valves on the equipment automatically release gas through piping to flare stacks. In the absence of safety flares, plants would be at higher risk for fires and explosions. Flares are also used as an outlet for gas during maintenance and equipment repairs. In these scenarios, the flare is operated temporarily until the emergency situation is resolved, or until maintenance activities have been completed.
- *For managing gas during compression and processing:* flare gas systems are used to manage small volumes of waste gas that cannot be efficiently captured and returned to the system for processing. For example, some natural gas compressor stations have small dehydrator units that remove water from the gas stream before it enters the pipeline system. There may be a small flare at the compressor station to burn off gas vapors captured by the dehydrator unit. These flares are typically small and not visible off site.

See Ohio Environmental Protection Agency, 'Understanding The Basics of Gas Flaring', 2012, available online at: http://epa.ohio.gov/portals/0/General%20pdfs/gas%20flaring.pdf accessed 13 Jul. 2017.

625. Engobo Emeseh, 'Gas Flaring in Nigeria: The Decision of the Federal High Court in Context' *Nigeria World*, 20 Dec. 2005. Available online at: http://nigeriaworld.com/Articles/2005/dec/204.html, accessed 16 Jul. 2017).
626. Raimi, L. et al., Redressing the Energy Challenge of Gas Flaring in Nigeria: The MEEs Approach, (2013) 2:2 *Journal of Sustainable Development Studies*, available online at www.infinitypress.info /index.php/jsds/Article/download/68/66, accessed 14 Jul. 2017.
627. National Energy Policy document, 2003. These energy resources are oil, natural gas, Tsar sands, coal, nuclear, hydropower, fuelwood, solar, biomass, wind, hydrogen, other renewable.

wind, hydrogen and other renewables. It needs to be mentioned that only three of the resources are currently being exploited, these include oil, gas and hydro.[628]

322. Gas flaring also persists in Nigeria because of the emphasis on crude oil to the neglect of gas for local use and exports. Nigeria has 36.2 billion barrels of proven oil reserves.[629] Lack of adequate industrial facilities required to commercialize abundant gas resource being flagrantly flared is another cogent reason. Reports indicate that Nigeria had an estimated 185 trillion cubic feet (tcf) of gas resources making it the eight largest natural gas reserve holder in the world and the largest in Africa.[630] The phenomenon of flaring gas exists in different oil fields in the Niger Delta because of apathy. Gas flaring is a by-product of crude oil production and is a common sight in the Niger Delta. Nigeria flares 40% of its annual natural gas production, while the World Bank estimates that Nigeria accounts for 12.5% of total flared natural gas in the world.[631]

323. The flares from Nigeria alone have contributed more greenhouse gases to the atmosphere than the combined flares from sub-Saharan African nations.[632] The energy challenge of gas flaring is socially and economically undesirable, as huge revenue loss and health hazards are engendered by this action. The quantity of gas has double the oil, and the availability of natural gas is longer than that of oil. Nigeria therefore can triple its foreign exchange earnings through effective and efficient exploitation of its natural gas instead of encouraging gas flaring.[633] The effects of gas flaring are multifaceted. The negative impacts of gas flaring are evident in the country particularly because of the dearth of technology for the utilization of such energy which is only recently just being employed at a slow pace. The impact on humans, the environment and the economy remain a global concern. Nigeria and Russia have been mentioned to be the highest gas-flaring countries.[634]

§7. Nigerian Environmental Laws and Gas Flaring

324. Nigeria's environmental laws can be classified into pre-environmental statutes and post-environmental era statutes.[635] The early legislations that can be said

628. Raimi, L. et al., *supra* note 626.
629. *Ibid.*
630. *Ibid.*
631. *Ibid.*
632. *See* Friends of the Earth, 'Gas flaring in Nigeria'. Media Briefing, 2004, http://www.foe.co.uk/resource/media_briefing/gasflaringinnigeria.pdf, last accessed 14 Jul. 2017.
633. Raimi, L. et al., *supra* note 626.
634. O. Saheed Ismail and G. Ezaina Umukoro, 'Global Impact of Gas Flaring', (2012) 4 *Journal of Energy and Power Engineering*, pp. 290–302, published online on July 2012 at: http://www.SciRP.org/journal/epe, also available online at: http://dx.doi.org/10.4236/epe.2012.44039, accessed 12 Jul. 2017.
635. Olanrewaju Fagbohun, *The law of Oil Pollution and Environmental Restoration; A comparative Review* (Lagos Nigeria, 2010) p. 285.

to be relevant to environmental protection were merely reactive, responding to the changing needs of the economy, industry and expanding urbanization in order to rectify immediate problems of health and safety.[636] The emergence of true macro-environmental planning and protection capable of being used as a tool for social engineering did not take centre stage until 1988 when the political pressure of the Koko incidence forced the government to reassess its role in environmental issues.[637]

325. Since the beginning of the environmentally-conscious era, other statutes have been enacted specifically for the protection of the Nigerian environment. These include the Federal Environmental Protection Agency (FEPA) Act of 1988,[638] now repealed by the National Environmental Standards and Regulations Enforcement Agency (Establishment) Act, 2007 (NESREA);[639] the Environmental Impact Assessment (EIA) Act of 1992;[640] Oil and Gas Pipelines Regulations, 1995;[641] the Environmental Guidelines and Standards for the Petroleum Industry 2002; and the National Oil Spill Detection and Response Agency (Establishment) Act, 2006.[642] The basis of this is the legal regime of energy resources in Nigeria found in the CFRN 1999.[643] It provides:

> Notwithstanding the foregoing, the entire property in and control of all minerals, mineral oils, and natural gas, in, under, or upon any land in Nigeria or in, under or upon the territorial waters and the Exclusive Economic Zone of Nigeria shall vest in the government of Nigeria.[644]

---

636. *Ibid.*
637. The attempts at protecting the Nigerian environment through the use of the statutes dates back to colonial times with the Oil Pipelines Act of 1956, Cap. 145 LFN 1958 now Cap. 07 LFN 2004; the Petroleum Regulation of 1967 L.N. 71 of 1967 (This is a subsidiary legislation to the Petroleum Act; Cap. P10, LFN 2004); Oil in Navigable Waters Act, 1968 No. 34 of 1968; Cap. 06 LFN, 2004 (and Oil in Navigable waters Regulation, 1968; L.N 101 of 1968, a subsidiary legislation to Oil in Navigable Waters Act); The Petroleum Act 1969, Petroleum Drilling and Production Regulations, 1969 L.N. 69 of 1969; Cap. P10 LFB. 2004 and it's Amendment Regulations in 1973 L.N. 26 of 1973; the Petroleum Refining Regulation, 1974 L.N. 45 of 1974.
638. Cap F10 LFN, 2004.
639. Act No. 25 of 2007.
640. Cap. E12 LFN 2004.
641. S. I. 14 of 1995. This is a subsidiary legislation to the Oil Pipeline Act, Cap. 07 LFN, 2004.
642. It should be noted that all matters relating to mines and minerals, including oil fields, oil mining, geological surveys and natural gas have always been under the exclusive legislative lists, thus, the unfettered power of the Federal Government of Nigeria to legislate thereon. It was recently that environmental issues are now directly addressed. *See* s. 20 44(3) of the Constitution of the Federal Republic of Nigeria 1999 Cap. C23 LFN 2004 (as amended).
643. *See Constitution of the Federal Republic of Nigeria* (CFRN) 1999.
644. *See* s. 44 (3) CRFN, *ibid.*

326. The above provision is also replicated under the *Petroleum Act*[645] and in the *Mineral and Mining Act*[646] among others. The *Petroleum Act* vests absolute ownership of the mineral oil[647] and related energy resources in the Government of Nigeria.[648]

§8. THE GAS FLARING (PROHIBITION AND PUNISHMENT) BILL, 2017

327. The Nigerian Senate announced that it has commenced legislative processes aimed at prohibiting gas flaring and imposing stiffer penalties on defaulting oil and gas firms, as proposed by the Gas Flaring (Prohibition and Punishment) Bill 2017. The bill is intended to address the inadequacies and shortcomings of the Associated Gas Reinjection Act of 1979, provide stiffer penalties in line with current economic realities, and ensure the achievement of the National Flares-out Target of 1 January 2030. The bill, which has passed through second reading, also makes it mandatory for operators to submit a gas utilization plan within ninety days of the commencement of the Act for effective monitoring.

328. The bill also makes specific provisions for the installation of requisite gas flare meters equipped with facilities that enable real-time, online data retrieval for independent reporting and monitoring by the industry regulator. The bill acknowledged serving as a legislative panacea to end gas flaring. The procedure of issuing gas flaring permits will now be set up in substantive legislation. Thus, the emerging

---

645. Section 1(1) of the Petroleum Industry Act, *supra* note 4 provides that:

> The entire ownership and control of all petroleum in, under or upon any lands to which this section applies shall vest in the State (State here mean the Federal Government of Nigeria).

646. For instance, s. 1(1) of the old *Minerals and Mining Act Cap M12 LFN 2004* (and also the 2007 Minerals and Mining Act) provides that:

> The entire property in and control of all minerals, in, under or upon any land in Nigeria, its contiguous continental shelf and of all rivers, streams and watercourse throughout Nigeria, any area covered by territorial waters or constituency, the Exclusive Economic Zone is and shall be vested in the Government for and on behalf of the people of Nigeria.

647. Petroleum Industry Act describes mineral oil in a broader context, as: '… mineral oil (or any related hydrocarbon) or natural gas as it exists in its natural state in strata, and does not include coal or bituminous shales or other stratified deposits from which oil can be extracted by destructive distillation'. *See also* G. Etikerentse, Nigerian Petroleum Law, 2nd ed. (Dredew, Lagos, 2004) at 6.
648. *See* L. Atsegbua, *Oil and Gas in Nigeria* (New Era, Lagos/Benin, 2004) at 5–7. While Nigeria's model of ownership of natural resources comes within the ambit of 'absolute ownership theory', it needs to be clarified that absolute ownership is not the only philosophical basis for ownership of energy resources. While 'absolute theory' advocates total, exclusive ownership by the resource owners, 'qualified theory' assumes that energy resources are incapable of being owned unless captured and possessed. Thus, the possessor of the energy resources is deemed to be the owner notwithstanding the fact that the lands upon which the resources are discovered belong to another person. To another school of thought, energy resources cannot conceivably be owned by anyone due largely to their fugacious nature. *See also* J.S. LOWE, *Oil and Gas* (Thomson: UK, 2003) at 36.

Act would serve the essence of prohibiting the development of oil and gas fields without a plan for utilization of the associated gas regime. The bill is also to address the inadequacies and shortcomings of the Gas Reinjection Act and bring gas flare penalty in line with current economic realities as well as to ensure the achievement of the international flares – out of deadline of 1 January 2030 and ensure the timely review of gas flaring regulations and monitoring mechanisms.[649]

§9. Gas Pricing Policy

329. End-user prices in the Nigerian domestic gas market have typically been set at levels significantly below international gas prices. Gas producers have either decided to flare the gas or sell to the LNG plant since the commercial benefits from LNG sales have been more attractive. The pricing policy is to ensure that gas is supplied at affordable and economic prices to different sectors of the domestic market.[650] The transitional pricing policy for natural gas will gradually move from the current low prices towards the export price. Under these conditions, it is assumed that suppliers will be indifferent as to where the gas is supplied since the price will effectively be the same. At the end of the transition, it is intended that future incremental gas additions will be predicated on market principles determined by 'willing buyers, willing sellers'.

330. Under the gas industrialization initiative, Nigeria intends to add value to its natural gas resource by engaging in gas-based industries like fertilizer, methanol and petrochemical. This will be achieved by directing gas that might otherwise have been flared towards the development of these gas-based industries. A key objective of the gas industrialization policy is to stimulate GDP growth through employment creation in associated secondary industries which are dispersed throughout the nation. The benefits to the nation will be maximized via the multiplier effects of the primary gas-based industries rather than via maximization of direct tax revenue. However, the success of this laudable initiative is largely dependent on appropriate pricing to avoid investors' apathy and divestitures from gas production projects.

---

649. Ahuraka I., Solomon A., *Gas Flaring: Senate to Enact Bill to end $2.5bn Annual Loss,* http://leadership.ng/2017/06/01/gas-flaring-senate-enact-bill-end-2–5bn-annual-loss/, accessed 17 Jul. 2017.

650. For challenges of gas pricing and energy access, *see* Yemi Oke, Power Generation and Energy Access in Western Africa: Perspectives From WAPP Countries *Paper Submitted to for* the Book Project titled *Em'Powering' Africa: New Energy For The African Century*, produced by OCP Policy Center ('OCP PC'), Rabat, Morocco in collaboration with the Istituto Affari Internazionali (IAI) of Rome, 2018, at 15–16. *See also* Babatunde Adeyemo 'West African Power Pool' *South Asia Regional Workshop on Competitive Electricity Markets*, Colombo, Sri Lanka: 18 Mar. 2014; International Renewable Energy Agency, 'West African Power Pool: Planning and Prospects for Renewable Energy', online at: https://www.irena.org/DocumentDownloads/Publications/WAPP.pdf, accessed 13 Jun. 2017. *See also* E. Gnansonuou, 'Boosting the Electricity Sector in West Africa: An Integrative Vision' (2008) *International Association of Energy Economies, Third Quarter*, at 23.*See* Africa Centre for Energy Policy, 'Challenges Facing Ghana's Power Sector: The Load Shedding Politics', online at: (http://www.aceplive.com/the-main-challenges-facing-the-power-sector-in-ghana/) access 13 May 2017.

§10. THE LIQUEFIED GAS REGIME

331. The reality in Nigeria was that prior to the regime of the Nigerian Liquefied Natural Gas (NLNG) project, around 3,000 million standard cubic feet of gas was produced annually. Due to a lack of gas utilization infrastructure, Nigeria flares 75% of the gas it produces and reinjects 12% to enhance oil recovery. A major export-oriented gas production in Nigeria is LNG. The export of liquefied natural gas commenced in 1999 with the establishment of the Nigeria Liquefied Natural Gas Company (NLNG). The company was registered under the Nigeria LNG Act[651] and designed to utilize Nigeria's enormous gas reserves. The NLNG is Nigeria's only operating LNG Company. It has six trains and is building the seventh.[652]

332. Prior to the NLNG regime, Nigeria was the world's highest natural gas flaring country with 42.6% of its total annual natural gas production being flared. NNPC had estimated that Nigerian flared natural gas accounts for approximately 20% of the world's total.[653] With the aim of increasing gas utilization, the NNPC set up a company, the Nigerian Gas Company limited in 1988, with the specific task of developing, harnessing and marketing natural gas from the domestic market. A number of projects are being developed to increase the utilization of gas and reduce gas flaring.[654] Chief among these is the NLNG regime.[655]

I. Regulatory Issues in NLNG Framework

333. Section 44(3) of the CFRN, 1999 and section 1(1) of the Petroleum Act, 1990 ('Petroleum Act') vest ownership and control of all petroleum which includes *natural gas* within the territorial boundaries and waters of Nigeria, and the Exclusive Economic Zone in the government. The Department of Petroleum Resources (DPR) is responsible for regulating both the upstream and downstream sectors of the oil and natural gas industry, while NNPC (through NGC) oversees gas transmission and distribution.[656] For instance, for an LNG project, an export or import

651. Nigeria LNG (Fiscal Incentives, Guarantees and Assurances) Act, Cap. N87 Laws of the Federation 2004.
652. Institute of Geosciences and Space Technology – IGST (1991), Nigeria LNG Project Development, Report on Historical Weather Data Analysis for Port Harcourt International Airport Weather Station (1980–1989), Volumes I–IV, Rivers State University of Science & Technology.
653. *Ibid., see also* Isabella E. Okagbue, 'The Law and Development of Natural Gas in Nigeria', Occasional Paper No.9. Published by *Nigeria Institute of Advanced Legal Studies.*
654. Mabro, R., (ed.), *Natural Gas: An International Perspective* (Oxford: Oxford University Press, 1986), at p. 5.
655. By way of summary, the description of the Nigeria Liquefied Natural Gas Limited is that it is a joint venture project between NNPC, Shell, TotalfinaElf and Agip with percentages as follows NNPC(49%), Shell Gas BV (25.6%), TotalfinaElf LNG Nigeria Limited (15%) and Agip International BV (10.4%). The combined total production capacity of trains 1–3 is 28,500 tonnes per day.
656. *See* Department of Petroleum Resources, 'Oil and Gas Industry Report 2015', online at: https://dpr.gov.ng/index/wp-content/uploads/2015/01/2015-Oil-Gas-Industry-Annual-Report.pdf, accessed 29 Aug. 2018.

licence for the exportation of liquefied natural gas must be obtained from the Ministry of Trade and Commerce. The licence is processed through DPR and is for a duration of three months. The licence contains the terms and conditions upon which the exportation of natural gas is permitted[657] which further reinforces the crucial roles of the DPR and other agencies in the regulation of liquefied natural gas.

334. There are also a series of government incentives to encourage gas-related activities. Legislation on gas incentives to date includes: tax-free dividends, accelerated capital allowances, non-applicability of WHT on interest payable on any loan obtained with the prior approval of the Minister of Finance for a gas project and tax-free period.[658] Also applicable is *Guarantees and Assurance to Nigeria LNG Limited and Its Shareholders No. 113 of 1993*, made Pursuant to section 9, Nigeria LNG (Fiscal Incentives Guarantees and Assurance) Act No. 39 of 1990. The preamble to the Act states that:

> The Federal Government of Nigeria … , in recognition of the magnitude of and in consideration of the investments which shall have to be made in order to prosecute the venture described in the Shareholders Contract dated 19th May, 1989 between *NNPC, Shell Gas B.V., CLEAG Limited and Agip International B.V.*, as amended, from time to time … , hereby grants to the company, it successor and to each of the shareholders, from time to time (in their capacity as such), the guarantees, assurances and undertakings following hereunder.

335. Treatment of the capital investment on facilities equipment to deliver associated gas in usable form at utilization or designated custody transfer points shall be treated for tax purposes as part of the capital investment for oil development. Capital allowances, operating expenses and basis of tax assessment shall be subject to the provisions of the above Act and the tax incentives under the revised Memorandum of Association. Investment required to separate crude oil and gas from the reservoir into usable products shall be considered as part of the oil field development.[659] In addition, the Natural Gas Strategy seeks to create a legal and regulatory framework for wholesale competition and multiple distributors with third-party access to the gas network and encourage private sector participation. There is also a push in the form of an independent regulator for the downstream natural gas sector, regulating the price of gas for local consumption and developing regulations for anticompetitive practices.[660]

657. *See* Isabella E. Okagbue, *supra* note 653.
658. Initial period is three years, which may be subject to the satisfactory performance of the business be renewed for an additional period of two years. *See* s. 39 of the *Companies Income Tax Act*, Cap the *Companies Income Tax Act* Cap C21, on downstream gas utilization operations.
659. *See* s. 11 of *Petroleum Profits Tax Act P 13,* Laws of the Federation of Nigeria (LFN) 2004.
660. *See* for example F.E. Adebowale, D. Agbelese, T. Olowu and R. Ajiamah, 'Overview of Proposed Petroleum Industry Bill' Contributed by Udo Udoma and Bello Osagie, 21 Mar. 2016, pp. 1–3, p. 1, available online at: http://uubo.org/downloads/overview-of-proposed-petroleum-industry-bill.pdf, accessed on 1 Nov. 2016.

II. The Brass Liquefied Natural Gas

336. The Brass Liquefied Natural Gas (LNG) project is another Lignified Natural Gas project in Nigeria, similar to the NLNG. Brass LNG is located in the Brass Island of Bayelsa State of South-South (Niger Delta) in Nigeria. The project, like others, is a vehicle through which the Federal Government aims to achieve its energy policy. Besides the production of LNG, the Brass LNG is also to produce tonnes of liquefied petroleum gas, otherwise known as cooking gas, i.e., the plant will have condensate recovery and LPG production. The activities of the project include the production of Liquefied Natural Gas through the gathering of natural gas for processing, transmission of gas by pipeline and transportation of produced LNG by LNG carriers for export. Even though the MOU of the project was executed by the Nigeria Federal Government through NNPC in September 2001 and the Brass LNG Limited was incorporated in December 2003, the Final Investment Decision (FID) is yet to be taken.[661]

337. Brass LNG was incorporated in 2003 as a company and four stakeholders signed the Shareholders Agreement for the Brass LNG Project in 2006. The shareholders were Nigerian National Petroleum Corporation (NNPC), ENI International, Phillips (Brass) Limited (an affiliate of ConocoPhillips) and Brass Holdings Company Limited – an affiliate of Total FinaElf. The financial investment decision was initially planned for the first quarter of 2011 with a total capital cost estimate of USD 15 billion. The Brass LNG plant is expected to produce five metric tons of LNG per year and consume 24 mmscm/d of natural gas. The first train is scheduled to start production in 2018 and a second train is expected to come up one year later. Frontend Engineering Design (FED) has already been completed, and the project, like the NLNG Train 7, is also awaiting Final Investment Decision (FID).

338. Betchel Corporation (which is a San Francisco Company) had earlier carried out conceptual studies for the project which assessed the viability of an onshore LNG facility to be built near the Brass Oil Terminal operated by Nigerian Agip Oil Company (NAOC) at Brass Island in Bayelsa.[662] The said Head of Agreement signed was for the development of the two-train LNG facility.[663] With the Head of Agreement signed, Brass LNG Limited moved a step further towards its shareholders' objectives of joining other stakeholders to monetize Nigeria's vast natural gas resources and to contribute to the reduction in gas flaring as well as meeting the global demand for clean energy.

661. U. Udok & E.B. Akpan, 'Gas Flaring in Nigeria: Problems and Prospects', 5:1 (Global Journal of Politics and Law Research (European Centre for Research Training and Development, UK: March 2017) p. 26; *see also* Amanze R. Ejiogu, 'Gas Flaring In Nigeria: Costs And Policy' (2013) 24:6 *Energy & Environment Journal*, (2013), pp. 983–998 online at: http://www.jstor.org/stable/43735213 accessed 16 Jul. 2017.
662. *Ibid.*
663. The Initial Shareholders to the project were NNPC 49%, Italy's Eni SPA, 17%, Chevron, 17% and Conoco Phillips, 17%.

339. The company witnessed another landmark event when it awarded the contract for the Front End Engineering and Design (FEED) of its LNG plant to Betchel Corporation which is an American Company.[664] The engineering work was due to be completed within twelve months period scheduled for the execution of the contract. The contract contains provisions for the National Engineering and Technical Company Limited a subsidiary of NNPC to participate in the execution of the FEED contract.[665] Bechtel Corporation of the United States completed the FEED of the plant in 2006.[666]

340. According to the 2017 National Gas Policy (2017 NGP)[667] Nigeria is presently facing significant challenges in its domestic environment. The challenges involved include: security of supply risks – gas supply restrictions for domestic gas projects; challenges in funding NNPC's cash call obligations in upstream projects; growing gas payment arrears in the power sector; and militancy and insurgency. Also constituting a challenge is the absence of enabling environment to attract Foreign Direct Investment (FDI) – slow pace of domestic gas projects; inadequate gas supply for the domestic market; and financing challenges from local financial institutions. Sector governance is also another challenge. The need for increased transparency and adherence to due process in business transactions; and conflicts of interest in government as a policymaker, legislator, regulator and commercial participant among others are key to the success of gas utilization ventures like the Brass NLG.

341. The 2017 National Gas Policy (NGP) is based on a fundamental review of the policy positions of the government over the last ten years in respect of Nigeria's gas resources. The previous policy positions emanated from the Gas Master Plan (GMP), which was designed to ensure the development of a full-blown domestic market by 2015.[668] According to the policy document, the vision of the 2017 NGP is:

> To be an attractive gas-based industrial nation, giving primary attention to meeting local gas demand requirements, and developing a significant presence

664. The signing of the agreement was witnessed by the top management of the company as well as the representatives of its shareholder.
665. The contract signing, which took place in Houston, Texas, by top members of management of the company as well as representatives of its shareholders. Mr Martin Hutchison, Managing Director of Brass LNG Limited signed on behalf the company, while Mr Jim Jackson, Senior Vice President of Bechtel signed on behalf of the engineering firm. *See* 'Brass LNG Project: Front End Engineering and Design Contract Awarded', 11 Nov.2004, online at: https://www.bechtel.com/newsroom/releases/2004/11/front-end-engineering-design-contract-awarded/.
666. *Ibid.*
667. *Ibid.,* at p. 31.
668. It was noted by the 2017 NGP that the GMP has not delivered on all its set targets. For instance, Nigeria still lacks critical gas infrastructure and continues to fall short of Domestic Gas Supply Obligations. Nigeria is experiencing a full-blown energy crisis in spite of its abundant gas resources. A new gas policy that is more effective and adjusted for the much harsher international business environment for gas is required to drive the reforms necessary to attract investment into the sector. *Ibid.,* at p. 13.

in international markets; and by its mission, it intends to move Nigeria from a crude oil export-based economy to an attractive oil and gas-based industrial economy.[669]

342. The policy acknowledges that the core principles upon which gas-based industrialization will be driven include: to separate the respective roles and responsibilities of government and the private sector; to establish a single independent petroleum regulatory authority; to implement international best practices for environmental protection; to establish strong linkages with electric power, agriculture, transport and industrial sectors; to ensure security of assets; among others.[670]

343. On the point of developing gas resources, the 2017 NGP intends to enable an environment that encourages exploration specifically targeting gas; achieve gas flare-out through gas utilization projects utilizing flare reduction technologies. The policy also intends to foster development in key gas infrastructure which would lead to an increase in gas supplies to its customers. However, knowing that the availability of gas without an available gas market is counterproductive, the policy also intends to focus on building the gas markets through continuing gas exports consistent with domestic gas market development; identifying and promoting domestic gas market development projects as well as set a suitable environment for financing of gas projects.[671] Gas financing and pricing are crucial aspects of the policy that impact directly the fruition or otherwise of the Brass NLG project.

344. The gas pricing policy is also embedded in the policy to create a structured and transparent framework for the pricing of gas driven by market prices while the gas supply obligation component seeks to ensure the availability of gas for domestic gas utilization projects. The ultimate aim of the plan which seeks to promote investment in pipeline infrastructure and new gas-fired power plants is to help reduce gas flaring and provide the much-needed resource for electricity generation.[672] This led to the pursuit of liquefied gas projects like the Brass NLG and others with the primary aim of stimulating gas utilization for export and ensuring diversification of national earnings.

345. The Nigerian gas industry has not enjoyed the same pace of development as the oil industry. Whereas oil exploration has had a long history spanning over five decades, gas has only recently been paid due attention.[673] The reason for the earlier neglect of the gas sector is not unconnected with the capital-intensive nature of the

---

669. *Ibid.*, at pp. 14 and 32.
670. *Ibid.*, at p. 14.
671. *Ibid.*, at p. 31.
672. *See* Banwo & Ighodalo, 'Synopsis of the 2017 National Gas Policy' http://www.banwo-ighodalo.com/resources/synopsis-of-the-2017-nationalgas-policy, accessed 29 Aug. 2018. *See also* online at: http://www.eia.gov/countries/cab.cfm?fips=NI, accessed 14 Jun. 2013.
673. Muhammed Ladan, 'Access to Environmental Justice in Oil Pollution and Gas Flaring Cases as Human Right Issue in Nigeria', Paper Presented at a Training Workshop for Federal Ministry of Justice Lawyers Organized by the Institute for Oil and Gas Law, Abuja, Nigeria, Nov. 28–30, 2011, http://papers.ssrn.com/sol3/papers.cfm?abstract_id=2336093, accessed 12 Dec. 2016.

gas industry and a lack of legal infrastructure. Other associated factors include; the domestic demand for gas was not high, gas transmission networks were grossly inadequate; and the international demand for gas was not firm enough to show a realistic short-term payout for such investment.[674]

346. There are several challenges facing the actualization and immediate take off of the Brass LNG project. The first is finance. Shareholders of the project were originally due to take the FID by the end of 2006 but it was put off to 2009. The FID was recently rescheduled from 2009 to 2010 and remains uncertain to date. The Brass NLG is bedevilled by several challenges, ranging from operational funding to logistics and other technical hitches. Generally, the NLG sector is an industry that is capital-intensive and relies hugely on foreign funding backed by generous local, institutional incentives.[675] For years, Nigeria lacked a gas utilization policy, hence gas flaring thrived. The lethargic attitude towards the National Gas Masterplan, domestic supply obligations and the pricing policy has affected the maximization of the potential of the gas industry. Gas utilization policies or plans are hardly implementable laws, as there are no sanctions for failure to comply or implement. What industry experts witnessed was recurrent cases of policy summersault and regulatory inconsistencies, which also affected the Brass NLG in several ways as outlined below.

347. There is also the challenge of weak regulatory oversight on the part of relevant bodies that seem to have decelerated the pace of gas utilization in Nigeria. There were hindrances of weak institutional capacity and discrepancies in the government's anti-flare policies.[676] Nigeria's gas infrastructure is grossly inadequate. The Nigerian government lacked the requisite infrastructure to harness and transport associated gas from oil wells to facilities where it can be stored, processed and distributed.[677] It needs to be acknowledged that the existing gas infrastructure has been largely improved in the last decade. However, there is a large room for improvement in this regard if Nigeria wishes to actualize the goal of domestic gas utilization and its attendant effects on electricity generation. Domestic Gas Supply Obligations (DGSO) exist, yet, gas is not readily available for domestic use by

---

674. Birnur Buzcu-Guven et al., Gas Flaring and Venting: Extent, Impacts and Remedies, Paper Prepared by the Energy Forum of the James A. Baker III Institute for Public Policy as Part of the Study: Energy Market Consequences of an Emerging U.S. Carbon Management Policy, online at: http://baker-institute.org/files/439/, accessed 12 Dec. 2016.
675. *See* for example, the NLNG incentives provisions, *supra* note 651. *See also* Occhiali, Giovanni; Falchetta, Giacomo Working Paper 'The Changing Role of Natural Gas in Nigeria: A Policy Outlook for Energy Security and Sustainable Development' (2018) *Working Paper, No. 010.2018*, online at https://www.econstor.eu/bitstream/10419/177262/1/ndl2018-010.pdf, accessed 29 Aug. 2018.
676. *See* Banwo & Ighodalo, 'Synopsis of the 2017 National Gas Policy' http://www.banwo-ighodalo.com/resources/synopsis-of-the-2017-nationalgas-policy, accessed 29 Aug. 2018. *See also* Ministry of Petroleum Resources, National Gas Policy 2017 (2017), available online at: http://www.petroleumindustrybill.com/wp-content/uploads/2017/06/National-Gas-Policy-Approved-By-FEC-in-June-2017.pdf, accessed 29 Aug. 2018.
677. *Ibid.*

power plants, generating companies, fertilizer plants and manufactures due to various factors, chief among which is pricing.

348. One of the main challenges of the Brass NLG is the inability to secure supply markets. This is because long-term gas purchase and supply contracts often entail extensive documentation and agreement with fixed pricing. In the United Kingdom, for instance, the country's gas industry was dominated by British Gas as the sole purchaser from upstream producers. Being a monopolistic buyer of gas, British Gas was able to manage the volume risk for which it was contracted to take or pay.[678] This market structure is also replicated in continental Europe and other markets, including under the NLNG structure in Nigeria.

349. Unlike oil which can readily be stored and transported to any destination, gas is difficult and costly to store and transport. The nature and complexities of the infrastructure linking the source of gas to its markets are capital-intensive. The volumetric size of gas makes storage and transportation difficult and very expensive.[679] It requires planning and significant preproduction capital expenditure which has been the challenge of the Brass LNG. Generally, developing an offshore gas field involves massive capital investment on the part of the developer from exploration through design to construction of the wells, the offshore platforms and pipelines and the modifications needed at the onshore terminals.[680] All these make it crucial to secure a long-term market or contract that enables the seller, in this case, the Brass NLG, to plan its supply on a long-term basis which makes the project bankable and sustainable.

III. The Olokola LNG (OK LNG)

350. The policy of increased gas utilization through Liquefied Natural Gas (LNG) was sustained upon return to democracy in 1999 with the Olusegun Obasanjo administration. The groundbreaking ceremony of the Olokola NLG project was laid by former President Olusegun Obasanjo, shortly before leaving office after his eight years as president in May 2007. By design, Nigeria had targeted earning about USD 10 billion a year by 2011 from this project. By its structure, the NNPC has 40% equity in OK-LNG, Chevron holds 19.50%, BG Group holds 14.25%, while the remaining 6.75% is reserved for strategic investors.[681]

---

678. *See* Marc Hammerson, *Upstream Oil and Gas* (Global Business Publishing Limited, London, UK: 2011) at 305.
679. *Ibid.*, at p. 293.
680. *Ibid.*, at 297.
681. The Olokola Liquefied Natural Gas Project is a world class player in the oil and gas sector of Nigerian economy. The project will initially develop a 2×6.3 million tonnes/year of LNG and ultimate capacity up to 35 million tonnes/year with 30,000 barrels/day of LPG and 15,000 barrels/day of Condensate. The OKLNG project seeks to capitalize on unprecedented and ever growing opportunities within the international gas market through socially and environmentally sound processes

351. Besides the foreign exchange to be realized from OK-LNG in 2012, the project had other potentials for the country and the cities or communities around the project within/around Ogun and Ondo States. Over 10,000 direct and indirect jobs were anticipated for Nigerians within the first four years of the existence of OK-NLG. This includes construction works, supplies and related pipeline projects that were anticipated to cost about USD 10 billion.[682] The power sector was also anticipated to be positively impacted by the project as the single largest consumer of natural gas in the domestic market, to power homes and industries in Nigeria.

352. In terms of energy utilization, Nigeria's energy requirements are met through oil (64%), natural gas (27%) and hydroelectricity (8%). Coal, nuclear energy and other renewable are not utilized. However, efforts are currently being made to deploy renewable energy sources as part of Decentralized Energy Options (DEOPs).[683] The relative low reliance on natural gas is due to the limited local gas projects in the country to utilize the natural gas produced. The present state of the gas infrastructure and the near absence of reliable integrated gas network systems are also contributory factors. It is important to note that this is being remedied, as natural gas is now being leveraged as fuel to power Nigeria's economy. Presently several new gas-fired plants are being constructed or planned and delivered or awaiting connection to the power grid. Demand for gas has been on a steady increase in the power sector, which underscores the potential for gas development and utilization through OKLNG and related gas projects in Nigeria.

---

that give back to the local communities, our investors, other stake holders and the great people of Nigeria. *See* 'The Olokola Liquefied Natural Gas Project' online at: oklng.com/, accessed 29 Aug. 2018.

682. At the ground ceremony, the former Governor of Ogun State, Gbenga Daniel said: 'With this project, we are hoping that a lot of benefits would be enjoyed by our people as well as investors who carry out their business in this Trade Zone'. *Ibid.*

683. Yemi Oke, 'Beyond Power Sector Reforms: The Need for Decentralised Energy Options ('DEOPs') for Electricity Governance in Nigeria', *Nigerian Journal of Contemporary Law*, 18:1 (2012), pp. 67–92. *See also* Yemi Oke 'Implications and Challenges of a Privatized Power Sector In Nigeria: Perspectives to Host Community Concerns', *Justice Journal*, Federal Ministry of Justice (2014), pp. 237–63, at p. 262; Yemi Oke, 'Manitoba Hydro and Electricity Undertakings in Developing Countries: The Case of Nigeria', *Manitoba Law Journal*, 36:1 (2012), pp. 37–65.

Chapter 5. Gas Administration, Exploitation and Distribution in Nigeria

§1. Introduction and Background to Gas Exploitation

353. The discovery of oil in commercial quantities in Nigeria preceded the enactment of the *Petroleum Act 1969*[684] and the *Petroleum (Drilling and Production) Regulations 1969*. Though there have been various amendments to these legislations, they are still in operation and are the principal laws regulating Nigeria's oil and gas industry. There are quite a number of legislations regulating the oil and gas industry.[685] However, the primary legislation regulating the said industry in Nigeria is the *Petroleum Act of 1969* and by virtue of section 9(1)(b)(iii) of the said Act, the minister has the power to make regulations providing for matters relating to licences, including prevention of pollution of the atmosphere.[686] However, as earlier observed, the Act was enacted mainly for crude oil operations and not gas operations.[687] This notwithstanding, the Act regulates the gas sector as the definition of petroleum under the Act includes natural gas. For instance, the *Petroleum (Drilling and Production) Regulations 1969*, passed pursuant to section 9 of the *Petroleum Act*, in Regulation 42 provides as follows:

> Not later than five years after the commencement of production from the relevant area, the licensee or lessee shall submit to the Minister, any feasibility study, programme or proposals that he may have for the utilisation of any natural gas, whether associated with oil or not, which has been discovered in the relevant area.

354. The nature of gas regulation that existed prior to the reinjection regime was such that even in cases where those statutes so provide, legal provisions that required oil companies to submit their strategies for gas utilization were not viewed as mandatory or obligatory and no penalty or punishment was meted out to the defaulters.[688] This is partly because oil companies were granted permission to flare

684. Cap. P12, Laws of the Federation of Nigeria, 2004.
685. The following regulations are issued pursuant to the *Petroleum Act*: Crude oil (Transportation and Shipping) Regulations 1984; Mineral Oils (Safety) Regulations 1963, as amended; Oil and Gas Pipelines Regulations 1995; Petroleum (Drilling and Production) Regulations 1969, as amended; Petroleum (Refining) Regulations 1974; Petroleum Regulations 1967, as amended; and Marginal Fields Fiscal Regime Regulations 2005.
686. *See* U. Udok & E.B. Akpan, 'Gas Flaring in Nigeria: Problems and Prospects' (2017) 5:1 Global Journal of Politics and Law Research Training and Development, UK, March 2017), at 18.
687. The Government of the Federal Republic of Nigeria, 'Nigeria National Gas Policy 2017', (Ministry of Petroleum Resources: 2017) p. 20. *See also* G. Etikerentse, 'Nigerian Petroleum Law', 2nd ed. (Dredew Publishers: 2006) pp. 212 to 213.
688. These state of affairs prevailed until subsequent years when amendments were made to include offences and penalties. For instance Regulation 60B of the 1996 Amendment to the *Petroleum (Drilling and Production) Regulations 1969* provides that 'any person who – (a) commits a breach of any provisions of these Regulations; or (b) fails to comply with any provisions of these Regulations or any directives given thereunder of any permit or licence issued thereunder;... commits an offence, and shall be liable on conviction to a fine not exceeding two hundred and fifty thousand

gas for a period of five years before submitting the feasibility report.[689] As a result of this regulatory gap, the Nigerian Government took much more radical, practical steps towards regulating gas flaring in Nigeria in the year 1979 with the enactment of the *Associated Gas Re-Injection Act 1979*.[690] The enactment of the law was a direct response to global concern on the issue of gas flaring. The law became handy given the fact that pre-existing legislations were practically silent on the question of gas utilization and management of consequential flaring of gas associated with oil operations.[691]

355. The *Associated Gas Re-Injection Act 1979* (as amended) became the first real legislative attempt to provide for and/or establish an anti-gas flaring regulatory framework in Nigeria. The primary intent and purpose of the Act was to phase out gas flaring in Nigeria.[692] The policy inherent in the *Associated Gas Re-Injection Act 1979* (as amended) was the protection of the environment as it was seen as the legislative or statutory response to the environmental impacts of gas flaring at the time. Section 1 of the Act states thus:

> Notwithstanding the provisions of Regulation 42 of the Petroleum (Drilling and Production) Regulations made under the Petroleum Act, every company producing oil and gas in Nigeria, shall not later than 1 April, 1980 submit to the Minister a preliminary programme for:
>
> (a) schemes for the viable utilization of all associated gas produced from a field or groups of fields;
> (b) project or projects to re-inject all gas produced in association with oil but not utilized in an industrial project.[693]

In addition to the above provisions, the Act further requires a 'detailed programme' as opposed to a 'preliminary programme' in section 2(1). Therefore, all oil

---

naira or to imprisonment, not exceeding six months or to both such fine and imprisonment, and in addition any permit, licence or lease granted to the offender of these Regulations or any regulations made pursuant to the Petroleum Act 1969 may be cancelled'. The feasibility and practical enforcement of these provisions are still highly doubtful due to many factors militating against just enforcement.

689. U. Udok & E.B. Akpan, 'Gas Flaring in Nigeria: Problems and Prospects', *supra* at note 589, p. 18.
690. Cap. A26, Laws of the Federation of Nigeria, 2004.
691. Oyewunmi, O.A. & Oyewunmi, A.E, 'Managing Gas Flaring and Allied Issues in the Oil and Gas Industry: Reflections on Nigeria' *supra* note 585, p. 643. *See also* Amanze R. Ejiogu, 'Gas Flaring in Nigeria: Costs and Policy' (2013) 24:6 *Energy & Environment Journal*, (2013), pp. 983–998 online at: http://www.jstor.org/stable/43735213 accessed 16 Jul. 2017.
692. O. Fagbohun, 'The Law of Oil Pollution and Environmental Restoration: A Comparative Review', (Odade Publishers, Lagos: 2010) p. 303; Yinka Omorogbe, 'Oil and Gas Law in Nigeria *Simplified*', (Malthouse Press Ltd., Lagos: 2001) p. 58; U. Udok & E.B. Akpan, 'Gas Flaring in Nigeria: Problems and Prospects', *supra* at note 589, p. 19.
693. *Ibid.*, p. 19.

and gas producing companies had six months from the submission of the initial 'preliminary programme' to submit the 'detailed programme'. The section provides thus:

> Not later than 1st October, 1980, every company producing oil and gas in Nigeria shall submit to the Minister, detailed programmes and plans for either:
>
> (a) the implementation of programmes relating to the re-injection of all produced associated gas; or
> (b) Schemes for viable utilization of all produced associated gas.[694]

356. In terms of meeting the objective of the law, the most significant provision of the Act is the provision on the prohibition or outlawing of gas flaring. Section 3 of the Act states that:

> (1) Subject to subsection 2 of this section, no company engaged in the production of oil and gas shall after 1st January, 1984 flare gas produced in association with oil without the permission in writing of the Minister.
> (2) Where the Minister is satisfied after 1st January 1984 that utilization or re-injection of the produced gas is not appropriate or feasible in a particular field or fields he may issue a certificate in that respect to a company engaged in the production of oil or gas:
> (a) Specifying such terms and conditions as he may at his discretion choose to impose for the continued flaring of gas in the particular field or fields.
> (b) Permitting the company to continue to flare gas in the particular field or fields if the company pays such sum as the Minister may from time to time prescribe for every 28.317 standard cubic metres (SCM) of gas flared: Provided that any payment due under this paragraph shall be made in the same manner and be subject to the same procedure as for the payment of royalties to the Federal Government by companies engaged in the production of oil.[695]

357. The Act, therefore, sets the date for the discontinuance of gas flaring. However, it also needs to be pointed out that the Act is inherently flawed to the extent that while providing for the application of permits to be granted by the minister upon the payment by the applicant of an amount to be prescribed by the minister, the provisions of the law gets needlessly watered-down and its effectiveness or potency undermined by the failure to make any strict provisions or measures to be observed in order to ensure its effectiveness.[696]

358. The *Associated Gas Re-Injection Act 1979* has been faulted by critics on the ground of not providing for very salient issues on gas reinjection. One of such

694. U. Udok and E.B. Akpan, *supra* note 589.
695. *Ibid.*, at p. 19.
696. *Ibid.*, at p. 20.

faults is that beyond providing for a feasibility report to be submitted by oil companies interested in the production of natural gas, the Act fails to provide for penalties for gas flaring.[697] It was the absence of a penalty clause or section that led a writer to opine that perhaps 'indirectly, it may not be out of place to conclude that the law does not make gas flaring illegal'.[698] This is one of the major weaknesses of the *Associated Gas Re-Injection Act.*

359. At the close of 1984, evidence revealed that no oil company had complied with the provisions of the *Associated Gas Re-Injection Act 1979* and there was no evidence to indicate that the minister had insisted that the oil companies complied with it.[699] Some reasons have been advanced for the lack of political will in enforcing the provisions of the Associated Gas Re-Injection Act. Some argue that aggressive implementation of the law would have halted oil production operations.[700] This presupposes a purely economic consideration bearing in mind that oil production is the mainstay of the nation's economy. In the words of a writer:

> A principal concern regarding the implementation of the Act is that both the government and the oil companies are not truly desirous of bringing an end to gas flaring. Government on its part is content with the money that it is making from oil while the companies are also concerned more with their economic interest.[701]

360. It has also been argued that the government's laxity in enforcing the gas reinjection law had to do with the absence of infrastructure for the utilization of associated gas. At the time the Act came into force, only one gas injection plant existed in the country, owned by Mobil. This is because, at the time in question, the LNG Project was stalled, and the Escravos-Lagos Pipeline (ELP) had not yet been completed.[702] There was also the issue of finance since the bulk of crude oil in Nigeria was produced under joint venture arrangements with the government, through the NNPC as the majority partner and liable to a share of costs according to its shareholding interest in the JVA. The Government of Nigeria, and invariably the NNPC has historically been having problems meeting its funding obligations through cash calls, which often impedes investment in gas re-injection and utilization facilities.[703]

---

697. *Ibid.*
698. *Ibid.*
699. *Ibid.*
700. *Ibid.*
701. O. Fagbohun, 'The Law of Oil Pollution and Environmental Restoration: A Comparative Review', *supra* at note 692, p. 738.
702. Y. Omorogbe, 'Oil and Gas Law in Nigeria *Simplified*', *supra* at note 692, p. 59.
703. *Ibid.*, It has been noted, according to a learned scholar, that the 'inability of the Nigerian Government to meet, as and when due, demands for counterpart funding in the petroleum sector, otherwise called 'cash call' is not necessarily due to the lack of funds or unwillingness. Rather, it is due largely to the nature of state politics and regulatory environments occasioned by budgetary formalities and legislative procedures for passing appropriation laws in Nigeria'. *See* Yemi Oke, 'Relevance of Derivatives and Related Debt Instruments to Public-Private Sector Financing of Energy Resources in Nigeria' (2012) 1 *NIALS Journal of Law and Public Policy*, p. 185.

361. Generally, the Nigerian National Petroleum Corporation (NNPC) is the principal institution vested with the statutory authority to discharge broadly speaking, the commercial and inspectorate functions for the entire oil and gas operations across the country. The NNPC also oversees the operations of the Nigeria Gas Company (NGC), one of its numerous subsidiaries, and the management of the country's participatory interests in the several joint venture arrangements with the multinational oil companies.[704] The issue of enforcement is a major challenge for Nigeria's regulatory authorities. This situation has been widely linked to non-compliance on the part of some of the Multinational Oil Companies (MNOCs) primarily because they perceive that the consequences of not carrying out their operations according to the stipulated regulations on gas flaring reduction as non-consequential. The NNPC would appear inherently conflicted to do a better job, being a participant in oil and gas production, directly and indirectly, coupled with being a sector regulator.

362. A further criticism of the regulation of gas flaring in Nigeria pertains to the nature of the existing Joint Venture Agreements (JVA) between the government and multinational corporations. The JVAs were constructed in such a way as to shift a greater amount of responsibility with regards to gas reinjection or utilization, to the NNPC. The greater responsibility, particularly in terms of cash calls, is implicit in its majority equity holding of 55% (income and cost of production) in some JVAs.[705] There is a paradigm shift from this form of contract, as the authorities are now more inclined towards the Production Sharing Contracts (PSCs) which exclude the government from bearing the costs associated with oil operations.

§2. Associated Gas Re-injection (Continued Flaring of Gas) Regulations

363. The oil companies continued to mount pressures on the government on the need to tone-down the velocity of gas reinjection law on the ground of hurting the Nigerian economy through a reduction in oil production. Due to this and other factors, the minister created another option amidst the dilemma between a choice to enforce or not to enforce the *Associated Gas Re-Injection Act 1979*. This eventually led to the *Associated Gas Re-Injection (Continued Flaring of Gas) Regulations 1984*[706] which provides for exemptions to the earlier general ban on flaring. With effect from January 1985, the *Associated Gas Re-Injection (Continued Flaring of Gas) Regulations 1984* provided as follows:

---

704. Oyewunmi, O.A. & Oyewunmi, A.E., 'Managing Gas Flaring and Allied Issues in the Oil and Gas Industry: Reflections on Nigeria', *supra* at note 585, p. 646.

705. *Ibid.*

706. Both the development and commercialization of gas in Nigeria have been described by a learned scholar as being at the centre of both the Associated Gas Re-Injection Act 1979 and the Associated Gas (Continued Flaring of Gas) Regulation 1984. M.M. Gidado, *supra* note 589, pp. 27 and 33.

(1) The issuance of a certificate by the Minister under section 3(2) of the Associated Gas Re-Injection Act, for the continued flaring of gas in a particular field or fields, shall be subject to any one or more of the following conditions, that is:
  (a) where more than seventy-five per cent of the produced gas is effectively utilized or conserved;
  (b) where the produced gas contains more than fifteen per cent impurities, such as N_2, H_2S, CO_2, etc. which render the gas unsuitable for industrial purposes;
  (c) where an on-going utilization programme is interrupted by equipment failure: Provided that such failures are not considered too frequent by the Minister and that the period of any one interruption is not more than three months;
  (d) where the ratio of the volume of gas produced per day to the distance of the field from the nearest gas line or possible utilization point is less than 50,000 SCF/KM: Provided that the Gas to Oil ratio of the field is less than 3,500 SCF/bbl, and that it is not technically advisable to re-inject the gas in that field;
  (e) where the Minister, in appropriate cases as he may deem fit, orders the production of oil from a field that does not satisfy any of the conditions specified in these Regulations.

(2) The Minister may, from time to time, review, amend, alter, add to or delete any provision of these Regulations as he may deem fit.[707]

364. It has been noted that the above regulations apply to ministerial certificates to permit flaring, regardless of whether or not payment is made under section 3(2) of the *Associated Gas Re-Injection Act 1979*.[708] The basis of the continued flaring has not been demonstrated or justified.[709] The payments made by the companies to continue to flare have not been effective, and would not be justifiable given the loss of revenue to Nigeria. The reality of the gas reinjection regime indicates that the monetary penalty for continued flaring of gas by oil companies is grossly inadequate and mischievously preferable to the oil companies, for obvious reasons, as opposed to complying with outright phasing out of gas flaring.[710]

§3. Judicial Interventions in Gas Reinjection

365. The essence of the *Associated Gas Re-Injection Act* and the *Associated Gas Re-Injection (Continuing Flaring of Gas) Regulation* became issues for judicial

707. U. Udok & E.B. Akpan, 'Gas Flaring in Nigeria: Problems and Prospects', *supra* at note 589, p. 22.
708. *Ibid.*
709. *Ibid.*
710. O.A. Osunbor, 'Environmental Law and Policy', in in Simpson & Fagbohun (eds,) *Environmental Law and Policy* (Law Centre, Faculty of Law, Lagos State University: 1998) p. 312.

intervention by the Federal High Court in *Gbemre v. Shell & Anor.*[711] The court made an order restraining Shell and the Attorney General of the Federation from further flaring of gas and ordered them to take immediate steps to stop the further flaring of gas in the applicants' community. The order was premised on the court's judgment that the actions of the first and second respondents (i.e., Shell and the Attorney General of the Federation) in continuing to flare gas in the course of their oil exploration and production activities in the applicants' community were a gross violation of the applicants' fundamental right to life including a healthy environment and dignity of human person as enshrined in the Constitution.

366. The court remarkably held that section 3(2)(a) and (b) of the *Associated Gas Re-Injection Act* and section 1 of the *Associated Gas Re-Injection (Continuing Flaring of Gas) Regulation* are null and void for being inconsistent with the applicants' rights to life and dignity of human person as enshrined in the Constitution.[712] The court had earlier per Hon Justice C. V. Nwokorie held thus:

> These constitutionally guaranteed rights inevitably include the rights to clean, poison-free, pollution-free healthy environment ... To flare gas in the course of oil exploration and production activities ... is a gross violation of their fundamental right to life (including healthy environment) and dignity of human person. Failure to carry out Environmental Impact Assessment concerning the effects of gas flaring activities is a clear violation of Section 2(2) of the Environmental Impact Assessment Act, Cap. E12 Vol. 6, Laws of the Federation of Nigeria 2004 and has contributed to a further violation of the said fundamental rights [emphasis added].[713]

367. The *Associated Gas Re-Injection (Continued Flaring of Gas) Regulation 1984* has been viewed as a reversal of the original intent of the *Associated Gas Re-Injection Act 1979*, which was aimed at prohibiting gas flaring as a measure of environmental protection. One striking feature of the Act is the permission given to oil companies to continue to flare gas on the payment of minimal fees. This was seen as contradictory to the overall objective of the gas reinjection regime. However, the set-back brought about by the 1984 Regulation was sought to be rectified with the amendment of the Act in 1985.

§4. Associated Gas Re-injection (Amendment) Act

368. The *Associated Gas Re-Injection (Amendment) Act*, which was amended by *Decree No. 7 of 1985* introduced a penalty of 2 kobo per 1,000 standard cubic feet (SCF) of gas flared at any place. This amount was increased to 50 kobo per 1,000

711. Unreported (Suit No. FHC/B/CS/53/05, Federal High Court Benin Judicial Division, 14 Nov. 2005).
712. U. Udok & E.B. Akpan, 'Gas Flaring in Nigeria: Problems and Prospects', *supra* at note 589, p. 21.
713. *Jonah Gbemre v. Shell Petroleum Development Company of Nigeria Limited* Suit, No. FHC/B/CS/2005.

standard cubic feet (SCF) of gas in 1990, and the amount was further increased to 10 Naira per 1,000 standard cubic feet (SCF) of gas in 1998. It has been contended that the amount fixed is minuscule and incapable of bringing about or acting as a deterrent to the seeming resolve of the oil companies to continue with gas flaring.[714] This is because, due to the paltry and insignificant penalty prescribed by law, oil companies prefer paying such penalties for gas flaring than incurring related costs in the reinjection of produced or associated gas.[715]

369. The status quo in the gas industry reveals a clear unwillingness on the part of the Nigerian Government to prohibit gas flaring in the country.[716] The rationales advanced for this state of affairs include the government's concern about the likely effect of such a prohibition on oil operations that may ultimately affect the Nigerian economy. The huge financial resources required for gas re-injection and the inability of the government to meet their financial obligations in the various joint ventures, coupled with the lack of required infrastructural facilities, among others, are cited as the basis of the insistence by the oil and gas companies of their inability to meet the various deadlines.[717]

§5. Fiscal Policies of Gas Reinjection

370. Financing is pivotal in achieving or actualizing Nigeria's policies on gas reinjection and utilization.[718] In this light, fiscal policies are mainly concerned with the framework laid down by the government to attract and encourage investment in the gas sector or industry. Like any other kind of energy investment, such as oil and electricity or power, investment in gas utilization is a capital-intensive one. Thus, Nigeria must be seen by potential investors as having a sound investment climate. As stated elsewhere, 'the investment atmosphere must be such as to be able to instil unflinching confidence in the investors that recouping the invested capital, with competitive yields, would not in any way be impeded'; and 'to attract investors in

---

714. U. Udok & E.B. Akpan, 'Gas Flaring in Nigeria: Problems and Prospects', *supra* at note 589 at p. 22.
715. *Ibid.*, at pp. 23 and 28.
716. Instances of this unwillingness can be garnered from previous policies by the government on the constant shifting of dates to finally end gas flaring. The 1 Jan. 1984 was set as the first date by the Associated Gas Re-Injection Act 1979. Next the *Associated Gas Re-Injection (Continued Flaring of Gas) Regulations 1984* was passed to stall the deadline set by the Associated Gas Re-Injection Act 1979. Then Nigeria's gas policy and agreements between the government and oil companies extended the date up to 2008. As a matter of fact the first Draft Bill on prohibition of gas flaring titled, 'Gas Flaring (Prohibition and Punishment) Bill 2009 (SB. 126) sponsored by Senator Osita Izunaso set the date for the ceasing of gas flaring by 31 Dec. 2008 but this date was later amended to reflect the 31 Dec. 2010. *See* the Report on Votes and Proceedings of Thursday, 2 Jul. 2009 of the 6th National Assembly Third Session, No. 6 of the Senate of the Federal Republic of Nigeria, at p. 26.
717. U. Udok & E.B. Akpan, 'Gas Flaring in Nigeria: Problems and Prospects', *supra* at note 589, p. 24.
718. Yemi Oke, 'Relevance of Derivatives and Related Debt Instruments to Public-Private Sector Financing of Energy Resources in Nigeria', *supra* at note 703, p. 195.

energy and allied sectors depends on how attractive the sector is in terms of incentives and ability to repatriate the invested funds with gains'.[719]

371. The Nigerian investment clime has quite a handful of investment incentives enshrined in the statutes that ensure the easy transferability of funds or investment,[720] and capital or investment rebate devices that offer general tax incentives as found in the general body of tax laws.[721] The issue of investing in the Nigerian business environment, inclusive of its gas industry, touches on many factors including political and social factors. Availability of energy is a prerequisite for economic growth and development. As the Federal Government of Nigeria strives to stimulate private sector investment in energy and infrastructural development, a major challenge is that government policies are bedevilled by needless bureaucratic bottlenecks that often make attracting private sector funding difficult, though not impossible.[722]

372. It is an immutable fact that energy investment, inclusive of gas investments, demands huge, long-term capital and Africa attracts very little project finance,[723] and due to this, investors are always cautious of the *booby trap* incentives provided in the statutes to attract them in making investments. Investors have always adopted a cautionary approach in this regard. This is largely because, as hinted elsewhere:

> An average investor knows that investment is easier made than unmade. This leads to piercing through the sometime deceptive incentives for a careful consideration of the political, social and other factors that would make investing in a country a reasonable business decision. It makes good business sense to

719. Yemi Oke, 'The Pathway to Energy Liberation in Nigeria: Lessons for Namibia', published in Yemi Oke, '*Essays on Nigerian Electricity Law*' (Princeton & Associates Publishing Co. Ltd., Lagos: 2016) pp. 10 and 11.
720. For instance, s. 22 of the *Nigerian Investment Promotion Act*, Cap N117, Laws of the Federation of Nigeria, 2004 provides an incentive for foreign investment by allowing for the unconditional transfer of funds through authorized agent, while ss. 22 and 25 provide respectively for incentives for special investments and guarantees against any expropriation.
721. Tax incentives can be found in the general body of tax statutes and they include: (1) the *Companies Income Tax Act*, Cap C21, Laws of the Federation of Nigeria, 2004 which makes provisions in s. 39 for incentives to companies engaged in downstream gas utilization in terms of a three-year initial tax-free period; investment allowance; capital allowances after the three-year tax-free period; tax-free dividends; among others. (2) the *Petroleum Profits Tax Act*, Cap P13, Laws of the Federation of Nigeria, 2004 which makes provisions in s. 11 for companies engaged in the utilization of associated gas in terms of incentives granted for investment required to separate crude oil and gas from the reservoir; capital investment on facilities equipment used to deliver associated gas in usable form; capital allowances and operating expenses, among others. (3) the *Value Added Tax Act*, Cap V1, Laws of the Federation of Nigeria, 2004 which makes provisions s. 3 and the first Schedule for goods exempt from VAT which include all exports; plant and machinery imported for use in the Export Processing Zone; and plant, machinery and equipment purchased for utilization of gas in downstream petroleum operations.
722. Yemi Oke, 'Relevance of Derivatives and Related Debt Instruments to Public-Private Sector Financing of Energy Resources in Nigeria', *supra* at note 703, p. 183.
723. *Ibid.*, at p. 187.

invest in a politically stable and socially reliable country with little or no incentives than embark on irrational and expensive decision of investing under a turbulent and politically volatile atmosphere on the guise of distorted, wooly 'incentives.[724]

373. The investment-related question usually asked by investors in this regard is termed the *bankability question,* especially in a volatile and politically unstable or rocky nation like Nigeria. Viewed from the standpoint of the Nigerian State, bankability readily denotes the 'commercial expectations and assurances that an investor will recoup the investment capital with gain'[725] in the country where the investment is made. For this reason, incentives are also provided in the gas regime for the utilization of associated gas.[726]

374. Under sections 11 and 12 of the *Petroleum Profit Tax Act* (PPTA),[727] incentives are provided for companies that utilize associated gas. It provides that: (a) investment required to separate crude oil and gas from the reservoir into usable products shall be considered as part of the oil field development; (b) capital investment on facilities equipment to deliver associated gas in usable form at utilization or designated custody transfer points shall be treated for tax purposes, as part of the capital investment for oil development; (c) capital allowances, operating expenses and basis of tax assessment shall be subject to the provisions of this Act and the tax incentives under the revised MOU. Section 12 of the Act similarly provides that all incentives granted in respect of investments in associated gas shall be applicable to investments in non-associated gas.

375. Another incentive is provided for gas utilization under the oil and gas export-free zone incentives. The enabling statute is the *Oil and Gas Export Free Zone (OGEFZ) Act*[728] of 1996. The Act[729] establishes an OGEFZ Authority at Onne, Rivers State, with the responsibility to administer the operation, granting of permits and issuing of licences to approved enterprises operating in the Export Free Zone. Under the Act,[730] approved oil and gas companies operating within the zone are initially exempted from all federal, state and local government taxes, levies and rates. All dividends distributed during the initial tax holidays shall be tax-free. The investment capital allowance period is also extended from three to five years and is renewable for another two years.[731]

---

724. Yemi Oke, 'Manitoba Hydro and Electricity Undertakings in Developing Countries: The Case of Nigeria', (2012) 36:1 *Manitoba Law Journal*, at 37–65. *See also* Yemi Oke, 'Essays on Nigerian Electricity Law', (Princeton & Associates Publishing Co. Ltd., Lagos: 2016) pp. 48 to 49.
725. *Ibid.*, at p. 47; Yemi Oke, 'Relevance of Derivatives and Related Debt Instruments to Public-Private Sector Financing of Energy Resources in Nigeria', *supra* at note 703, p. 193 & 198.
726. Lolade Ososami, 'Nigeria: Developments in Nigeria's Tax Regime for Gas Utilization Projects' online at www.mondaqcom.uk, accessed 30 Jun. 2014.
727. *See* Petroleum Profits Tax Act Cap P13 LFN 2004.
728. Oil and Gas Export Free Zone Act, No. 8 of 1996.
729. Sections 2 and 5, Oil and Gas Export Free Zone Act.
730. Section 8, Oil and Gas Export Free Zone Act.
731. The following are the other incentives available to approved enterprises within the zone under the Act:

§6. Gas Reinjection and the 2017 National Gas Policy

376. The issue of corruption may very well be one of the reasons why the recent Nigerian National Gas Policy, 2017 reiterated that Nigeria is currently facing significant challenges in its domestic environment. This created the ineluctable need for increased transparency and adherence to due process in business transactions.[732] According to the 2017 National Gas Policy (2017 NGP),[733] Nigeria is presently facing significant challenges in its domestic environment. The challenges involved include:

(i) Security of supply risks – gas supply restrictions for domestic gas projects; challenges in funding of NNPC's cash call obligations in upstream projects; growing gas payment arrears in the power sector; militancy and insurgency.
(ii) Absence of enabling environment to attract FDI – slow pace of domestic gas projects; inadequate gas supply for the domestic market; financing challenges from local financial institutions.
(iii) Governance – vast gulf of understanding between the private and public sectors (especially between the government and the International Oil Companies (IOCs)); need for increased transparency and adherence to due process in business transactions; conflicts of interest in government as a policymaker, legislator, regulator and commercial participant.

377. The background of the 2017 National Gas Policy (NGP) is based on a fundamental review of policy positions of the Nigerian Government over the last ten years in respect of gas resources. The previous policy positions emanated from the GMP, which was designed to ensure the development of a full-blown domestic market by 2015. However, as was noted by the 2017 NGP, the GMP has not delivered on all its set targets. The vision of the 2017 NGP is 'to be an attractive gas-based

---

(i) Exemption from foreign exchange regulations.
(ii) Permission of 100% repatriation of foreign capital investment.
(iii) Permission of 100% repatriation of profits and dividends earned by foreign investors in the zone.
(iv) No pre-shipment inspection of goods imported into the zone.
(v) No expatriate quota.
(vi) Removal of import and export licences.
(vii) Permission of up to 100% foreign ownership of business, and Permission of employment of foreign managers and qualified personnel by the companies operating in the zone.

Section 11, Oil and Gas Export Free Zone Act.

732. The Government of the Federal Republic of Nigeria, 'Nigeria National Gas Policy 2017', *See* The Government of the Federal Republic of Nigeria, 'Nigeria National Gas Policy 2017', (Ministry of Petroleum Resources: 2017).

733. *Ibid.*, at p. 31.

industrial nation, giving primary attention to meeting local gas demand requirements, and developing a significant presence in international markets'. It also intends to move Nigeria from a crude oil export-based economy to attractive oil and gas-based industrial economy.[734]

378. A critical analysis of the investment guarantees and incentives in the Nigerian gas industry reveals that while a company engaging in petroleum operations is taxed under the PPTA and is precluded from claiming incentives under the CITA, a company dealing strictly in gas production is excluded from being taxed under the PPTA. A case in view is *Nigerian Agip Oil Company Ltd (NAOC) v. Federal Inland Revenue Service (FIRS)*[735] decided before the Tax Appeal Tribunal (TAT), Lagos Division based on the issue of applicability of WHT on dividend paid out of profits from gas operations.

§7. Taxation of Gas Operations: A Review of AGIP Versus FIRS

379. In the suit, the FIRS issued notices of additional assessment on the Appellant for the 2006–2009 tax years. The assessments were raised on the premise that NAOC is required by the CITA to deduct WHT on dividend paid out of profits generated from its gas operations (gas income). Dissatisfied with the position of the respondent, the appellant submitted the issue to the TAT for determination. The appellant, in its defence, argued that the incentive granted under the Petroleum Profits Tax Act (PPTA) with respect to the taxation of gas income, is limited to establishing the tax rate applicable to profits generated from that source, and does not eliminate the fact that the PPTA remains the governing legislation for gas income. Therefore, the dividends paid out of its gas income should enjoy the WHT exemption.

380. The respondent maintained that the implication of section 11(2)(d) of the PPTA is that all income generated from gas operations should be taxed in accordance with the provisions of CITA. Exemption from dividend WHT should only apply to dividend paid out of profits from which tax is charged, assessed and paid under the provisions of the PPTA. Therefore, a dividend paid out of gas income is not exempted from WHT, as the profits from which the dividend payments were made are taxable under CITA.

381. In its judgment, the tribunal ruled as follows:

> Section 11 (2) (d) of the PPTA implies that gas income should be taxed in accordance with the provisions of CITA and does not merely provide an incentive for the taxation of gas income at the rate of 30%.

734. *Ibid.*, at pp. 14 and 32.
735. Judgment delivered on the 10 Dec. 2014 at the TAT, Lagos Division.

382. It needs to be stated, for clarity, that section 60 of the PPTA does not apply to dividend paid out of gas income. The TAT interpreted sections 11(2) and 60 of the PPTA. According to the tribunal, the provision of section 11(2) is unambiguous. The section requires a company to set aside expenses incurred for associated gas utilization while the gas income and profit should be taxed under CITA. The TAT ruled that the phrase:

> Under CITA puts gas income completely under the full provisions of CITA such that its other provisions would apply to such income. The TAT indicated that if the PPTA intended to apply only the CITA rate, as against the whole Act, it would have been expressly stated so. Therefore, the subsection of the PPTA provides that gas income would be fully taxed under CITA and not merely that the CIT tax rate would govern the taxation of such income.[736]

383. The TAT held that since Agip's gas income is liable to tax under CITA, Agip is subject to all the provisions of CITA in assessing its gas income. Therefore, Agip is liable to WHT on dividends paid out of its gas profits as provided under sections 80 and 9(1)(c) of CITA. The ruling has far-reaching implications on the issue of incentives under CITA by a company engaged in gas operations as it provides some clarity on the hitherto divergent interpretations of sections 11(2) and 60 of the PPTA by stakeholders in Nigeria's upstream petroleum and gas industry. By determining that gas income is taxable in its entirety under the provisions of CITA, the TAT's ruling effectively removes gas operations from the scope of the PPTA.

384. Furthermore, section 9(1)(c) of the PPTA provides for the profits of a company subject to tax (PPT) to include, 'all income of the company of that period incidental to and arising from any one or more of its petroleum operations … '. The PPTA defines 'petroleum operations' and 'petroleum', respectively, as 'the winning or obtaining and transportation of petroleum or chargeable oil in Nigeria … ' and 'any mineral oil or relative hydrocarbon and natural gas existing in its natural condition in Nigeria'.

§8. The Chevron's Case

385. In another decision of the TAT delivered on 28 October 2015, the Tax Appeal Tribunal Lagos Zone held in *CHEVRON NIGERIA LIMITED v. FIRS*[737] on whether an upstream company engaged in gas projects is entitled to claim investment allowance at the rate of 35% set out in section 39 of the Companies Income Tax Act. The TAT ruled in favour of Chevron Nigeria Limited by holding that despite being a company in the upstream operation it is still entitled to claim investment allowance at the rate of 35% set out under CITA – the EGTL being a downstream project and ordinarily taxable under the CITA.

736. *Ibid., See also* s. 11(2) of the *Petroleum Profits Tax Act, supra* note 727.
737. (TAT/LZ/023/2012).

386. The tribunal held that the applicable Petroleum Investment Allowance (PIA) rate for assets situated onshore is 5% for companies engaged in petroleum operations and that the applicable rates for offshore petroleum operations vary depending on the water depth. The position of TAT is clearly that a company is only entitled to claim Petroleum Investment Allowance at the rates set out in the PPTA where the company is engaged in petroleum operations. The PIA rates set out for companies engaged in petroleum operations will not apply to the appellants' EGTL gas project. This implies that a company cannot be allowed to claim incentives from both the PPTA and CITA within the same accounting period. The TAT held that section 39(1)(b) of the CITA applies to the EGTL project. Section 39 sets out the incentives for upstream gas utilization and entitles companies engaged in upstream gas utilization to claim an additional investment allowance at the rate of 35%.

§9. Gas Distribution and Marketing

387. The transport of natural gas from a gas flow station to homes and businesses mainly requires an extensive network of interconnected pipelines designed to move natural gas quickly and effectively, sometimes over great distances.[738] There are essentially three main types of transportation pipelines: gathering pipelines, transmission pipelines and distribution pipelines. Natural gas produced from wells can be collected through a series of low-pressure pipelines referred to as a gathering system and in turn processed to the city gate from where it can be distributed in large volume, to residential and commercial consumers.[739]

388. From the transmission pipelines, the gas flows into a low-pressure distribution system. Local natural gas distribution pipelines are usually smaller in diameter than natural gas transmission pipelines and many are constructed out of plastic rather than steel. They consist of smaller service lines that are normally installed underground, usually along or under streets and roadways. The initial condition of the gas from the wellhead determines to a large degree the type and extent of processing undertaken before transmission to the city gate, from where the gas can be distributed to residential and commercial consumers. Thus gas containing; free liquids such as crude oil, water and condensates, condensable hydrocarbon vapours, water vapour, and undesirable components such as hydrogen sulphide, carbon dioxide, etc., would require more complex processing in order to meet sales gas specifications.

389. The Nigerian Gas Company (NGC) currently runs a number of gas pipelines in Nigeria to aid and stimulate gas distribution and utilization across the nation.[740] All these facilities comprise over 1,250 kilometres of pipelines ranging from 10 inches to 36 inches in diameter with an overall design capacity of more than

738. *See* Agbonifo E., 'Opportunities and Obstacles to Economic Growth and Sustainable Development through Natural Gas in Nigeria' (2015) 17:5 *Journal of Sustainable Development in Africa.*
739. *Ibid.*
740. The list of such pipelines include, without being limited to:

2.5 billion standard cubic feet of gas per day (bscf/d), sixteen compressor stations and eighteen metering stations. The facilities represent a current asset base of more than NGN 21 billion. The distribution of gas through low-pressured pipelines to the end-users in Nigeria is done majorly by two companies, Shell Nigeria Gas (SNG) and Gaslink Nigeria Limited (Gaslink). Gaslink has built about 100 kilometres of pipelines in Lagos State for the supply of natural gas to industrial and residential users. While SNG also targets the supply of gas to power plants and industrial users, it operates several systems including Agbara-Ota, which has a supply capacity of 42 million standard cubic feet per day.

---

(1) The Aladja Gas Pipeline System which supplies the Delta Steel Company, Aladja.
(2) The Oben-Ajaokuta-Geregu Gas Pipeline System, which will form the backbone of the proposed Northern Pipeline System, supplies Gas to Ajaokuta Steel Company, Dangote's Obajana Cement Company and PHCN Geregu Power Plant.
(3) The Sapele Gas Supply Systems which supplies gas to Power Station at Ogorode, Sapele.
(4) The Imo River-Aba System for gas supply to the International Glass Industry Limited PZ, Aba Textile Mills and Aba Equitable Industry.
(5) The Obigbo North -Afam system caters for Power Station at Afam.
(6) The Alakiri to Onne Gas pipeline system supplies gas to the National Fertiliser Company of Nigeria (NAFCON) now Notore Chemicals for fertilizer production.
(7) The Alakiri -Obigbo North -lkot Abasi system for gas supply to the former Aluminum Smelting Company of Nigeria (ALSCON) Plant now Rusal Industries in Ikot Abasi.
(8) The Escravos-Lagos Pipeline (ELP), which supplies gas to Egbin Power Plant near Lagos. Subsequent spur lines from the ELP supply in the West African Portland Cement Company (WAPCO) Plants at Shagamu and Ewekoro, PZ Industries at Ikorodu, City Gate in lkeja Lagos, PHCN Delta IV at Ughelli, and Warri Refining and Petrochemical Company at Warri.
(9) Ibafo – Ikeja Gas Supply Pipeline System supplies gas to Ikeja City Gate from where Gaslink distributes to the Lagos Industrial Area (LIA).
(10) Ikeja – Ilupeju – Apapa Gas Pipeline System currently operated by Gaslink for Gas Supplies to Greater Lagos Industrial Area.
(11) Ajaokuta – Geregu Gas Pipeline System which supplies gas to the Geregu PHCN Power Plant.
(12) Ajaokuta – Obajana Gas Pipeline System which supplies gas to Dangote's Obajana Cement Plant (OCP).

See the List of available pipelines run by the Nigerian gas company available online at: http://www.nnpcgroup.com/NNPCBusiness/Subsidiaries/NGC.aspx, accessed on 24 May 2016.

Chapter 6. Renewable Energy Law and Regulation in Nigeria

§1. Introduction

390. Nigeria is yet to tap the benefit of abundant renewable energy for its socio-economic development despite the fact that the recently concluded bid round for the privatization of state power companies witnessed an unprecedented influx of foreign companies bidding either directly or in collaboration with local companies as technical partners.[741] A private sector-driven electric power sector is anticipated in the unfolding electric power sector industry in Nigeria.[742] Energy is a catalyst for national development[743] and explains the reason why the current regime leaves no doubtful impression as to the need for the restructuring of the Nigerian electricity sector through privatization of state power companies.[744]

391. Beyond privatization, the reformed power sector of Nigeria requires some operational and regulatory restructuring to bring about a socially sustainable and community-friendly electricity regime in the country. The electricity industry is very complex. Rigorous competition as a result of privatization could discourage investment in renewable energy in developing countries like Nigeria where the government desires to attract private investors, particularly for the purpose of production of renewable energy. Maximizing the benefit of renewable energy requires proper planning, as unsuccessful outcomes could result in losses that tend to discourage investment.[745] Given this background, this segment reviews the global trend in the area of promoting renewable energy alternatives to stimulate economic growth and development through stable electricity in Nigeria. It provides an overview of the policy framework and related legislative and regulatory interventions or measures that have been adopted in other jurisdictions as the basis for promoting

741. *See* the Public Enterprises (Privatization and Commercialization) Act, Cap P 38, Laws of the Federation of Nigeria 2004 (Revised 2010). Pursuant to this Act, the NCP recently privatized some generation and distribution successor companies (GENCOS and DISCOS) respectively. *See* Presidential Power Reform Transaction signing Summit, *The Punch Newspaper*, Friday 19 Apr. 2013, at 36.
742. For Nigeria, as any developing country, electricity is indispensable to national growth and economic development. For detailed discussion on the role of energy in national development. *See* Yemi Oke, 'Beyond Power Sector Reforms: The Need for Decentralized Energy Options (DEOPs)' (2012) 18:1 *Nigerian Journal of Contemporary Law, University of Lagos*, 67 at 68–71. *See also* Yemi Oke, 'National Grid or National Greed', The Punch Newspaper (7 Dec. 2011) 14 and (8 Dec. 2011) 16.
743. *See* F.T. Sparrow; William A. Masters and Brian H. Bowen, 'Electricity Trade and Capacity Expansion Options in West Africa' Purdue University Institute for Interdisciplinary Engineering, online at: http://www.ecn.purdue.edu/IIES/SUFG, at p. 5, accessed 15 Apr 2015.
744. *See* Yemi Oke, 'Beyond Power Sector Reforms: The Need for Decentralized Energy Options (DEOPs)', *supra* note 683.
745. Deunden Nikomborirak and Wanwiphang Manachotphong, 'Electricity Reform in Practice: The Case of Thailand, Malaysia, Indonesia and the Philippines', *'Intergovernmental Group of Experts on Competition Law and Policy'*, Geneva, 17–19 2007, at 1–3.

energy efficiency through renewable energy in Nigeria. The section also identifies the challenges of renewable and efficient energy for electricity in Nigeria.[746]

§2. Overview of Renewable Energy Governance in Nigeria

392. The *Nigerian Electricity Regulatory Commission* (NERC) is saddled with power sector governance including facilitating electricity generation in Nigeria through conventional and renewable sources. The Commission is also charged with duties to create, promote, and preserve the efficient industry and market structures, and to ensure the optimal utilization of resources for the provision of electricity by promoting and facilitating consumer connections to distribution systems in both rural and urban areas, among others.[747]

393. Conventional energy sources are not sustainable in the long run, being perishable and unrenewable.[748] Renewable energy constitutes one of the means of attaining the objective of DEOPs argued elsewhere by the author.[749] The trends of renewable energy have already taken deep roots in some countries in Africa.[750] No similar policy exists in Nigeria although the *National Energy Policy* (NEP)[751] advocates and encourages renewable energy sources. This is yet to translate into a matter of 'national priority'.

394. The availability of renewable energy alternatives is vital to the provision of low-cost, affordable and regular electricity for industrial development, employment generation and poverty alleviation in Nigeria. It also underscores the importance of renewable energy to the country from the standpoint of sustainable electricity including climate change adaptation.[752] Renewable energy[753] came to the limelight

746. *See* for example, the Federal Ministry of Power and Steel, Federal Republic of Nigeria: 'Renewable Electricity Policy Guidelines' December, 2006, (International Centre For Energy, Environment and Development (ICEED), online at www.iceednigeria.org, accessed 20 May 2014.
747. *See* s. 32(1) of the *Electric Power Sector Reform Act*, 2005, Cap E7, Laws of the Federation of Nigeria (LFN), 2004 (updated to the 31 Dec. 2010).
748. Julia Kennedy-Darling, Nick Hoyt, Kyle Murao and Allison Rose, 'The Energy Crisis of Nigeria' -An Overview and Implications for the Future, (LL.M Thesis, The University of Chicago, 6.3.2008), pp. 2–5.
749. *See* Yemi Oke, 'Beyond Power Sector Reforms: The Need for Decentralised Energy Options ('DEOPs') for Electricity Governance in Nigeria', *supra* note 400 at pp. 67–92.
750. R.H. Acker, 'The Quiet (Energy) Revolution: Analysing the Dissemination of Photovoltaic Power Systems in Kenya' (1996) 24:1 *Energy Policy,* pp. 81–111 at 81.
751. *See* the *Federal Republic of Nigeria*, 'National Energy Policy', the Presidency – Energy Commission of Nigeria, April 2003, at p. 1.
752. *See* Yemi Oke, 'Adapting to Climate Change: Sustainable Mitigation Options for Developing Countries in Sub-Saharan Africa' (2011) 1 *NAILS Journal of Environmental Law* (Nigerian Institute of Advanced Legal Studies), at pp. 59–101.
753. 'Renewable electricity' refers to electric power obtained from energy sources whose utilization does not result in the depletion of the earth's resources. Renewable electricity also includes energy sources and technologies that have minimal environmental impacts, such as less intrusive hydro and certain biomass combustion. *See Policy Guidelines on Renewable Electricity in Nigeria*, December 2006, para. 2.0.

in Nigeria due to energy challenges in the country occasioned largely by an epileptic supply of electricity to consumers and partly as a result of the global trend of reducing the emission of carbon dioxide to curtail the devastating effects of the use of fossil energy resources which have led to climate change.

395. Renewable energies are derived from sources that are essentially inexhaustible, unlimited and naturally renewable and replenishable, such as wind, water, sun, wave, refuse, biofuel, among others. Captured in the *Policy Guidelines on Renewable Electricity in Nigeria* are solar, biomass and wind which formed the focus of this segment.[754] For a country like Nigeria, the challenge of maximizing the potential of renewable energy is one of lack of technological ability and innovation required to tap, utilize and manage renewable energy sources.[755] Although attaining the goal of national energy security through an efficient energy delivery system is one of the cardinal principles of the NEP;[756] realizing this lofty objective has proved very difficult, though not impossible in Nigeria.[757]

396. The NEP aims at guaranteeing an adequate, sustainable and reliable supply of energy at appropriate costs and in an environmentally friendly manner to various sectors of the economy for national development. It also emphasizes the need for promoting the use of alternative energy sources by conserving and using the environment and national resources for the benefit of present and future generations. The overall objective of this Policy Guideline is to expand the role of renewable electricity in sustainable development through effective promotional and regulatory instruments.[758]

---

754. *Ibid.*, The Policy defines 'biomass electricity', 'solar energy' and 'wind energy' thus:

- *Biomass electricity* – Green plants converting sunlight into plant material through photosynthesis produce biomass energy.
- *Solar energy* – Electricity is generated from solar energy predominantly through photovoltaic materials (cells or modules) that converts sunlight directly into electricity.
- *Wind energy* – The energy contained in the movement of air in form of wind is used to turn the blades of windmills or wind turbines which in turn could be used to drive electrical generators to produce electricity.

755. Akinbami J.F.K, *Renewable Energy Resources and Technologies in Nigeria: Present Situation, Future Prospects, and Policy Framework, Mitigation, and Adaptation Strategies for Global Changes* (Kluwer Academic Publishers, Netherlands, 2001) at pp.155–181 and pp. 162–164.

756. *See* 'National Energy Policy', *supra* note 751.

757. *Ibid.*

758. The Policy Guideline seeks to achieve the following specific objectives:

(i) expand electricity generating capacity to meet national economic and social development goals;
(ii) encourage the diversification of sources of electricity supply through renewable energy, and as such improve the energy security of the country;
(iii) increase access to electricity services nationwide, especially in rural areas;
(iv) stimulate growth in employment generation through an expanded renewable electricity industry;

397. The above policy instrument also captures the need for effective implementation through the coordination of rural electrification expansions with economic development objectives that encourage states, local communities as well as the private sectors to partner in the development of renewable energy sources. The *Policy Guidelines* is the Federal Government of Nigeria's integrated renewable energy policy. The Policy Guidelines sets out the Federal Government's vision, policies and objectives for promoting renewable energy in the power sector.[759] It acknowledges that access to electricity services is critical to achieving the economic and social development targets of the Federal Government of Nigeria.[760] However, beyond the seemingly vague and general powers given to the NERC on renewable energy, the country appears to lack enforceable legal and/or regulatory frameworks to govern and manage renewable energy utilization for national growth and socio-economic development.

§3. The NERC and Renewable Energy

398. The policy requires NERC to promote the generation of electricity through renewable sources by providing suitable commercial and technical measures for

---

(v) enhance technological development through increased domestic manufacturing of renewable electricity components;
(vi) stimulate competition in the delivery of renewable electricity;
(vii) promote rapid expansion of renewable-based electricity market through cost-reducing supply side and demand side incentives;
(viii) develop regulatory procedures that are sensitive to the peculiarities of renewable energy based power supply;
(ix) create stable and predictable investment climate in renewable electricity market;
(x) provide effective protection of electricity consumers through effective regulation; and
(xi) reduce household and outdoor air pollution as well as contribute to the abatement of greenhouse gas emissions, and thus contribute to improved health and overall social development.

Ibid. See also Adegoroye Adegoke, 'The Challenges of Environmental Enforcement in Africa: The Nigerian Experience' – *The Third International Conference on Environmental Enforcement*, at pp. 43–45.

759. *See Policy Guidelines on Renewable Electricity in Nigeria*, December 2006. The Policy Guidelines is drawn primarily from the Constitution of the Federal Republic of Nigeria (1999), the National Energy Policy (2003), the National Electric Power Policy (2001), Electric Power Sector Reform Act (2005), the Renewable Energy Master Plan (2005), the draft Rural Electrification Policy and the National Economic Empowerment and Development Strategy (NEEDS).

760. The Federal Government of Nigeria seeks the implementation of the policy on renewable electricity for the following specific reasons: first, renewable energy represents an important tool in the government's overall effort to expand access to electricity services nationwide. Second, rural electricity access in Nigeria is less than 20%. By their nature, renewable electricity technologies are generally ideal for improving rural electricity access situations in the country, as grid power extensions over long distance to serve low load densities are usually technical and financially involving compared with a decentralized renewable electricity option. Renewable electricity provides more diversity and improves the reliability of electricity supply through the grid, especially in times of localized disruption of sources of power supply. It is environmentally friendly being mostly carbon neutral and reduces indoor and urban pollution as well as emission of greenhouse gases that cause global warming. *Ibid.*, para. 1.0 background.

connectivity to the grid and the sale of electricity to any person.[761] Under the Guidelines, the NERC shall also develop an appropriate standard or model for PPAs and shall also determine the delivery location, power characteristics, price, quality, schedule and terms of agreement and penalties for breach. It shall among other things, ensure that prices provide an adequate return on investments in renewable electricity; standardizes and simplifies contractual relationships; and protects investors, utilities and consumers.[762] Subject to the provisions of the Policy Guideline, the NERC shall also specify the terms and conditions for the determination of tariff, and in so doing shall be guided by the promotion of renewable sources in electricity production.[763]

399. The Guidelines emphasize that off-grid renewable energy operations are vital to meeting the Federal Government's policy on the electric power sector and expanding access to rural areas, in particular.[764] This is to be supplemented by mini-grid concessions.[765] In developing mini-grid concessions, NERC shall select a company to exclusively serve a specific geographical location with an obligation to serve all customers that request service. The agency shall provide subsidies and shall regulate the fees and operations of the concession. Electricity service concessions may employ a mixture of energy sources to serve customers.[766] The Guidelines also provide that the Federal Government will develop innovative, cost-effective and practical measures to accelerate access to electricity services in rural areas through renewable sources.[767]

400. Policy 5 of the Guidelines provides for financing renewable electricity through Renewable Electricity Trust Fund (RETF) which shall be set up under the *Rural Electrification Fund.*[768] The purpose of RETF shall be to promote, support and provide renewable electricity through private and public sector participation.[769]

---

761. *See* para. 5.2.2 for NERC's roles regarding access to the grid.
762. *See* para. 5.2.3 for the role of NERC on Development of a Standard for Power Purchase Agreements.
763. *See* para. 5.2.4 on Tariff regulation.
764. Paragraph 5.3, off-grid operations. Under Policy 3 of the Guidelines, the Federal Government supports the construction of independent renewable electricity systems in areas not covered by the electricity grid to provide power service for local economic activities and sustainable living. *Ibid.*
765. Paragraph 5.3.1.
766. *Ibid.*
767. *See* Policy 4, para. 5.4 on rural electrification.
768. *See* Policy 5, para. 6.0 on financing renewable electricity.
769. The RETF seeks to provide support to the following: (i) construction of independent renewable electricity projects, especially in rural and remote areas; (ii) establishment of domestic production of technologies for the development and utilization of renewable electricity; (iii) provision of resources for micro financing to stand-alone systems under 20 kilowatt capacity; (iii) support to research and development and construction of pilot projects; (iii) promote training and capacity building in renewable electricity technology and business development; (iv) encourage public awareness initiatives; and (v) provision of surveys and assessments of renewable electricity resources and other relevant information. *See* generally para. *6.1 Renewable Electricity Trust Fund.*

In discharging its regulatory functions in respect of renewable electricity, the NERC undertakes specified duties under the Guidelines.[770]

401. One of the strategies devised by the Federal Government for promoting renewable electricity is *Grid-connected operations.*[771] Grid-based renewable electricity is crucial in promoting the development and utilization of electricity, diversifying the sources of electricity supplies, strengthening energy security, expanding electricity access and improving the environment. To ensure a stable pricing policy, the Federal Government introduces feed-in tariffs for small hydro schemes not exceeding 30 megawatts, as well as for biomass co-generation power plants, solar and wind-based power plants, irrespective of their sizes.[772]

§4. Renewable Energy Options for Nigeria

402. A number of renewable energy options are presently available in Nigeria, though largely unexplored including wind, solar and biomass. This segment aims at amplifying the three renewable energy sources, being the sources captured by the *Policy Guidelines on Renewable Electricity*, as highlighted above.

I. Wind Energy

403. Renewable energy literature indicates that wind energy is the oldest source of power applied by mankind, used together with other sources of energy.[773] Nigeria's energy resources potential still suffer from over-dependence on hydropower which is largely susceptible to seasonal variations in the amount of water levels at dams. This is one of the rationales offered for the nation's commitment to establishing wind energy projects as power generation alternatives.[774] Nigeria's wind and other renewable energy initiatives are inspired by various international processes.[775] By placing reliance on renewable energy that is naturally inexhaustible in nature, the country is able to develop renewable energy resources for its economic

770. This includes: (i) develop simplified licensing procedures for renewable energy investments; (ii) develop a framework for power purchase agreement that ensures access to grid-based renewable electricity; (iii) ensure preferential prices for renewable electricity to cover additional costs due to size, technology, location and the intermittent nature of the particular renewable electricity resource base; (iv) lower licensing charges for renewable electricity licensees; (v) develop and maintain quality standards for renewable electricity equipment and installations; (vi) lessen the regulatory compliance and reporting burden; (vii) ensure that appropriate Environmental Impact Assessments are conducted prior to award of licences; and (viii) report specifically on the status of the renewable electricity industry in its quarterly report to the president and the National Assembly. *See* para. 7.3 of the Guidelines.
771. Paragraph 5.2.
772. *See* para. 5.2.1 on feed-in tariffs.
773. *See* The Early History of Wind Energy, Global Sources, online at: http://www.brighthub.com/environment/renewable-energy/Articles/71440.aspx, accessed 17 Apr. 2014.
774. *Ibid.*
775. *See* for example the United Nations Conventions and Programmes, the G8 process and the high level Ministerial Conference Series and International Renewable Energy Conference dedicated to

development while also contributing to the improvement of the global world efforts through the pursuit of greener energy devoid of greenhouse gases that deplete the ozone layers.[776]

404. Wind energy is a global phenomenon. For instance, in its submission to the United Kingdom National Grid on the future operation of the Electricity Transmission Network, wind energy is seen as a crucial backup to the nation's electricity needs.[777] Similarly, China's total exploitable capacity for both land-based and offshore wind energy is higher when compared to other leading global wind power markets that are closer to that of the United States and greatly above the resource of India, Germany or Spain. This further amplifies the importance of wind energy to countries and underscores the need for Nigeria to fully exploit its wind energy resource in the quest for a stable, private sector-driven electricity in the country.[778] For Nigeria, renewable sources for power generation portend enormous, untapped and sustained opportunities for meeting enormous electricity demands in the country.

II. Solar Energy

405. Solar radiation, being abundantly present in Nigeria, is one area of focus among renewable energy resources, though technologies for solar energy applications are yet to be fully accepted as household commodities in the country.[779] Solar energy portends hope for the majority of the people of Nigeria who live in rural communities where there are difficult terrains, no good roads, electricity grids or lack of access to fossil fuel energy resources.[780] Solar energy is one of the veritable sources of renewable electricity in Nigeria.[781] The *Renewable Energy Policy of Nigeria* 2006[782] merely acknowledges the fact that 'renewable electricity offers cost-effective, options for extending electricity and stimulating sustainable development in the rural areas'. The Guidelines also set out the Federal Government's vision, policies and objectives for promoting renewable energy in the power sector, including electricity from solar energy sources.[783]

---

renewable energy which forms platforms for positioning and promoting renewable energy as a potential win-win option in both the environmental and development arenas.

776. Renewable Energy and Electricity: 'World Nuclear Association'. Online http://www.world-nuclear.org/info10.html, accessed 13 Apr. 2011, at p. 3.
777. Rajveer Mittal, K.S. Sandu and D.K. Jain, 'Battery Energy Storage System of Variable Speed Driven PMSG for Wind Energy Conversion System' (2010) 1:3 *International Journal of Innovation, Management and Technology*, at pp. 9–11.
778. *Ibid.*
779. *See* P.A. Ilenikhena, 'Sola Energy Applications in Nigeria' WEC, Montreal, Paper No. 135 (Revised), 2010 online at: http://www.worldenergy.org/documents/congresspapers/135.pdf, accessed 15 Oct 2012.
780. *Ibid.*
781. Other sources of electricity include; solar energy, wind power; geothermal; bioenergy or biofuel or biomass co-generation; hydrothermal, tide; wave and hydrogen energy, among others.
782. *See* the *Policy Guidelines on Renewable Electricity in Nigeria*, 2006, *supra* note 753.
783. *Ibid.*

406. Nigeria is squarely located in the tropics, with its land mass stretching between latitudes of 5 degrees south and 15 degrees north of the equator. As a consequence, the country enjoys abundant amounts of sunshine.[784] The opportunities offered by decentralized, rural/community-based solar-powered electrification programmes have been well documented.[785] For Nigeria, these benefits include but are not limited to community water pumping; enhanced health care delivery to rural areas and remote villages; and exposure to modern education technology and lighting. Solar energy sources could therefore enable the development of social infrastructures in Nigeria to enhance the health and well-being of rural communities; catalyse the development of small-scale enterprises and cottage businesses; and stem the trends of rural-urban migration. However, despite efforts to create awareness of the effective use of solar energy, the technologies for solar energy applications are yet to gain acceptance in most Nigerian households.[786]

407. The use of solar electricity is particularly suitable for rural electrification due to the inability to connect to the national electricity power grid.[787] Nigerian researchers have made an attempt to justify the need for rural, community electrification through solar, by applying photovoltaic to convert solar energy radiation to electricity.[788] The development of renewable energy for rural communities through solar cannot be overemphasized though, regrettably, there is no specific legal framework for solar energy in Nigeria. One may concede that the policy framework of solar energy is enshrined in the NEP and the *Policy Guidelines on Renewable Electricity in Nigeria* which list 'solar' as one of the focal points of the government's renewable electricity policy and guidelines respectively.[789]

III. Biomass

408. As a renewable energy source, biomass is biological in nature and derived from living, or recently living organisms.[790] Biomass can either be used directly such as biopower, or converted into other energy products such as biofuel.[791] Examples of sources of biomass include forest residues, (such as dead trees,

---

784. The average solar insulation in Nigeria is estimated to vary between 4.0 KWh/m2/day at the southern coasts to 7.0 KWh/m2/day at the northern coasts of the country. The daily average is estimated at 5.5 KWh/m2/day. The availability of abundant sunshine is a positive indicator that Nigeria is an ideal candidate for investment in solar energy resource development.
785. Freling, R. & Lahl, J. *Renewable Energy Technology: Optimizing Energy Sources for the Development of Millennium Project Villages*; Solar Electric Light Fund (SELF): Washington, DC, USA, 8 Jul. 2005.
786. *See* P.A. Ilenikhena, 'Sola Energy Applications in Nigeria', *supra* note 779.
787. *See* Adenike Boyo, 'Development of Solar Energy in Lagos State, Nigeria' online at: http://www.wcpsd.org/posters/environment/Boyo_Adenike_2.pdf, accessed 15 Oct. 2015.
788. *Ibid.*
789. *See* for example para. 2.0 of the *Policy Guidelines on Renewable Electricity in Nigeria*, *supra* note 753.
790. *See* Arnosti, D. and Abbas, D. 'Harvesting Fuel: Cutting Cost and Reducing Forest Fire Hazards through Biomass', (2008) *Institute for Agriculture and Trade Policy*, at p. 1.
791. Volk, T.A. *Developing a Willow Biomass Crop Enterprise for Bioenergy and Bio-products in United States*, (Buffalo Press, New York, 2000), at 15.

branches and stumps), yard clippings, wood chips, etc. The other category of biomass includes plant or animal matter that can be converted into biofuels and those derived from other types of plants such as switchgrass, corn, sugarcane, oil palm, etc.[792]

409. Biomass is one of the oldest sources of renewable energy in Nigeria used since its ancestors learned the secret of fire.[793] Biomass is a renewable low carbon fuel that is already widely available in all the parts of the world. Its production and use also bring additional environmental and social benefits to Nigerians. If properly managed, biomass is a sustainable fuel that can deliver a significant reduction in net carbon emissions when compared with fossil fuels.[794] Unlike biomass, the burning of fossil fuel dirties the air, consumes and pollutes water, hurts plants and animals, creates toxic wastes and causes global warming.[795] This makes biomass a preferable option in the quest for greener energy sources in Nigeria. Biomass energy has the potential to greatly reduce greenhouse gas emissions.

410. Traditionally, biomass is the most commonly used source of rural energy in Nigeria because fuelwood is the cheapest and most accessible source of fuel even in urban households. Despite the availability of conventional domestic fuels, fuelwood as a traditional fuel source remains in very high demand at the expense of Nigerian forests. In the quest for rural electrification, the pursuit of biomass will ensure uninterrupted electricity to rural areas; enhance rural energy efficiency; promote technological innovations and transfer of renewable energy technologies to rural communities; and generally improve lives and livelihoods of the Nigerian masses, particularly those in the rural areas and local communities.

§5. Nigerian Renewable Energy Policies, Strategies and Institutions

411. One of the greatest challenges faced by Nigeria is its energy sector. Nigeria is an oil-rich country, and most of its energy consumption comes from non-renewable sources, such as coal, natural gas, and, most importantly, oil.[796] The challenges of energy security and access are compounded by inefficiency and poor environmental governance. Oil accounts for about 20% of GDP, 95% of export earnings, and 85% of budgetary revenues. However, while oil plays a large role in

792. *Ibid.*
793. Miller Alan and Serchuk Adam, 'The Environmental Imperative: A Driving Force in the Development and Deployment of Renewable' (1996) No. 1 *REPP Issue Brief*, p. 5.
794. Brown, L.R. 'Plan B: Mobilizing to Save Civilization'. *(2008) Earth Policy Institute*, W.W. Norton and Company, New York, p. 398.
795. Holmberg, J. and Dornburg, V. 'Using Biomass for Climate Change Mitigation and Oil Use Reduction' (2007) 35 *Energy Policy*, p. 671.
796. Akuru and Okoro postulate that one of the reasons why the Nigerian energy sector is highly vulnerable to shocks is due to its overdependence on fossil sources. *See* U.B. Akuru, O.I. Okoro, 'Renewable Energy Investment in Nigeria: A Review of the Renewable Energy Master Plan', J. Energy South, Afr. 25, 3, (2014).

the Nigerian economy, energy poverty is still rampant in the country.[797] While Nigeria possesses an abundance of access to renewable energy sources and a master plan for renewable energy, the country is still behind in renewable energy development and usage. This may be attributed to the cost of renewable resources when compared to costs associated with fossil-based fuels. Interests in shifting renewable energy to mainstream sustainable development are recently growing, due in part to the expanding commercial markets for renewable energy that are shifting investment patterns away from traditional government and international donor sources towards a greater reliance on private firms and banks.[798]

412. While renewable energy still cannot compete with fossil fuels on price, the margins are narrowing: major improvements in energy efficiency and renewable energy production costs have decreased the amount of capital needed for key applications. There is still a need for capital investment, but costs have often fallen by more than 75% in the last decade. Because Nigeria's fossil fuel-based economy will undoubtedly come to an end, searching for alternatives early is of utmost importance. With an abundance of renewable resources and growing government support, the ability of Nigeria to incorporate renewable energy into its power grid is ever-increasing.

413. Renewable energy has considerable potential in Nigeria, as it could bridge major energy gaps in rural areas. The growing opportunities for renewable energy in Nigeria are becoming more evident as new grid technologies, like concentrated solar power, are emerging as competitors with conventional, oil-based power generation. Similarly, an intuitional framework of renewable energy governance has continued to expand, as further highlighted below.

I. National Electric Power Policy, 2001

414. The NEPP was the first of its kind in the wake of reform in the Nigerian power sector. Its development was due to the recommendations of the Electrical Power Implementation Committee (EPIC), which was the body in charge of reforms and transformation of the power sector in 1999. The NEPP was created in March 2001 and presented three bold steps in achieving the goal of reforming the power sector. The first step was to privatize NEPA which was state-owned and introduce Integrated Power Producers (IPPs) of electricity. The next step was to increase competition between participants in the market, gradually remove subsidies and sell excess power to the DISCOs. In the last step, it was expected that the market and

797. About 85 million Nigerians – representing approximately 60% of the population – have no access to electricity services. [1] Of the 40% of Nigerians who have ready access to electricity, less than 20% of them are located in rural areas. *Ibid.*

798. Gigi Nwagbo, 'Renewable Energy in Nigeria' 12 Dec. 2017, available online at: http://large.stanford.edu/courses/2017/ph240/nwagbo2/, accessed 12 Jan. 2019.

competition would have been more intense and allow for full cost pricing of supply, and liberalization of the electricity market would have been complete at this stage under the EPIC implementation agenda.

II. National Energy Policy, 2003, 2006, 2013

415. The Nigerian NEP started from a conference in 1978 when Olusegun Obasanjo, a military leader, controlled all affairs in the country.[799] The Energy Policy of 2003 has a number of objectives pertaining to renewable energy sources. These objectives include: increasing the percentage of hydroelectric sources and their extension to the rural areas; conservation of the forest resources of the nation; development of the solar capability of the nation's energy mix: promotion of biomass as an alternative energy source for the rural areas; development of the local capability of the wind energy technology; and keeping abreast of the international trends in hydrogen production as well as its application. It has become clear from the situation on the ground that the political will on the part of the government to apply the above policies is totally absent. This is due to the fact that there is no competent legal and institutional framework on the ground to implement these policy objectives.

III. National Renewable Energy and Energy Efficiency Policy, 2014

416. The National Renewable Energy and Energy Efficiency Policy (NREEEP) aggregate and amplify the global thrust of the policies and measures for the promotion of renewable energy and energy efficiency. NREEEP seeks to bring to the attention of policymakers the economic, political and social potential of renewable energy. It recommends that an appropriate strategy should be developed to harness these potentials in order to add value to the ongoing changes in Nigeria's power sector. The document also stipulates that existing policies lack a coherent and all-encompassing framework that drives the sector. It, therefore, calls for an integrated renewable energy and energy efficiency policy which will serve as a useful vehicle that limits conflicts in the future and promotes the development and deployment of renewable energy technologies in Nigeria. The overall focus of the policy is on the optimal utilization of the nation's energy resources for sustainable development.[800]

---

799. *See* Energy Policy of Nigeria, 2003, available online at: www.onlinenigeria.com/geology/?blurb=514, accessed viewed on 12 15 Jul. 2017.

800. The purpose of this policy on renewable energy and energy efficiency is to:

(1) set out a framework for action to address Nigerians' challenge of inclusive access to modern and clean energy resources, improved energy security and climate objectives;
(2) incorporate provisions for renewable energy and energy efficiency generation activities into government policy statements and plans, and recognizes the importance of enabling framework conditions for private investment in renewable energy and energy efficiency;
(3) recognize that poverty mitigation and environmental protection are hindered by the continued predominance and inefficient use of oil and natural gas in meeting our energy needs;

IV. Renewable Electricity Policy Guidelines, 2006

417. The Renewable Electricity Policy Guidelines (REPG) which was developed by the Federal Ministry of Power and Steel in December 2006 mandated the Nigerian government the expansion of electricity generation from renewables to at least 5% of the total electricity generated and a minimum of 5 TWh of electricity generation in the country. This policy document presents the Nigerian government's plans, policies, strategies and objectives for the promotion of renewables in the power sector.

V. Renewable Electricity Action Programme, 2006

418. The Renewable Energy Action Programme (corresponding to the REPG) was issued by the Federal Ministry of Power and Steel in 2006. The Renewable Electricity Action Programme (REAP) sets out a roadmap for the implementation of the REPG. The document presents an overview of the Nigerian electricity sector and relates it to renewable energy development. The documents also review government targets and provide strategies for renewable energy development, such as: levelling the playing field for renewable electricity producers, multi-sector partnerships, demonstration projects, supply chain initiatives, etc. The study also made provision for financing renewable programmes and explored the roles of government ministries and agencies, then concludes with a risk assessment, monitoring and evaluation.[801]

VI. Renewable Energy Master Plan 2005 and 2012

419. The Renewable Energy Master Plan (REMP) was developed by the Energy Commission of Nigeria (ECN), in collaboration with the United Nations Development Programme (UNDP) in 2005 and was later reviewed in 2012. The REMP expresses Nigeria's vision and sets out a roadmap for increasing the role of renewable energy in achieving sustainable development. The REMP is anchored on the mounting convergence of values, principles and targets as embedded in the National Economic Empowerment and Development Strategy (NEEDS), NEP, National Policy on Integrated Rural Development (NPIRD), the Millennium Development Goals (MDGs) and international conventions to reduce poverty and reverse global environmental change. The REMP does not specifically differentiate between

(4) take a step in the right direction and broaden the definition of energy security to include renewable energy and energy efficiency as equally important indigenous sources of energy, in addition to oil and gas; among other objectives.

801. The core focus of the document is on utilizing all forms of renewable energy sources for electricity generation and highlights potential gaps, technical assessments and financial implications, benefits and limitations of Nigeria's renewable energy sources potentials. However, this programme seems to be abandoned with the restructuring of the Ministry of Power and Steel to the new Ministry of Power.

on-grid and off-grid generation, however, it refers to integrating renewable energy into buildings, electricity grids and other distribution systems stressing the need for the integration of renewables in buildings, electricity grids and for off-grid electrical systems. Further, the importance of solar power in the country's energy mix was also highlighted in the policy document.

Chapter 7. Energy and Environmental Laws in Nigeria

§1. Introduction

420. One of the negative effects of petroleum exploration in Nigeria is that it is hazardous to the environment.[802] The exploration of natural resources by man is symbiotically related to man's exploitation of the environment, as there can be no natural resource without the environment as its platform. Environment, in this context, includes 'water, air, land and all plants and human beings or animals living therein and the interrelationship which exists among these or any of them'.[803] How the environment is managed has a direct bearing on the quality of life of every living being. Thus, a poor degenerated and polluted environment is bound to do irreparable damage to human existence and could make the earth uninhabitable to man if measures are not implemented to control the effect of pollution on the environment.

§2. Environmental Standards and Regulation in the Petroleum Industry

421. Environmental guidelines and standards for the petroleum industry in Nigeria are issued by the DPR. The Petroleum Act generally empowers the minister in section 9-(1)(b)(iii) to make regulations for the prevention of pollution of water courses and the atmosphere.[804] The Petroleum Regulations 1969 issued by the minister contain provisions on environmental pollution.[805] Petroleum operations give rise to various types of pollution, such as air, water, land, noise or thermal, and these occur at exploration and production stages up to the refining and transporting of products to end users.[806] This is one of the basic reasons why the Petroleum Regulations of 1969 provide for environmental pollution in its regulation. There is an omnibus provision on pollution in Regulation 25, which provides that:

> The licensee or lessee shall adopt all practicable precautions including the provision of up to date equipment approved by the Director of Petroleum Resources to prevent pollution of inland waters, rivers, water course, the territorial waters of Nigeria or the high seas by oil, mud or other fluid or substances which might contaminate the water bank or shore line which might

802. Atsegbua L. Akpotaire, V. Dimowo F., Environmental Law in Nigeria: Theory and Practice, Lagos; Ababa Press Ltd., 2004, p. 3.
803. Environment has also been defined as 'The system of abiotic, biotic, and socio-economic components with which man interacts, and simultaneous to which he adapts and transforms and uses in order to satisfy his needs'. *See* generally Yemi Oke, 'Intergenerational Sustainability and Traditional Knowledge in Africa: Natural Resource Management Perspective' *in* Sustaining Life on Earth: Environmental and Human Health Though Global Governance (C.L. Soskolne, et al., eds) Lexington Books Maryland, USA. (2007) at 227–239.
804. *See* s. 9(1)(b)(iii) *of the Petroleum Act, Cap P10 Laws of the Federation of Nigeria 2004.*
805. Duru O.W., 'An Appraisal of the Legal Framework for the Regulation of Nigerian Oil and Gas Industry, with Appropriate Recommendations' available at http://ssrn.com/abstract=2137979 accessed on 01.1.14.
806. *Ibid.*

cause harm or destruction to fresh water or marine life and where any such pollution occurs or has occurred, shall take prompt steps to control and, if possible, end it.[807]

422. The above provision suffers from two major defects. The duty imposed a very vague legal duty, as all the operators are enjoined to do no more than take prompt steps 'to control and, if possible, end' the pollution in question. Second, it does not provide for land pollution at all.[808] *Regulation 36* enjoins the operator to carry out his operations in a proper and workmanlike manner in accordance with good oil field *practices, and to take 'reasonable steps' to control the flow and prevent the escape of waste of petroleum discovered in or obtained from the relevant area.*[809] *Regulations 38 and 39* of the Petroleum Act provide for the use of approved methods and practices for the production of oil and gas respectively.[810] It should be noted that these and similar regulations are loosely worded and very weak as they contained unrealistic provisions incapable of resulting in serious legal consequences like revocation if contravened by an operator.

423. The Petroleum Regulations 1967 deal with downstream activities of the petroleum industry and contain provisions against leakage of petroleum products. Penalties for non-compliance are *revocation, and a fine of NGN 100 with the option of imprisonment.* The Petroleum Refining *Regulations 1974* also, among other things, deal with environmental standards applicable in Nigerian refineries.[811] *Regulation 43*, for example, deals with effluent and drainage disposal and imposes a duty on the manager to ensure that disposal is in accordance with good refining practices.[812] The manager is also obliged to prevent pollution and 'where it occurs, take prompt steps to control, and if possible, end it'.[813] The penalty for this, if found guilty under this provision, is a fine *of NGN 100* or imprisonment, which are not feasible in practice since revocation is unlikely unless it is a major environmental offence[814] if it ever gets remediated. The above provisions place a greater responsibility on the government bureaucracy in the DPR, to define and delimit the scope of terms such as *good Oilfield practice,* and approved methods and practices.

424. Marine oil pollution is also one of the fatal consequences of energy or petroleum pollution. Although international conventions take the lead in the legal regime underpinning the prevention and compensation of marine oil pollution damage, national legal systems differ considerably in how they interpret and apply their

807. *Ibid.*
808. *Ibid.*
809. What amount to a reasonable step and its determination remains a mystery in the mind of scholars till this moment as the definition is a continuum and remained very elastic as it is none specific.
810. For instance, how do we measure *prompt steps 'to control and, if possible, end' the pollution in question, also what is good oil practice when most officers of the DPR lacks the expertise to measure and determine what is a good mining practice?.*
811. *Ibid.*
812. Reg. 43 (1).
813. Reg. 43 (3).
814. *Ibid.*

monitoring and enforcement responsibilities. The highest degree of pollution comes from offshore sources and coastal states are the greatest victims. Added to the problem of coastal states is the constraint placed on local jurisdiction or authority to monitor and punish vessels which cause pollution.[815] In international law, the jurisdictional competence of a coastal state ends at the outer limits of its territorial waters, save for the power of such a coastal state to penalize its nationals and the vessels that are registered under its jurisdiction. Thus, a coastal state that suffers damage is helpless and incapacitated from apprehending an offending vessel that plies the high seas outside the territorial waters despite committing serious environmental offences by way of marine pollution.[816] The only option open to any such state is to wait for the offending vessel to come within its territorial waters and effect an arrest thereafter.

425. In light of this, the international conventions have made an attempt to address this unsatisfactory situation. The main source of the law regulating pollution from offshore causes can be traced to international treaties and conventions. For example, the United Nations Convention of the Law of the Sea (adopted in 1958) and its updated version in 1982 (UNCLOS) provide useful guides in this regard.[817] Article 1(4) defines the pollution of the marine environment to mean:

> The introduction by man, directly or indirectly of substances or energy into the marine environment, including estuaries, which result or is likely to result in such deleterious effects as harm to living resources and marine life, hazards to human health, hindrance to marine activities, including fishing and other legitimate uses of the sea, impairment or quality for use of sea water and the reduction of amenities.

426. In addition UNCLOS, the International Convention of Civil Liability of Oil Pollution Damage of 1969[818] places strict liability (within certain limited exceptions) on shipowners for pollution damage caused by their ships. In this Convention, the required maximum level of liability of shipowners relating to insurance coverage as to compensation is specified in the Convention. In addition, the International Convention and Establishment of an International Fund for Compensation for Oil Pollution Damage 1971[819] also provide compensation for victims. The purpose of this Convention is twofold: (1) to compensate victims of oil pollution who have not received full satisfaction from the shipowner under the International Convention of Civil Liability for Oil Pollution Damage; and (2) to spread the increased financial burden beyond shipowners to importers and/or receivers of crude or refined oil.

---

815. G. Etikerentse, *Nigerian Petroleum Law* (Andrew Publishers, 2004), p. 144.
816. *Ibid.*
817. *Ibid.*
818. International Convention of Civil Liability of Oil Pollution Damage of 1969.
819. *See* the International Convention and Establishment of an International Fund for Compensation for Oil Pollution Damage 1971.

427. Article 194(3) of the Law of the Sea (UNCLOS), 1982, demands that States should take measures for combating all sources of pollution including:

> Pollution from installations and devices used in the exploration or exploitation of the natural resources of the seabed and the sub-soil in particular measures of preventing accidents and dealing with emergencies, ensuring the safety of operations at sea and regulating the design, construction equipment, operation and manning of such installations or devices.[820]

428. A number of legal, regulatory and institutional provisions also touch upon the environmental pollution resulting from operations in the petroleum industry in Nigeria. These include the *Associated Gas Re-injection Act;*[821] EIA *Act*;[822] *Harmful Waste (Special Criminal Provisions,* etc.*) Act*;[823] *Oil in Navigable Waters Act*;[824] *Oil Pipelines Act (Cap 338)*;[825] and *Petroleum Act.*[826] These also include the various states' laws on environmental Protection as well as a number of regulations such as the National Environmental Protection (Effluent Limitation) Regulations 1991 contained in Statutory Instrument No. 8 of 1991; National Environmental Protection (Pollution Abatement in Industries and Facilities Generating Wastes) Regulations, 1991, in Statutory Instrument No. 9 of 1991; Oil and Gas Pipelines Regulations 1995 in Statutory instrument No. 14 of 1995; and Petroleum (Drilling and Production) Regulations – a subsidiary legislation of the Petroleum Act.

§3. National Environmental Standards and Regulations Enforcement Agency

429. The Federal Government in line with section 20 of the 1999 CFRN, established the NESREA, a parastatal of the Federal Ministry of Environment.[827] NESREA has responsibility for the protection and development of the environment, biodiversity conservation and sustainable development of Nigeria's natural resources in general and environmental technology including coordination, and liaison with, relevant stakeholders within and outside Nigeria on matters of enforcement of environmental standards, regulations, rules, policies and guidelines. The NESREA Act empowers the agency to be responsible for enforcing all environmental laws, guidelines, policies, standards and regulations in Nigeria, as well as enforcing compliance with provisions of international agreements, protocols, conventions and treaties on the environment to which Nigeria is a signatory.[54]

820. Yemi Oke, *Impacts of International Law and Global Best Practices on Energy Resources Governance in Nigeria* (2012) 8 *University of Ilorin Law Journal*, 156–180.
821. Associated Gas Re-injection Act, Cap A 25, LFN, 2004.
822. Environmental Impact Assessment Act, Cap E 12, LFN, 2004.
823. Harmful Waste (special Criminal Provisions, etc.) Act, Cap H1, LFN, 2004.
824. Oil in Navigable Waters Act, Cap O6, LFN, 2004.
825. Oil Pipelines Act, Cap O7 LFN, 2004.
826. Petroleum Act, Cap P10, LFN, 2004.
827. By the NESREA Establishment Act 2007, the old regime under the Federal Environmental Protection Agency Act Cap F 10 LFN 2004 has been repealed.

§4. National Oil Spill Detection & Response Agency

430. The establishment of the National Oil Spill Detection & Response Agency (NOSDRA) by Act No. 15 of 2006[828] by the Federal Government of Nigeria has been a major breakthrough for the government and the victims. The agency is charged with responsibilities for regulating and coordinating oil spill response activities throughout Nigeria, among others.

§5. Associated Gas Re-injection Act

431. The spirit and letters of this law point to the total cessations of the flaring of associated gas in the Nigerian Oil industry, which would result in the improvement of the country's air and atmospheric quality. As highlighted above, a fiscal penalty is imposed on gas flaring not approved by the Minister of Petroleum Resources which presupposes that under the law, the minister may approve certain levels of gas pollution in the course of oil production subject as provided in the law.

§6. Environmental Impact Assessment Act, 1992 No. 86

432. The Act makes it mandatory for an EIA study of a project (which is likely to significantly impact the environment), to be prepared at the early stage of the project often before the project is undertaken.[829] Any project which falls under the headings provided for by the Act is subjected to the Federal Ministry of Environment for approval. Any project which is disapproved by the agency cannot be undertaken.[830] Projects by private and public entities are covered by the Act. The procedures for assessing an EIA, including a public hearing are set out in this law.

§7. Harmful Waste (Special Criminal Provisions, Etc.) Act

433. This law became effective on 25 November 1988. This law prohibits and imposes penalties for carrying, dumping and importing harmful waste (without lawful authority) on any land, territorial waters, contiguous zone and the Exclusive Economic Zone of Nigeria. Breaches of this law constitute a crime in respect of which the Federal High Court has exclusive jurisdiction to try.[831] This law also provides for civil liabilities by virtue of which a victim may proceed to recover damages and compensation under section 12 of the Act.

---

828. *See* National Oil Spill Detection & Response Agency (NOSDRA), Cap N157, LFN, 2004.
829. *See* s. 2 of this Act.
830. *See* Environmental Impact Assessment Act, Cap E 12, LFN, 2004.
831. *See* Harmful Waste (special Criminal Provisions, etc.) Act, Cap H1, LFN, 2004.

§8. Oil in Navigable Waters Act

434. This law is one of the oldest anti-pollution laws in Nigeria. It became effective in 1968. It implements terms of certain international conventions to which Nigeria is a signatory such as the 1954–1962 Conventions for Prevention of Pollution of the Sea by Oil and the Convention for Prevention of Pollution from Ships (signed in 1973). This prohibits pollution, *inter alia*, of the navigable waters (territorial waters and inland waters) of Nigeria by crude oil, fuel oil, lubricating oil, heavy diesel oil and any mixture of oil discharged from a ship. The Act covers not only the owners or masters of the Nigerian ships and the high seas within 80 kilometres of Nigeria's territorial waters but also Nigerian registered vessels in such faraway places. Under this Act, a defaulting Nigerian vessel or master can therefore be prosecuted even if the breach of the provisions of the Act occurred in locations outside the shores of Nigeria.

§9. Oil Pipelines Act

435. Under this Act, the holder of a pipeline licence is not permitted to construct works near a public road, a dam or a government building. This is provided for in section 14 of the Act.[832] The Minister of Petroleum Resources (who issues the licence) may prescribe regulations for the prevention of pollution of any land or water, *See* section 33(c).[833]

§10. Petroleum Act

436. One of the subjects in respect of which the Minister of Petroleum Resources is empowered to prescribe regulations under section 9 of the Petroleum Act is the prevention of Pollution of water courses. Pursuant to the regulation made by the minister, most leases contain standard provisions which enjoin lessees to adopt '*all practicable precautions' in their operations for the prevention of environmental pollution.* Such standard provisions are common to grants covering Land and Territorial Waters areas. This also extends to Continental Shelf areas; and by deductive reasoning, the Exclusive Economic Zone too in light of the formal inclusion of this zone in the coverage of the Petroleum Acts section 1(2) by the Petroleum (Amendment) Act, 1968 No. 22.[834]

832. *See* s. 23, Oil Pipelines Act, Cap O7 LFN, 2004.
833. *Ibid.*, s. 33(c).
834. *See* Petroleum Act. 1968 No. 22, s. 1(2) as (Amended).

§11. Overview of Pollution Control Regulations

437. Under the Nigerian regime of petroleum governance, a number of regulations have also been put in place for curtailing the challenges of environmental pollution in the energy sector. These include:

(a) National Environmental Protection (Effluent Limitation) Regulations No. 8 of 1991.
(b) National Environmental Protection Pollution (Abatement in Industries and Facilities Generating Wastes) Regulations No. 9 of 1991. These regulations prohibit the release of hazardous or toxic substances into the air, water or land of Nigeria's ecosystems beyond the limit approved by FEPA (*see* Regulation 1).[835]
(c) Oil and Gas Pipelines Regulations No. 14 of 1995. Regulations 5(d)(ii) of this instrument specifically provide that pipeline construction shall be carried out in a way that causes the least disturbance to the environment. Regulation 8(b) states that where a pipeline passes within 100 metres of a water course, the operator shall assure DPR that adequate contingency plans have been made for protecting the environment. Regulation 9(b)(ii) states that holder of a pipeline licence must establish emergency plans to ensure prompt and remedial action for the protection of property and the environment.

§12. Petroleum (Drilling and Production) Regulations

438. The above regulations provide more direct, sector-specific governance for petroleum drilling and extraction. In Regulations 17(b)(iii) and (iv) of the *Petroleum (Drilling and Production) Regulations*, it is provided that a licensee or lessee (of OPL or OML) may not enter upon land within a village, town, market, cemetery or within 20 metres of a reservoir, public road, railway or any land in actual cultivation without the prior written permission from the Petroleum Resources Minister. Regulation 18 states further that the lessee shall comply with all applicable town and country planning laws and regulations while Regulation 25 enjoins the lessee to adopt all practicable precautions (including the provisions of up-to-date equipment) for the prevention of pollution by oil, mud or other fluid.

439. Regulation 40 imposes an obligation on the lessee to drain all waste oil, brine and sludge or refuse from all storage vessels, boreholes and wells into proper receptacles constructed in compliance with the safety regulations made under the Act or any other applicable regulations. Lessees are to dispose thereof in a manner approved by the Director of Petroleum Resources or as provided by any other applicable regulations. Regulation 45(1)(c) makes it obligatory that the lessee shall

835. National Environmental Protection Pollution Abatement in Industries and Facilities Generating Wastes) Regulations 1991 in Statutory Instrument No. 9 of 1991.

within two months (or such further period approved by the minister) after the termination of a lease, take reasonable steps to restore as far as possible the surface of the operational area to its original condition.[836]

§13. EXTRATERRITORIAL ENFORCEMENT OF ENVIRONMENTAL STANDARDS

I. *SERAP v. Federal Republic of Nigeria*

440. This case originated from a complaint brought on 23 July 2009 by the Registered Trustees of the Socio-Economic Rights and Accountability Project (SERAP) pursuant to Article 10 of the Supplementary Protocol A/SP.1/01/05 against the President of the Federal Republic of Nigeria, the Attorney General of the Federation, Nigerian National Petroleum Company, Shell Petroleum Development Company (SPDC), ELF Petroleum Nigeria Ltd, AGIP Nigeria Plc, Chevron Oil Nigeria Plc, Total Nigeria Plc and Exxon Mobil.[837] The Plaintiff alleged violation by the Defendants of the rights to health, adequate standard of living and rights to economic and social development of the people of Niger Delta and the failure of the Defendants to enforce laws and regulations to protect the environment and prevent pollution.

441. Upon receipt of the application, the third to ninth Defendants raised preliminary objections to the jurisdiction of the court to entertain the application on various grounds. After careful consideration of the issues raised in the preliminary objections, the court, in Ruling No. ECW/CCJ/APP/07/10 delivered on 10 October 2010, ruled that the Plaintiff is a legal person and has the *locus standi* to institute the action. The court also held that it has no jurisdiction over the third to ninth Defendants who are corporations and struck out their names in the suit.

442. The Plaintiffs argued that Niger Delta has suffered for decades from oil spills, which destroy crops and damage the quality and productivity of soil that communities use for farming, and contaminate water that people use for fishing, drinking and other domestic and economic purposes. These spills which result from poor maintenance of infrastructure, human error and a consequence of deliberate vandalism or theft of oil have pushed many people deeper into poverty and deprivation, fuelled conflict and led to a pervasive sense of powerlessness and frustration. The Plaintiff prays the court to make a number of orders including an Order directing the Defendants individually and/or collectively to pay adequate monetary compensation of USD 1 billion to the victims of human rights violations in the Niger Delta, and other forms of reparation that the Honourable Court may deem fit to grant.

443. The Federal Republic of Nigeria maintained that the court has no jurisdiction to examine the alleged violations of the International Covenant on Civil and

836. *See* Petroleum (Drilling and Production) Regulations cap 350, Regulation (45)(1)(c).

837. *SERAP v. Federal Republic of Nigeria*, the Court of Justice of The Economic Community of West African States (ECOWAS) General List N°ECW/CCJ/App/08/09 Judgment N° ECW/CCJ/Jud/18/12 (14 Dec. 2012).

Political Rights (ICCPR) and the International Covenant on Economic, Social and Cultural Rights (ICESCR). The Federal Republic of Nigeria further affirmed that the Plaintiff does not have *locus standi* to bring the instant action. It contended that by virtue of the provisions of the new Article 9(3) of the Protocol on the court as amended by the 19 January 2005 Protocol, certain facts brought by the Plaintiff have come under the three-year statute bar, and therefore its action is foreclosed. The Federal Republic of Nigeria concluded that the Plaintiff's application is unfounded and must be dismissed.

444. In its judgment, the ECOWAS Court adjudged that it has jurisdiction to adjudicate on the alleged violations of the ICCPR and the International Covenant on Economic, Social and Cultural Rights. It also ruled that SERAP has *locus standi* in the case and that the report by Amnesty International is admissible. The court concluded that the Federal Republic of Nigeria has violated Articles 1 and 24 of the African Charter on Human and Peoples' Rights. It, therefore, ordered Nigeria to:

(i) take all effective measures, within the shortest possible time, to ensure restoration of the environment of the Niger Delta;
(ii) take all measures that are necessary to prevent the occurrence of damage to the environment;
(iii) take all measures to hold the perpetrators of the environmental damage accountable.

445. The ECOWAS court also ruled that the Federal Republic of Nigeria shall fully comply with and enforce the decision of the Community Court of Justice, ECOWAS, in accordance with Article 15 of the Revised Treaty and Article 24 of the 2005 Supplementary Protocol on the Court. This is the main snag of the above ruling. It remains mere diplomatic declarations lacking the force of law. The court has no cognizable means of enforcing its decision on Nigeria and other countries. The court also deliberately refused to grant monetary compensation to the Plaintiff against the Federal Government of Nigeria.

446. The implication of this is that the Plaintiff has been denied justice and left without any remedies which it had sought through the court on behalf of the people of the Nigeria Delta for environmental harm done to specific communities in the region. Second, the Plaintiff might not be able to bring the same set of claims before the local (regular) court having unsuccessfully litigated the same at the ECOWAS Court. The victory is mere declaration. In actual fact, unless there are/is institutional mechanism(s) of coercing the Federal Republic of Nigeria to comply and monetary compensation given to the affected communities through the Plaintiff or other representatives, it would amount to injustice irrespective of the fact that some of the reliefs were granted in favour of the Plaintiff.

II. *Friday Alfred Akpan v. Royal Dutch Shell Plc & Anor*

447. The Plaintiff is a resident of Ikot Ada Udo, Akwa Ibom State, Nigeria who sued in the name of an association with a corporate personality, named *Vereniging Milieudefensie*, domiciled in Amsterdam, Netherlands.[838] The defendants are: *Royal Dutch Shell Plc,* having its registered office in London, United Kingdom, but its principal place of business in The Hague, Netherlands, and *Shell Petroleum Development Company Of Nigeria Ltd.*, having its registered office in Port Harcourt, Rivers State, Nigeria. The suit involves two specific oil spills in 2006 and 2007 from oil facilities of operator SPDC near the village of Ikot Ada Udo in Nigeria where Akpan lives.

448. In its judgment which is declared provisionally enforceable, the District Court held that Shell et al. committed tort against Akpan and are jointly and severally liable towards Akpan for the damage that he suffered and will suffer in the future as a result of these torts on the part of Shell et al., which damage is to be assessed by the court and to be settled in conformance with the law. The court also declared that Shell et al. are liable for the infringement of Akpan's physical integrity by living in a contaminated environment. It also renders a declaratory judgment to the effect that Shell et al. are jointly and severally liable for the damage to the environment near Ikot Ada Udo in Nigeria as a result of these torts on the part of Shell et al.

449. The District Court observes that many oil spills occur each year in Nigeria but the instant spill has far-reaching consequences for the local population and for the environment. However, the court is of the view that SPDC's policy constitutes insufficient reason to rule that under Nigerian law, Royal Dutch Shell (RDS) assumed a duty of care in respect of the people living in the vicinity of the oil pipelines and oil facilities of SPDC. The court observes that those circumstances do not mean that any proximity was created between RDS in The Hague and those people living in the vicinity in Nigeria. The court reasoned that it would not be fair, just and reasonable to assume that RDS had a specific duty of care in 2006 and 2007 near Ikot Ada Udo. In view of these, the District Court is of the opinion that under applicable Nigerian law, the parent company RDS in The Hague did not commit any tort of negligence against Milieudefensie and Akpan. For this reason, the District Court dismissed all the claims initiated against RDS.

450. The court ruled that SPDC has a general duty of care in respect of people living in the vicinity such as Akpan to prevent sabotage of its oil pipelines and oil facilities by taking additional and better preventive measures. It observed that the SPDC should have foreseen this obvious risk of sabotage and should have taken

838. *Friday Alfred Akpan v. Royal Dutch Shell Plc & Anor.* (District Court of The Hague) Commercial team; Judgment dated 30 Jan. 2013; in the matter with case number/ docket number: C/09/337050/ HA ZA 09-1580.

more and better preventive measures against this risk. Thus, the District Court is of the opinion that under the special circumstances of this case, the requirement of proximity has been satisfied.

451. On liability on account of infringement of Akpan's human rights, the court alluded to the *Nigerian case of Gbemre v. Shell Petroleum Development Company and others (2005).*[839] The District Court finds that a fundamental difference can be pointed out between that case and the subject issue. In *Gbemre v. Shell Petroleum Development Company and others*, the court ruled that SPDC had infringed a human right by its active conduct, namely by deliberately flaring gas during a long period. However, in the case at issue, SPDC cannot be blamed for any active conduct but for negligence and consequently dismissed this head of claim.

452. On the issue of costs compensation, the District Court ruled that each of the parties bear its own costs of the proceedings. The court feels that the principal nature of this dispute and the legal complexity of the points in dispute are sufficient grounds for not making an order to pay compensation which is to be assessed by the Court. Nonetheless, it orders SPDC to compensate Akpan for the damage he suffered as a result, to be assessed by the court and to be settled in conformance with the law.

453. In effect, the District Court partially allowed the declaratory judgment and order to pay compensation, to be assessed by the court as claimed by the Plaintiff but dismissed the other (main) claims in the suit. While the actual amount is not declared, the case under review remains one of the attractions of increasing resort to extraterritorial forums to pursue environmental claims against multinational oil companies. This is due to difficulties and related technical obstacles hurled on the way to justice in the Nigerian jurisdiction by way of proof of special damages, paucity or inadequacy of monetary compensation awarded by courts and other technical issues in securing justice.

§14. Applicable International Regimes Pollution Governance

454. In Nigeria, pollution control is the primary responsibility of a number of regulatory institutions.[840] However, it appears victims of pollution are wary of approaching the domestic court, as they hardly get adequate remedies. Victims of pollution damage have better chances of remedy in foreign courts. A graphic

839. *Jonah Gbemre v. Shell Petroleum Development Company of Nigeria Limited* Suit, no. FHC/B/CS/2005.

840. NESREA Act established the agency under the Federal Government of Nigeria as a parastatal of the then Federal Ministry of Environment, Housing and Urban Development. NESREA This Act establishes NESREA 2007 and is currently the major federal body charged with the protection of Nigeria's environment. NESREA Act repealed the Federal Environmental Protection Agency (FEPA). Section 7(a) states that the agency is authorized to enforce compliance with laws, guidelines, policies and standards of environmental matters.

example is the case of *A.F. Akpan v. Royal Dutch Shell Plc*[841] in respect of oil spillage.[842] While some have argued that lack of political will on the part of the government is responsible for gas being flared, others believe it is a result of the unavailability of the infrastructure required to control gas flaring.[843]

I. Geneva Convention on Long-Range Transboundary Air Pollution

455. In 1979, thirty-two countries in the pan-European region decided to cooperate to reduce air pollution by signing the United Nations Economic Commission for Europe (UNECE) Convention on Long-range Transboundary Air Pollution, creating the first international treaty to deal with air pollution on a broad regional basis.[844] The Convention entered into force in 1983, laying down the general principles of international cooperation for air pollution abatement and setting up an institutional framework which has fostered research and policy in this regard.[845] Article 1 of the Convention defines 'Air Pollution':

> the introduction by man, directly or indirectly, of substances or energy into the air resulting in deleterious effects of such a nature as to endanger human health, harm living resources and ecosystems and material property and impair or interfere with amenities and other legitimate uses of the environment, and 'air pollutants' shall be construed accordingly.[846]

456. The Convention is under the purview of the European Monitoring and Evaluation Programme (EMEP). Since 1979, the Convention has addressed some of the major environmental problems of the UNECE region through scientific collaboration and policy negotiation. The Convention has been extended by eight

---

841. C/09/337050. The contention in this case which The Hague Court had to resolve bothered on 'duty of care' to the victims of environmental harm. *See Environmental Law Alliance Worldwide*, https://elaw.org/af-akpan-v-royal-dutch-shell, accessed 12 Jul. 2017. In this case, a farmer from Ikot Ada Udo, Akwa Ibom State sued Royal Dutch Shell (Shell) and its Nigerian subsidiaries in a Dutch court in the Netherland seeking compensation for damage claimed to have been caused by leaking oil pipelines and an oil well in Nigeria. Overturning a lower court decision, the Court of Appeal of The Hague ruled that Dutch courts have jurisdiction to consider the claims. Damages were awarded to the farmer from Ikot. This case has set a precedent on environmental activities as companies can be charged in their home countries for their actions in the host countries.
842. *Ibid.*, at p. 31.
843. A.W. Reitze, 'Federal Control of Carbon Dioxide Emissions: What Are the Options?' (2009) 36:1, *Boston College Environmental College Law Review* pp. 1–79.
844. *See* the *United Nations Economic Commission for Europe (UNECE) Convention on Long-range Transboundary Air Pollution*, (1979) TIAS 10541; 1302 UNTS 217; 18 ILM 1442 (*1979*), online at https://www.unece.org/fileadmin/DAM/env/lrtap/full%20text/1979.CLRTAP.e.pdf, accessed 28 Aug. 2018.
845. *See* 'Environmental Policy' online at: http://www.unece.org/environmental-policy/conventions/env lrtapwelcome/the-air-convention-and-its-protocols/the-convention-and-its-achievements.htm, accessed 8 Jul. 2017.
846. *See* Art. 1 *Convention on Long-range Transboundary Air Pollution* (1979), *supra* note 844.

protocols[847] that identify specific measures to be taken by parties to cut their emissions of air pollutants. The aim of the Convention is essentially to enjoin parties thereto to endeavour to limit and, as far as possible, gradually reduce and prevent air pollution including long-range transboundary air pollution.[848]

II. Global Gas Flaring Reduction Initiative

457. The World Bank Group has assumed a leadership role in gas flaring reduction through the *Global Gas Flaring Reduction Partnership* (GGFR), a public-private initiative comprising international and national oil companies, national and regional governments and international institutions.[849] GGFR works to increase the use of natural gas associated with oil production by helping remove technical and regulatory barriers to flaring reduction, conducting research, disseminating best practices and developing country-specific gas flaring reduction programmes.[850]

458. The Initiative was launched formally at the World Summit on Sustainable Development (WSSD), in Johannesburg, South Africa, on 30 August 2002, with the objective of reducing carbon emissions and the environmental impact of flaring, monetization of wasted resources and improving energy efficiency and access to energy. It seeks to achieve its objectives through research, seminars and reports by providing data on gas flaring in countries and reporting on commitments and efforts of these countries in support of the initiative.[851] The GGFR has made remarkable efforts in reducing flaring in Nigeria.[852] The GGFR work programme is managed and facilitated by a World Bank team, and focuses on four key areas to overcome the obstacles to gas flaring reduction in partnership with target countries namely;

847. These include: Protocol on Long-Term Financing of the Cooperative Programme for Monitoring and Evaluation of the Long-range Transmission of Air Pollutants in Europe (EMEP) (1984);1985 Helsinki Protocol on the Reduction of Sulphur Emissions, Nitrogen Oxide Protocol (1988),Volatile Organic Compounds Protocol (1991)1994 Oslo Protocol on Further Reduction of Sulphur Emissions, Protocol on Heavy Metals (1998),Aarhus Protocol on Persistent Organic Pollutants (1998) Gothenburg Protocol to Abate Acidification Eutrophication and Ground-level Ozone (1999). *See* generally online at: https://www.unece.org/env/lrtap/status/lrtap_s.html accessed 8 Jul. 2017.

848. Article 2 of the Convention.

849. Online at: http://www.worldbank.org/en/programs/gasflaringreduction retrieved 8 Jul. 2017.

850. *Ibid.*

851. *Ibid.* For example a data released in 12 Dec. 2016 by the GGFR revealed an increase over the past five years in the amount of gas flared at oil production sites worldwide, and emphasized the need for reversing a trend of flaring reduction. The flaring increase is mainly attributed to an overall growth in oil production, particularly in Iraq and the United States. Also a ranking of countries on the amount of gas flared by the initiative between 2013–2015 lists Russia, Iraq, Iran and the US as the top countries with highest amount of gas flared within this period. Nigeria occupies the seventh position on the gas flaring chart, online at: http://www.worldbank.org/en/news/press-release/2016/12/12/new-data-reveals-uptick-in-global-gas-flarin, accessed 15 Jul. 2017.

852. This includes the endorsement of a 'Global Standard for gas flaring reduction, through the implementation of demonstration projects for associated gas utilization in seven countries, namely: Nigeria, Equatorial Guinea, Cameron, Algeria, Kazakhstan, and Qatar in meeting flaring out targets by specific dates. This has increased the potentials for avoidable gas, through GGFR facilitated carbon projects, which is approximately 12 billion cubic metres per year; and development of a web-based tool to report flared and vented data on country basis. *Supra* note 73 p. 23.

commercialization of associated gas; regulation of associated gas; implementation of the global flaring and venting standard; and capacity building to obtain carbon credits for gas flaring and venting projects.[853]

III. United Nations Framework Convention on Climate Change

459. This is an international environmental treaty adopted on 9 May 1992 and opened for signature at the Earth Summit in Rio de Janeiro from 3–14 June 1992 and came into force on March 1994 ninety days after the fiftieth country's ratification had been received. By December 2007, it had been ratified by 192 countries.[854] Article 2 of The United Nations Framework Convention on Climate Change (UNFCCC) provides that:

> Ultimate objective of this Convention and any related legal instruments that the Conference of the Parties may adopt is to achieve, in accordance with the relevant provisions of the Convention, stabilization of greenhouse gas concentrations in the atmosphere at a level that would prevent dangerous anthropogenic interference with the climate system. Such a level should be achieved within a time-frame sufficient to allow ecosystems to adapt naturally to climate change, to ensure that food production is not threatened and to enable economic development to proceed in a sustainable manner.

460. The framework sets no binding limits on greenhouse gas emissions for individual member countries and contains no enforcement mechanisms. The framework however outlines how specific international treaties (called 'protocols' or 'agreements') may be negotiated to specify further action towards the objective of the UNFCCC[855]

IV. The Kyoto Protocol and Paris Agreement

461. The Kyoto Protocol extends the frontiers of the UNFCCC, which commits parties thereto by setting internationally binding emission reduction targets. Recognizing that developed countries are majorly responsible for the current high levels of GHG emissions in the atmosphere as a result of more than 150 years of industrial activity, the protocol places a heavier burden on developed nations under the principle of common but differentiated responsibilities. The Kyoto Protocol was adopted in Kyoto, Japan, on 11 December 1997 and entered into force on 16 February 2005.

---

853. *Ibid.*
854. Further details on ratification of the United Nations Framework Convention on Climate Change (UNFCCC) online at: http://enb.iisd.org/process/climate_atm-fcccintro.html, accessed on 8 Jul. 2017.
855. Online at: https://www.revolvy.com/main/index.php?s=United%20Nations%20Framework%20Convention%20on%20Climate%20Change, accessed 8 Jul. 2017.

462. The detailed rules for the implementation of the protocol were adopted at COP 7 in Marrakesh, Morocco, in 2001, and are referred to as the 'Marrakesh Accords'. Its first commitment period started in 2008 and ended in 2012.[856] The protocol constitutes the most important move by the international community to strengthen undertakings embodied in the UNFCCC.[857] The protocol's major feature is that it has mandatory targets on greenhouse gas emissions for the world's leading economies which have accepted it. These targets range from -8% to +10% of the countries' individual 1990 emissions levels with a view to reducing their overall emissions of such gases by at least 5% below existing 1990 levels in the commitment period 2008–2012.[858] The Doha Amendment is the second commitment to Kyoto Protocol running till 2012. It is known as the Doha Amendment to the protocol in which thirty-seven countries have binding targets. As of 2016, a total of sixty-six countries have ratified the instrument. This commitment ends in 2020.[859]

463. One important element of the Kyoto Protocol is its flexible mechanisms that enable nations to achieve their emission target by means other than reducing their domestic emission of greenhouse gases.[860] Such mechanisms are the Clean Development, Join Implementation, and Emission Trading Mechanisms.[861] Article 2 of the protocol provides that:

> Each Party included in Annex I, in achieving its quantified emission limitation and reduction commitments under Article 3, in order to promote sustainable development, shall:(a) Implement and/or further elaborate policies and measures in accordance with its national circumstances, such as: (i) Enhancement of energy efficiency in relevant sectors of the national economy; (ii) Protection and enhancement of sinks and reservoirs of greenhouse gases not controlled by the Montreal Protocol, taking into account its commitments under relevant

856. *See United Nations Framework Convention on Climate Change* (U. N. Doc. A/AC.237/18 (Part II) (Add. 1), Misc 6 (1993), Cm 2137; 31 I.L.M. 848. *See also Kyoto Protocol to the United Nations Framework Convention on Climate Change*, 31 ILM 849 (1992). In Doha, Qatar, on 8 Dec. 2012, the 'Doha Amendment to the Kyoto Protocol' was adopted. The amendment includes: new commitments for Annex I Parties to the Kyoto Protocol who agreed to take on commitments in a second commitment period from 1 Jan. 2013 to 31 Dec. 2020. For a revised list of greenhouse gases (GHG) to be reported on by Parties in the second commitment period; and amendments to several articles of the Kyoto Protocol which specifically referenced issues pertaining to the first commitment period and which needed to be updated for the second commitment period. *See* generally http://unfccc.int/kyoto_protocol/items/2830.php, accessed 8 Jul. 2017.
857. *Ibid.*
858. *See also* UNFCCC online at: http://unfccc.int/kyoto_protocol/background/items/2879.php, accessed 8 Jul. 2017.
859. L. Justin. 'Rooting the Concept of Common But Differentiated Responsibilities in Established Principles of International Environmental Law'. (2015) 17:1 *Vermont Journal of Environmental Law*, pp. 27–50.
860. *See* for example, Christopher Carr, 'Structuring and Financing Projects' in Paul O. Watchman (ed.) *Climate Change: A Guide to Carbon Law and Practice* (London, Globe Business Publishing, 2008), at 39.
861. L. Justin, *supra* note 859, at p. 22.

international environmental agreements; promotion of sustainable forest management practices, afforestation and reforestation; (iii) Promotion of sustainable forms of agriculture in light of climate change considerations; (iv) Research on, and promotion, development and increased use of, new and renewable forms of energy, of carbon dioxide sequestration technologies and of advanced and innovative environmentally sound technologies; (v) Progressive reduction or phasing out of market imperfections, fiscal incentives, tax and duty exemptions and subsidies in all greenhouse gas emitting sectors that run counter to the objective of the Convention and application of market instruments; (vi) Encouragement of appropriate reforms in relevant sectors aimed at promoting policies and measures which limit or reduce emissions of greenhouse gases not controlled by the Montreal Protocol; (vii) Measures to limit and/or reduce emissions of greenhouse gases not controlled by the Montreal Protocol in the transport sector; (viii) Limitation and/or reduction of methane emissions through recovery and use in waste management, as well as in the production, transport and distribution of energy.

464. Nigeria became a signatory to the Kyoto Protocol on 23 October 1998 and ratified the protocol on 30 September 2004. Nigeria, as a non-Annex I country has the possibility and the potential to benefit from the market-based mechanism created by the protocol. Nigeria has indeed collaborated with the United Nations Industrial Development Organization (UNIDO) and CDM Secretariat in accessing some projects targeted at reducing gas flaring such as the West African Gas Pipeline project and other gas utilization projects.[862]

465. The *Kyoto Protocol*[863] deals essentially with environmental management challenges arising from emissions of greenhouse gases by countries.[864] However, the emission of greenhouse gases impacts developing countries more due to reliance on energy and other forms of natural resource extraction, activities which are prone to the emission of GHGs. However, beyond the menace of oil-induced climate change, global concern for controlling GHGs emission might remain a façade, as the world continues to prefer economic interests over and above climate change and related environmental concerns. The Rio+20 Summit[865] is anything but a success. The global players appear receding than accelerating in their commitments to climate change governance. According to an observer:

> As the global economic crisis has consumed more and more time and attention, focus on the global warming crisis has waned. So it wasn't surprising when President Barack Obama chose not to attend the Rio+20 … , and it also was unsurprising when there was little progress reported there. … And with the world economy on everyone's mind, global warming has taken a back

862. *Ibid.*
863. *See Kyoto Protocol, supra* note 856.
864. *See* Art. 3. *Ibid.*
865. *See* 'At Rio+20 Summit, Little Actual Disappointment over Lack of Progress', online at http://www.pri.org/stories/science/environment/tt-at-rio-20-summit-little-actual-disappointment-over-lack-of-progress-10382.html, accessed 24 Jun. 2012.

> seat … the summit was a bit of a disappointment, but only marginally so, because no one was really expecting anything to come out of it.[866]

466. The lacklustre outcome of the Rio 20+ Earth Summit had been predicted by those who contend, in relation to climate change, that these types of mass international conferences have become an incredible distraction that actually undermine rather than support efforts to reduce greenhouse gas emissions.[867] Edis and others are of the view that such global conferences reinforce a false belief that reducing carbon emissions must be closely and internationally coordinated.[868] The above notion would appear justified in the sense that the Rio+20 and the Paris Agreement might not offer much respite for developing countries like Nigeria in terms of global consensus and readiness to mitigate the climate change effects of energy exploitation.

467. Similarly, in 2009, the Copenhagen Summit failed to produce a binding climate change agreement, as large target goals on carbon dioxide emission reductions were dropped, and the Summit ended in failure. This reinforces the arguments that local policy and action are more likely to succeed than globally binding agreements.[869] The Paris Agreement also seems to offer no comfort given the decision of the US to back out of the accord. The agreement demonstrates the effort of governments, on a larger scale, to take measures to limit emissions of carbon dioxide and other greenhouse gases. The Paris Agreement is a voluntary agreement among 118 nations ratified on 4 November 2016, in an effort to combat climate change on a global scale.[870] As part of the agreement, each country agreed to take measures to combat climate change, with the ultimate goal of keeping the post-industrial global temperature rise below 2°C.[871]

V. International Convention on Civil Liability for Oil Pollution Damage (Civil Liability Convention), 1996

468. The Convention recognizes the right of members to exploit the natural resources of the sea subject however to the obligation not to degrade the environment. The legal regime of this Convention which came into force in 1972 was developed by the International Maritime Organization (IMO). The Convention

---

866. *Ibid.*
867. *See* Tristan Edis, 'Climate Spectator: Ignore Rio, Copenhagen and Kyoto', *Business Spectator*, online at http://www.businessspectator.com.au/bs.nsf/Article/Why-you-should-ignore-Rio-Copenhagen-and-KyotoPerp-pd20120622-VH3AC?OpenDocument&emcontent_spectators&src=rot, accessed 24 Jun. 2012.
868. *Ibid.*
869. Alex O. Awiti, 'Rio=20 Must Focus on Local Action', http://www.mwanabidii.com/showthread.php?1502-Rio-20-Must-Focus-On-Local-Action, accessed 25 Jun. 2012.
870. Online at: https:// www.nationalgeographic.com, accessed 11 Jul. 2017.
871. *Ibid.*

entered into force on 30 May 1996. The Convention laid down a regime of strict liability by shipowners for oil pollution damage subject to insurable limits based on the tonnage of the ship.

469. Under the Convention, a shipowner shall be liable for any pollution damage caused by the ship unless he is able to show that the incident was caused by war, hostilities, civil war, insurrection or a natural phenomenon of an exceptional, inevitable or irresistible character or the act or omission of a third party done with an intent to cause damage or was caused by government negligence or other authority responsible for navigational aids. Under this provision, no claim can be brought against the servants, agents, or independent contractors of the shipowner except if it can be shown that the damage occurred through deliberate, intentional or recklessly negligent conduct of such servant, agent or independent contractor.

470. A shipowner is exempted from liability once he has constituted a fund as in Article V and the claimant has access to the court where the fund is kept. The Convention makes it mandatory for all ships of contracting states carrying more than 200,000 tonnes of oil to be covered by insurance or other financial security in the sums fixed by applying the limits of liability prescribed in Article V(1). This is to cover liability for pollution damage under the Convention and a certificate of compliance shall be issued by a contracting state in case of a ship registered by it or by any contracting state in case of a ship registered in a non-contracting state.[872]

471. The contracting states must put in place laws to enforce compliance with the insurance requirements. Actions under the Convention are brought in courts of contracting states where the damage occurred or is threatening to occur including damages or threat of damage in the territorial waters of such states and contracting states are to ensure that their national courts have the jurisdiction to entertain such cases. However, where a fund has been constituted in a court of contracting states in line with Article V, such a court shall have exclusive jurisdiction over the case. The right to compensation under the Convention shall lapse after three years from the date of the pollution incident or not later than six years in respect of other matters.[873]

472. Any judgment given by the court of a contracting state in respect of matters covered by the Convention is enforceable in all contracting states and shall not be subject to review in any contracting state except for formalities for enforcement of foreign judgment unless it is shown that such a judgment was obtained by fraud or that the defendant was not given a fair hearing. It needs to be emphasized that warships used for non-commercial purposes are excluded from the application of

872. *See* International Convention on Civil Liability for Oil Pollution Damage (Civil Liability Convention), 1996, online at: www.imo.org/.../Conventions/ListOfConventions/.../International-Conventi on-on-Civi, and treaties.fco.gov.uk/docs/pdf/1996/TS0086.pdf, accessed 29 Aug. 2018.
873. *Ibid.*

the Convention. However, ships owned by the government and used for commercial purposes are within the force of the Convention and are deemed to have waived all pleas of sovereign immunity in respect of action in connection with such ships.

473. The above Convention is intricately related and linked to the International Convention for the Establishment of an International Fund for Compensation for Oil Pollution Damage Caused by Sea Going Vessels Carrying Oil as its Cargo,[874] which requires members to take individually or jointly all measures using the best practicable means at their disposal to reduce, prevent and control the pollution of the marine environment.[875] Under this Convention, States are required under the Convention to adopt laws to prevent, minimize and control pollution of the marine environment from land-based sources including estuaries, rivers, pipelines and other structures taking into account internationally agreed rules and standards.[876]

§15. Some Applicable International Law Principles

474. A number of principles have evolved which are applicable in international environmental disputes in the oil and gas sector and by extension gas pollution damages in Nigeria. These include the precautionary principle of sustainable development and 'polluter pays principles' as highlighted below.

I. The Precautionary Principle

475. The Precautionary Principle urges a willingness to take action in advance of scientific proof of evidence of the need for the proposed action on the grounds that further delay could prove ultimately most costly to society and nature and in the longer term, selfish and unfair to future generations. Central to the application of the Precautionary Principle is the concept of proportionality or cost-effectiveness.

476. The Precautionary Principle was incorporated into the 1992 Rio Declaration on Environment and Development, stating that, 'Where there are threats of serious or irreversible damage, lack of full scientific certainty shall not be used as a reason for postponing cost-effective measures to prevent environmental degradation'. According to the Wingspread Statement on the Precautionary Principle, formulated by an international group of scientists, government officials, lawyers and environmental activists in January[877] 1998 at Wingspread in Racine, Wisconsin, USA, the principle of precautionary action has four parts:

---

874. *See International Convention for the Establishment of an International Fund for Compensation for Oil Pollution Damage Caused by Sea Going Vessels Carrying Oil as its Cargo*, online at www.cep.unep.org/meetings-events/11th-igm/oil-spill-compensation-funds.../file, accessed 29 Aug. 2018.

875. *Ibid.*

876. *Ibid.*

877. *Ibid.*

(i) People have a duty to take anticipatory action to prevent harm.
(ii) The burden of proof of harmlessness of a new technology, process, activity, or chemical lies with proponents, not with the general public.
(iii) Before using a new technology, process, or chemical, or starting a new activity, people have an obligation to examine 'a full range of alternatives' including the alternative of doing nothing.
(iv) Decisions applying the precautionary principle must be 'open, informed, and democratic' and 'must include affected parties'.[878]

II. Polluter Pays Principle

477. This is a principle of international law where a polluter is made responsible for the pollution occasioned by its activities. The 'polluter pays' principle is the commonly accepted practice that those who produce pollution should bear the costs of managing it to prevent damage to human health or the environment. It is a normative doctrine of environmental law.[879] The central thesis of this principle stems from the fundamental, logical and fair proposition that those who generate pollution should bear the cost of cleaning it up.[880] This normative principle is one of the considerations for the emission-trading venture which is aimed at encouraging investment in projects to reduce greenhouse gases in developing nations.[881] The polluter pays principle first appeared in a legal text in a document prepared by the OECD[882] but received its widest expression as an international environmental law principle in the Rio Declarations, which provides:

> National authorities should endeavor to promote the internationalization of environmental costs and the use of economic instruments, taking into account the approach that the polluter should, in principle, bear the cost of pollution, with due regard to the public interest and without distorting international trade and investment.[883]

878. *Ibid.*
879. *See* Principle 16 Rio Declaration. Declaration of the Right to Development, G.A. Res. 41/128, U.N. GAOR Supp. (No. 53) at 186, U.N. Doc. A/41/53 (4 Dec. 1986); U.N. Conference on Environment and Development, Rio de Janeiro, Braz., 3–14 Jun. 1992, Rio Declaration on Environment and Development, at prin. 4, U.N. Doc. A/CONF. 151/26 (12 Aug. 1992), reprinted in 31 I.L.M. 874 [hereinafter Rio Declaration] (non-binding but recommends states develop laws of liability and compensation for environmental damage).
880. *See* J.R. Nash, 'Too Much Market? Conflict Between Tradable Pollution Allowances and the "Polluter Pays" Principle' (2000) 24 *Harvard Environmental Law Review*, 465 at 466.
881. *Ibid. See also* J.J. Fialka, 'World Bank Emissions-Trading Venture May Expand to Accommodate Interest' *Wall Street Journal*, 24 Apr. 2000 at A18.
882. OECD, Environment and Economics: Guiding Principles Concerning International Economic Aspects of Environmental Policies, 26 May 1972, annex para. 1 Doc. No C (72) 128, 1972 WL 24710 (hereinafter OECD Recommendation).
883. Principle 16, *See* the UN Conference on Environment and Development 1992 (Rio) A/CONF.151/26 Vol. I), 8:31 I.L.M 874 (1992).

478. The principle has been applied more specifically to emissions of greenhouse gases which cause climate change.[884] The principle serves as an economic rule according to which a portion of the profits accruing to polluters as the result of their activities must be returned to the public authorities responsible for inspecting, monitoring and controlling the pollution.[885] The principle usually takes the form of a tax collected by the government and levied per unit of pollution emitted into the air or water. The principle has received support from most countries of the Organisation for Economic Co-operation and Development (OECD) and from the European Community (EC).[886]

479. There are other principles that may become applicable in the settlement of international environmental disputes from Nigeria's perspective. These include: source principle, the principle of common but differentiated responsibility, the principle of international and intergenerational equity, environmental procedural rights, common concern of humankind, common heritage and the principle of stakeholder participation and partnership. These principles also imply a number of environmental duties such as the duty of conducting a comprehensive EIA, the duty to warn other states promptly about environmental emergencies and the environmental damages to which they may be exposed.

480. It needs to be pointed out that an important trend in gas pollution cases is that the law does not leave a victim without compensation either in the domestic or international court or tribunal. The quantum of damages awarded, applicable law or principles, the ability of the victim to successfully plead and argue the suit, and the appropriate forum among other factors often determine the success or otherwise of seeking remedies for gas pollution and other related claims in Nigeria and other jurisdictions.

§16. Framework for Environmental Claims in Nigeria

481. In the past and present, many indigenes of petroleum-related pollution have attempted to use the courts of law to seek redress. For many Nigerian victims who have decided to tow this path, no doubt, there have been many hurdles on the way. Environmental claim litigants have faced several technical legal issues such as the proper forum (court) to seek redress, the proper parties to sue in such actions, and the proper reliefs to seek. For this reason, many have even resorted to bringing court actions in foreign courts.

482. The Nigerian Court clarified all issues on the right to sue in environmental actions in the case of *Adediran and Another v. Interland Transport Limited*,[887]

884. *Ibid.*
885. *See* Nicolas de Sadeleer, *The Polluter-pays Principle in EU Law – Bold Case Law and Poor Harmonisation* (H.C. Bugge, Forurensningsansvaret, Oslo, Tano Aschehoug, 1999), p. 405.
886. Online at: http://www.ejolt.org/2013/05/polluter-pays-principle/, accessed 13 Jul. 2017.
887. [1992] 9 NWLR (Part 214), 155.

where the appellants as residents of a particular area instituted the action for nuisance due to noise, vibration, dust and obstruction of the roads in the area. The Supreme Court of Nigeria held that in the light of section 6(6)(b) of the 1979 CFRN,[888] a private person can commence an action on public nuisance without the consent of the Attorney General or without joining him as a party where the plaintiff proves he has suffered injury above that of the public.

483. In *Jonah Gbamre v. S.P.D.C. Nigeria Ltd.*[889] the Plaintiff sued for himself and on behalf of the people of Iwherekan Community asking the Federal High Court, Benin Division to declare that Gas Flaring is illegal, harmful to their health and environment and therefore constitutes a violation of their right to life as guaranteed by the CFRN 1999 and reinforced by the African Charter on Human and People Rights. In his judgment, Justice V.C Nwokorie held in favour of the applicants that the Continuing Flaring of Gas by the defendant is a violation of the rights provided by the Constitution and the African Charter on Human and People Rights. The judgment has been lauded in several local and international quarters and up until now stands as one of the most far-reaching decisions given by a court in Nigeria on issues relating to the environment.

484. The above is one of the few cases involving pollution by gas. The desire of the Nigerian Government to increase gas production and supply may have invariably increased instances of environmental pollution arising from gas drilling, with a few communities suing the operators for damages arising from pollution by the escape of gas.[890] The Nigerian courts have been limited in their award of compensation. The proof of sabotage is a defence which negates compensation. Section 11(5)(c) of the Oil Pipelines Act states that compensation for spills need not be paid if the spills are a result of the default of the affected person or a malicious act of a third party. Most operators use this as a defence in incidents of environmental pollution as done in *Umudje v. Shell BP Nig. Ltd.*[891] Although the onus is on the operator who claims sabotage to prove that sabotage has in actual fact occurred, the experience in practice has so far shown that the mere claim of sabotage as a defence by the operator, in most times, effectively closes the issue as far as the Nigerian courts are concerned.

---

888. Now s. 6(6)(b) of the 1999 Constitution of the Federal Republic of Nigeria.
889. Suit No. FHC/CS/B/152/2005.
890. Suit No: [FHC/CS/1033/12] J. *Fabby Young v. Chevron Nigeria Limited & Anor*; Suit No: [FHC/CS/314/2012] J. *His Royal Majesty, King Alfred Pappareye Diete Spiff and 16 Others v. Nigerian National Petroleum Corporation and 2 Others*, where the plaintiffs in both suits have sued Chevron Nigeria Limited for damages arising from a gas explosion that occurred on the Chevron operated Funiwala Gas well on the North Apoi Fields in Bayelsa State, Nigeria.
891. (1975) 11SC. 15.

Chapter 8. Energy Law and Taxation in Nigeria

§1. Taxation of Petroleum Operations and Petroleum Industry Fiscal Framework

485. The *Petroleum Industry Act (PIA), 2021*[892] makes comprehensive provisions for the petroleum industry fiscal framework in Chapter 4. The PIA sets clear objectives for the provision of Chapter 4 of the Act on Petroleum Industry Fiscal Framework. The objectives of the chapter are to establish a progressive fiscal framework that encourages investment in the Nigerian petroleum industry, balancing rewards with risk and enhancing revenues to the Federal Government of Nigeria. It also seeks to provide a forward-looking fiscal framework that is based on core principles of clarity, dynamism and fiscal rules of general application. It also aims to establish a fiscal framework that expands the revenue base of the Federal Government, while ensuring a fair return for investors; simplifying the administration of petroleum tax; and promoting equity and transparency in the petroleum industry fiscal regime.[893]

486. The PIA institutionalizes and centralizes petroleum revenue collection in Nigeria. All moneys collected from the petroleum industry that are due to the government shall be transferred to the Federation Account in a timely manner. The affected revenue includes taxes, royalties, production shares, profit shares, signature bonuses, production bonuses, renewal bonuses, rents, fees, fines, and other levies due in relation to the grant, assignment, termination, and breach of licences, leases and permits.[894]

487. Administration and collection of government revenue in the petroleum industry remain vested in the Federal Inland Revenue Service (the Service/FIRS) and the Commission.[895] In terms of stricture, the PIA provides that the Service shall be responsible for the assessment and collection of: (i) hydrocarbon tax and enforcement of the provisions of the Act as it relates to hydrocarbon tax assessment and revenue collection; and (ii) company's income tax and tertiary education tax in accordance with this Act as it relates to taxable petroleum operations.[896] The Commission on the other hand shall be responsible for the determination and collection of: (i) royalties, signature bonus, rents, and related payments and their enforcement under; and (ii) related payments or production shares, where the model contract

892. *See* the *Petroleum Industry Act, (PIA) No. 6 of 2021*. According to the Long Title to the PIA, it is 'An Act to Provide Legal, Governance, Regulatory and Fiscal Framework for the Nigerian Petroleum Industry, the Development of Host Communities; and For Related Matters'. The PIA commenced on the 16 Aug. 2021.

893. *See* s. 258(1)(a–e).

894. *Ibid.*, subs. (2).

895. *See* s. 259(a) of the PIA.

896. *Ibid.*, para. (a)(i–ii).

includes provisions related to production sharing, profit sharing or risk service provisions,[897] while the Authority shall be responsible for the determination and collection of the gas flare penalty arising from midstream operations and its enforcement under the Act.[898]

I. Hydrocarbon Tax

488. The provisions of the PIA on Hydrocarbon Tax apply to companies engaged in upstream petroleum operations in the onshore, shallow water and deep offshore. Payment of hydrocarbon tax shall apply to crude oil as well as field condensates and natural gas liquids derived from associated gas and produced in the field upstream of the measurement points.[899]

489. Hydrocarbon tax shall not apply to: (i) associated natural gas, including gaseous natural gas liquids produced in the field and contained in the rich gas, and non-associated natural gas. Application of the hydrocarbon tax is also excluded from condensates and natural gas liquids produced from non-associated gas in fields or gas processing plants. For this exception to apply, the related volumes must be determined at the measurement points or at the exit of the gas processing plant, regardless of whether the condensates or natural gas liquids subsequently commingled with crude oil. Hydrocarbon tax is also excluded in respect of any condensates and natural gas liquids produced from associated gas at gas processing or other facilities downstream of the measurement points.[900]

490. The Act makes further categorization for the purpose of application of hydrocarbon tax to the effect that the costs of production of associated gas, upstream of the measurement point shall be allocated to crude oil for the purposes of calculating hydrocarbon tax. This exception is subject to the fact that capital and operating costs for wells solely producing associated gas-cap gas shall not be allocated to crude oil, but shall be claimed under the Companies Income Tax Act.[901] The Act expressly excludes the application of Part II of Chapter 4 of the PIA on hydrocarbon tax to a frontier acreage until it is reclassified under section 68 (3) of the Act[902] and to deep offshore.[903] For the purpose of determining royalties, condensates shall

897. *Ibid.*, subs. (b)(i–ii).
898. *Ibid.*, subs. (c).
899. *See* s. 260(1)(a) of the PIA.
900. *Ibid.*, subs. (b)(i–iii).
901. *Ibid.*, subs. (2) of the PIA.
902. *See* s. 68 (3) of the PIA provides thus: Where a significant petroleum discovery is made in a frontier basin, the Minister may, on the recommendation of the Commission, reclassify all or part of the basin from frontier acreages to a general onshore area and the fiscal terms applicable to onshore under this Act shall apply to (a) new licences and leases in the basin after reclassification; and (b) any existing lease upon renewal, provided that it shall not be applied to licences and leases existing at the moment of reclassification.
903. *See* s. 260(3) of the PIA.

be treated as crude oil and natural gas liquids and shall be subject to upstream petroleum operations taxation as may be assessed under the Companies Income Tax Act.[904]

II. Charge to Hydrocarbon Tax

491. The PIA imposes a charge by way of hydrocarbon tax on upstream petroleum operations. It states that:

> There shall be levied upon the profits of any company engaged in upstream petroleum operations in relation to crude oil a tax to be known as hydrocarbon tax, which shall be charged and assessed upon its profits related to the operations and payable during each accounting period in accordance with this Act.[905]

492. Ascertainment of crude oil revenue, adjusted profit, assessable profits and chargeable profits for the purpose of hydrocarbon tax are matters of law as provided under the PIA. In any accounting period, the crude oil revenue of a company shall be the value of any chargeable oil adjusted to the measurement points, based on the proceeds of all chargeable oil sold by the company and the value of all chargeable oil disposed by the company.[906] The value of any chargeable oil disposed of is regarded as the aggregate of the value of that crude oil determined for royalties for all fields in accordance with the Act or any applicable law.

493. The adjusted profits of an accounting period shall be the profits of that period after the deductions allowed by section 263 (1) of the Act. The assessable profit of an accounting period is the adjusted profit of that period after any deduction allowed by section 265 of the Act while the chargeable profits of an accounting period are the assessable profits of that period after the deduction allowed by section 266 of the Act.

III. Allowable Deductions and Chargeable Profits, Loses or Allowances

494. Allowable deductions are statutory exceptions to the application of hydrocarbon tax. Generally, tax rules allow the particular expense to be deducted from trading income when calculating the business' profits on which it will pay applicable tax to upstream petroleum operations. Under the PIA, the adjusted profit of a company in upstream petroleum operations related to crude oil for any accounting period is computed by factoring in a number of issues.[907]

---

904. *Ibid.*, subs. (4) and (5).
905. Section 261 provides basis for charging hydrocarbon tax on upstream petroleum operations in Nigeria.
906. *See* s. 262(1) of the PIA.
907. *See* generally s. 263(1)(a–h).

495. Where a deduction has been allowed to a company under this section in respect of the liability of the company and the liability or part of the liability is waived, released or recovered, the amount of the deduction corresponding to the liability or part thereof shall, for the purpose of section 262 (1) of the Act, be treated as income of the company of its accounting period, in which such waiver or release was made or given.[908]

496. The Act also provides a detailed list of items in respect of which deductions are not allowed for the purpose of calculating the liability of a company for hydrocarbon tax under the PIA.[909] The assessable profits for each company or petroleum mining lease for any accounting period shall be the amount of the adjusted profit of that period after the deduction of the amount of any loss incurred by that company during any previous accounting period. However, the assessable profit shall be determined separately for each of the two classes of chargeable tax identified in section 267 (a) and (b).[910] The Act states that a deduction under subsection (1) shall be made from the amount if any, of the adjusted profit of the first accounting period after that in which the loss was incurred. In the alternative, it can be made from the amount of the adjusted profit of the next succeeding accounting period and so on until such loss is fully deducted.[911] The Act allows for deferred deductions till the subsequent accounting period when such an application is made to the FIRS in writing by the company.[912]

497. The chargeable profits of any company for any accounting period shall be the amount of the assessable profits of that period after the deduction of any amount to be allowed including: (a) the aggregate amount of capital allowances due to the company under the provisions of the Fifth Schedule to the Act for the accounting period; (b) the aggregate amount of all production allowances due to the company under the provisions of the Sixth Schedule for the accounting period; and (c) in the case of acquisition costs of petroleum rights, the value of the rights and the value of the assets acquired shall be reported separately to the Service, provided that the value of the rights shall be eligible for an annual allowance of 20% per annum and the value of the assets shall be depreciated based on the applicable depreciation rates for the respective assets, and there shall be a retention of 1% in the last year until the asset is disposed of.[913]

---

908. *Ibid.*, subs. (2).
909. *See* generally the provisions of s. 264(a–q) of the PIA on 'Deductions not allowed'.
910. Section 265(1) and (2) of the PIA.
911. *Ibid.*, subs. (3).
912. Subsection (4) provides that:

> Within five months after the end of any accounting period of a company, or within such further time as the Service may permit in writing, the company may elect in writing that a deduction or any part to be made under this section shall be deferred to and be made in the succeeding accounting period, and may so elect in any succeeding accounting period.

913. *See* generally s. 266(1)(a–c) of the PIA. The Act further provides under subs. (2) and (3), thus:

IV. Ascertainment of Chargeable Tax

498. The PIA specifies chargeable tax for any accounting period of a company to be a percentage of the chargeable profit for that period aggregated, as follows:

(a) 30% of the profit from crude oil for petroleum mining leases selected under section 93 (6) (b) and (7) (b) of this Act with respect to onshore and shallow water areas; and
(b) 15% of profit from crude oil for onshore and shallow water and for petroleum prospecting licences selected under section 93 (6) (a) and (7) (a) of this Act.[914]

499. Additional chargeable tax may be payable in certain circumstances where, for any accounting period of a company, the amount of the chargeable tax for that period, calculated in accordance with the provisions of the Act is less than the amount mentioned in subsection(2). Where this occurs, the company shall be liable to pay an additional amount of chargeable tax for that period equal to the difference between those two amounts.[915] The amount of additional chargeable is the amount which the chargeable tax for crude oil for that period, calculated in accordance with the Act, would come to, in the case of crude oil exported from Nigeria by the company. This is cross-referenced with the provision of section 262 (1) (a), by multiplying the number of barrels of that crude oil determined at the measurement point by the fiscal oil price per barrel.[916]

500. For the purpose of the above provisions, the Commission shall establish the fiscal oil price at each measurement point on an export parity basis under paragraphs 8(1) and (2) of the Seventh Schedule[917] and the total value of the chargeable oil for a company shall be the sum of the multiplications of volume and fiscal oil

---

(2) In determining the chargeable profit, the total cost shall not exceed the cost-price ratio as determined in the Sixth Schedule to this Act.
(3) The chargeable profits and allowances shall be determined separately for the two classes of assessable profits under section 267 (a) and (b) of this Act.

914. *See* s. 267(a) and (b) of the PIA.
915. *Ibid.*, s. 268(1).
916. *Ibid.*, subs. (2).
917. Paragraph 8(1) and (2) of the Seventh Schedule of the PIA provides for 'determination of price for royalty', thus:

(1) The royalties applicable to crude oil and condensates shall be based on the fiscal oil price determined for the field at the measurement points under applicable regulations or guidelines, and this price shall be determined by the Commission on the basis of information supplied by the lessees and from non-confidential independent publications, making such adjustments for quality and transport costs as appropriate to prices of comparable crude oils and condensates sold in the international market, as determined by the Commission, for which appropriate information is available and with the objective to approximate as reasonably as possible the average fair market value of the month of the crude oil and condensates for such month for such field.

price at all measurement points as established by the Commission.[918] All additional chargeable tax for crude oil and associated gas payable by a company in any accounting period shall be payable concurrently with the final instalment of the chargeable tax payable for that period.[919]

501. The PIA acknowledges that fiscal oil prices might not be feasible in a particular crude oil stream. To bridge the gap when it does occur, the Act provides that the Commission shall establish fiscal oil price for such stream and every fiscal oil price per barrel established shall bear a fair and reasonable relationship to the established fiscal oil price of Nigerian crude oil streams of comparable quality and specific gravity. In the alternative, it shall bear a fair and reasonable relationship to the official selling prices at main international trading centres for crude oil of comparable quality and gravity, due regard being had in either case to freight differentials and other relevant factors.[920] Where any crude oil of a particular company be it chargeable oil is exported from Nigeria by another company, that crude oil shall be deemed to be exported from Nigeria by that particular company and appropriate principles of chargeability shall apply as further amplified below.[921]

V. Ascertainment of Chargeable Profits

502. The PIA gives the FIRS powers to disregard artificial or fictitious transactions[922] where in its opinion any transaction which reduces or would reduce the amount of any tax payable is artificial or fictitious. In such cases, FIRS may ignore such disposition by way of trust, grant, covenant, agreement or arrangement, and direct that such adjustments shall be made with respect to the companies' liability to tax as FIRS considers appropriate to counteract the reduction of liability and the companies concerned shall be assessed accordingly.[923] The Act accords the right of appeal to the affected company on FIRS assessment in like manner as provided in

---

> (2) The fiscal oil price for each field shall consider any quality differentials related to international crude oils and condensates and shall be an export parity price taking into consideration the deduction of transportation costs within Nigeria from the measurement points as determined by the Authority to export terminals.

918. Section 268(3) of the PIA, *supra* note 4.
919. *Ibid.*, subs. (4).
920. *Ibid.*, subs. (5)(a–b).
921. *Ibid.*, subs. (6).
922. Section 269(3) provides that:

> For the purpose of this section, the following transactions shall be deemed to be artificial or fictitious, namely, transactions between persons one of whom has control over the other or between persons both of whom are controlled by some other person which, in the opinion of the Service, were not made on terms which might be expected to have been made by independent persons engaged in the same or similar activities dealing with one another at arm's length.

923. *Ibid.*, subs. (1) and (2) of the PIA.

respect of the provisions of Part III of Chapter 4 of the PIA, but the provisions of the Income Tax (Transfer Pricing) Regulations 2018 shall apply for the purpose of this segment.

503. The PIA allows the amortization of pre-production cost where a company has not yet commenced the production and sale or disposal of chargeable oil. For this purpose, all costs incurred wholly, reasonably, exclusively and necessarily for the purpose of coming into upstream petroleum operations shall be amortized. Subject to sections 263 and 264 of the Act on allowable and unallowable deductions, such pre-production cost shall upon commencement of production and sale or disposal of chargeable oil be deemed to have incurred a qualifying pre-production capital expenditure and shall be amortized in line with paragraphs 5 and 17 of the Fifth Schedule to the Act.[924]

504. Transfer of trade or business of upstream petroleum operations carried on in Nigeria by a company may not affect applicable tax liabilities unless done for the purposes of better organization of that trade or business. Where the FIRS is satisfied that one of those companies has control over the other or that both companies are controlled by some other person or are members of a recognized group of companies and have been so for a consecutive period of at least three years prior to the date of reorganization, it may benefit from certain exceptions under the PIA.[925]

505. In respect of transfer of business or trade, the FIRS may at its discretion, direct that the first accounting period of the company acquiring that trade or business shall commence on the date on which the sale or transfer of the trade or business takes place and end on 31 December of that same year.[926] The asset sold or transferred to the company acquiring that trade or business by the company selling or transferring the trade or business shall be deemed to have been sold for an amount equal to the residue of the qualifying expenditure on the asset on the day following the day on which the sale or transfer occurred. Similarly, the company acquiring the asset sold or transferred shall be deemed to have received all allowances given to the company.[927]

506. The Act provides that any concession enjoyed under the above clause shall be rescinded and the company shall be treated as if it did not qualify for the concession as on the date of the initial reorganization where the acquiring company makes a subsequent disposal of the assets thereby acquired within the succeeding three years after the date of acquisition.[928] The Act makes further clarifications under subsection (5) in respect of transferred trade or business of petroleum operations being carried on in Nigeria by a company incorporated under any law in Nigeria. It states:

---

924. *See* s. 270 of the PIA.
925. Section 271(1) of the PIA.
926. Subsection (2)(a) of the Act.
927. *Ibid.*, para. (b).
928. *Ibid.*, subs. (4).

> Where a trade or business of petroleum operations carried on in Nigeria by a company incorporated under any law in force in Nigeria is sold or transferred to another company and any asset employed in that trade or business is so sold or transferred, and the Service is satisfied that the companies are not connected and that none has control over the other or both are not controlled by another company, the:
>
> (a) transaction shall be dealt with under section 266 (1) (c); and
> (b) accounting period of the new trade or business shall be as provided for in subsection (2).[929]

507. The accounting period of the company acquiring that trade or business shall commence on the date on which the sale or transfer took place or within the calendar month in which the sale or transfer took place as may be elected by the company with the approval of the FIRS. But no merger, take-over, transfer or restructuring of the trade or business carried on by a company shall take place without the approval and having obtained direction of the FIRS on any tax that may be due and payable.[930]

VI. Persons Chargeable

508. The Act declares that illegal sharing of benefits from any profits on upstream petroleum operations shall be subject to hydrocarbon tax and companies income tax on the profits as well as penalty provided under section 297[931] of the Act.[932] Where two or more companies are engaged in upstream petroleum operations either in partnership, in a joint venture or in concert under any scheme or arrangement, tax shall be charged and assessed on them in accordance with subsection (4).

509. The rate of apportionment of profits, outgoings, expenses, liabilities, deductions, qualifying expenditure and the tax chargeable upon each company shall be in line with the equity interest of the parties. The Act requires that any jointly executed agreement shall be made available to the FIRS. Where no jointly executed agreement is made available, the Commission shall advise the FIRS of the approved equity interest of the parties and it shall be binding on the parties.[933]

510. The Act permits two or more companies to be engaged in upstream petroleum operations either in partnership, in a joint venture or in concert under any scheme or arrangement. But the FIRS regulation for the ascertainment of tax to be

929. *Ibid.*, s. 271(5)(a–b) of the PIA.
930. *Ibid.*, subs. (6–7). By virtue of subs. (8) reference to a 'trade or business' in this section shall include references to any part of the trade or business.
931. Section 297 of the PIA generally provides for 'Penalty for default'.
932. Section 273(2) of the PIA.
933. *Ibid.*, subs. (4).

charged or assessed upon each company so engaged shall be applicable.[934] The relevant FIRS regulation in this regard may stipulate the apportionment of profits, outgoings, expenses, liabilities, deductions, qualifying expenditures and tax chargeable upon each company. The regulation may also provide for the computation of any tax as if the partnership, joint venture, scheme or arrangement were carried on by one company and apportion that tax between the companies concerned. It may list the basis or other conditions for ascertaining the tax chargeable upon each of the companies, among others.[935] The regulation may generally apply or be applicable only to a category without conferring disproportionate benefits or burden on any company, partnership, scheme or arrangement.[936]

511. In case of winding-up of a company or under a court-appointed receivership by the holders of any debentures issued by the company or otherwise, such a company may be assessed and charged to tax in the name of the liquidator of the company, the receiver or any agent in Nigeria of the liquidator or receiver. The company under this category (wound-up or under receivership) may be assessed and charged tax for any accounting period whether before, during or after the date of the appointment of the liquidator or receiver with respect to companies income tax and hydrocarbon tax.[937]

512. Under the PIA, and to the extent of a company's winding-up or receivership, the appointed liquidator, receiver or agent shall be answerable for any acts required to be done under the Act regarding assessment, charging and payment of such tax. No liquidator or receiver shall distribute any asset of the Company to the shareholders or debenture holders unless he has made provision for the payment in full of any tax which may be found payable by the company.[938]

513. The PIA is very strict on tax avoidance by transfer. Therefore, in a situation where a company which is or was engaged in petroleum operations transfers a substantial part of its assets to any person without paying companies income tax or hydrocarbon tax, assessed or chargeable upon the company, its liability shall be carried over and removed from the transferee. Put differently, where the FIRS discovers that the main reason for such transfer by the company is to avoid payment of such tax, the tax assessed or charged upon the company may be recovered from that person (the transferee) in a manner similar to a suit for any other tax under section 294[939] of the Act.[940] The PIA enshrines institutional and statutory indemnification for representatives or person who withholds a company's money for purposes of paying companies income tax or hydrocarbon tax on behalf of a company.[941]

---

934. *Ibid.*, subs. (5).
935. *Ibid.*, subs. (6)(a–c).
936. *See* subs. (7) and (8) respectively for general or peculiar application of the regulation made under the subs. (6).
937. *See* s. 274(1) of the PIA.
938. *Ibid.*, subs. (2) and (3).
939. Section 294(1) and (2) of the PIA provides for 'Suit for tax by the Service' (FIRS), thus:

> (1) Hydrocarbon tax may be sued for and recovered in a court of competent jurisdiction at the place at which payment shall be made by the Service.

VII. Applicability, Accounts and Particulars

514. The PIA makes detailed provisions for the applicability of hydrocarbon tax and account and related particulars for purposes of tax payment under Part VI of Chapter 4 of the Act. In the preparation and delivery of accounts and particulars, every company engaged in upstream petroleum operations related to crude oil shall for each accounting period of the company as it relates to its profits or losses accounts contain certain particulars for the purpose of determining hydrocarbon tax. These particulars must include: (a) a statement of accounts of its profits or losses; (b) computations of its actual adjusted profit or loss and actual assessable profits of that period; (c) in connection with the Fifth Schedule to the Act, a schedule showing: (i) the residues at the end of that period in respect of its assets; (ii) all qualifying petroleum expenditure incurred by it in that period; (iii) the values of any of its assets disposed of in that period; and (iv) the allowances due to it under that schedule for that period.[942]

515. The profits and losses accounts shall also furnish particulars by way of a schedule showing total production allowance from each and every field of its upstream petroleum operations related to crude oil; a computation of its actual chargeable profits for that period for the two classes of chargeable profits identified in section 267 (a) and (b) of the Act as well as a statement of amounts repaid, refunded, waived or released to it pursuant to section 263 (2) of the Act, during that period. The account shall also provide a computation of its chargeable tax for that period and where associated gas is being sold or otherwise delivered through the measurement point or the methodology used to determine the chargeable tax; duly completed self-assessment form attested to by the principal officer of the company and evidence of payment of the final instalment.[943]

516. By virtue of subsection (2), every company engaged in upstream petroleum operations related to crude oil shall, within or after five months in any accounting period or five months after the effective date of the Act, whichever is later, deliver to the FIRS a copy of its accounts. The details must bear an auditor's certificate of that period. If not an estimate, each copy must contain a declaration

---

> (2) In any suit under subsection (1) the production of a certificate signed by any person duly authorised by the Service giving the name and address of the defendant and the amount of tax due by the defendant shall be sufficient evidence of the amount due.

940. *See* s. 275 of the PIA.
941. *See* the provisions of s. 276 of the PIA on indemnification of representatives. It specifically provides that:

> Every person answerable under this Act for the payment of companies income tax or hydrocarbon tax on behalf of a company may retain out of any money in or coming to his hands or within his control on behalf of such company so much as shall be sufficient to pay the tax and shall be indemnified against any person for payments made by him in accordance with this Act.

942. *See* general s. 277(1)(a–c)(i–iv) of the PIA.
943. *Ibid.*, subs. (d–g)(i–ii).

signed by the authorized officer of the company or by its liquidator, receiver or the agent of the liquidator or receiver, that the same is true and complete. If based on estimates, it shall contain a declaration, similarly signed, that the estimate was made to the best of the ability of the person signing the same.[944]

517. The PIA grants a qualified exception to every company which is yet to commence bulk sales or disposal of chargeable oil. Any company in this category shall file with the FIRS its audited accounts and returns within eighteen months from the date of its incorporation, in the case of a newly incorporated company. In the case of any other company, it shall file within five months after any period ending on 31 December. A caveat applies to the extent that where there is an interval between 31 December of the preceding year and the date on which the company commences the bulk sale or disposal of chargeable oil, natural gas or condensate, the interval shall be deemed to form part of the preceding period.[945]

518. The Act imposes stiff penalties for failure to comply with the above provisions as they relate to subsections (2) or (3). It states:

> A company which fails to comply with subsection (2) or (3) is liable to pay as penalty for late filing:
>
> (a) N 10,000,000 on the first day the failure occurs and N2,000,000 for each and every subsequent day in which the failure continues; or
> (b) other sum as may be prescribed by the Minister of Finance by order published in the Federal Government Gazette.[946]

519. The PIA grants the FIRS enormous powers. This includes powers to request further information by notice in writing to any company engaged in upstream petroleum operations related to crude oil. The notice shall, among others, require the company to furnish further information within a reasonable time as may be specified, in relation to any matter referred to in section 277 of the Act or any other matter which it may consider necessary.[947]

520. Additional powers vested in the FIRS include the power to call for returns and books by notice to a company requiring it within a period not less than twenty-one days from the date of service of the notice, to complete and deliver any information so required. It may also require an authorized representative of such company or its liquidator, receiver or the agent of such liquidator or receiver, to produce for examination any books, documents, accounts and particulars which the FIRS may deem necessary or require.[948] Failure or refusal to keep adequate books or accounts by a company assessable to hydrocarbon tax may form the basis of a

944. *Ibid.*, subs. (2)(a) and (b).
945. *Ibid.*, subs. (3)(a) and (b).
946. *Ibid.*, subs. (4)(a) and (b).
947. *See* s. 278 of the PIA.
948. *Ibid.*, s. 279(1).

stern directive in writing by the FIRS directing the company to keep the specified records, books and accounts as may be directed in the notice.[949] This is without prejudice to the right of appeal to the Tax Appeal Tribunal from any direction of the FIRS made pursuant thereto.[950]

VIII. Returns of Estimated Tax

521. The Act makes it compulsory that, not later than two months after the commencement of each accounting period of any company engaged in upstream petroleum operations related to crude oil, the company shall submit to the FIRS an estimated return of its profits or losses for that accounting period for the purpose of hydrocarbon tax. This shall include a computation of its estimated adjusted profit or loss and of its estimated assessable profits for that period.[951] It shall also contain a schedule showing the estimated residues at the end of that period in respect of its assets, all estimated qualifying petroleum expenditure incurred by it in that period, the values of any of its assets, estimated by references to the provisions of that schedule, to be disposed of in that period, and the allowances due to it under that schedule for that period. The schedule shall also show the estimated total production allowance from all its upstream petroleum operations related to crude oil on a field-by-field basis; a computation of its estimated chargeable profits for that period as well as a computation of its estimated tax for that period.[952]

522. Failure of a company to provide the estimates will leave the FIRS with no option but to exercise its statutory right to determine such estimates on the best-of-judgment basis and impose the same on the company. The defaulting company shall also be liable to pay as penalty for late filing the sum of NGN 10,000,000 on the first day the failure occurs and NGN 2,000,000 for each and every subsequent day in which the failure continues; or other sum as may be prescribed by the Minister of Finance by order published in the Federal Government Gazette.[953] However, subject to good reasons, the FIRS may grant in writing an extension of that time as it may consider necessary for making returns.[954]

IX. Assessment and Additional Assessments of Tax Payable

523. The PIA gives the FIRS general powers to proceed to assess a company with the hydrocarbon tax for any accounting period immediately after the expiration of the time allowed to such company for the delivery of self-assessment. A

949. *Ibid.*, subs. (2).
950. *Ibid.*
951. *See* generally s. 280(1)(a) of the PIA.
952. *Ibid.*, para. (b)(i–iv) and (c–e).
953. *Ibid.*, subs. (5) and (6)(a–b).
954. Section 281 of the PIA allows the FIRs to consider and grant extension of periods for making return by a company engaging in upstream petroleum operations for the purpose of applicable hydrocarbon tax.

self-assessment of a company for any accounting period of the company may be accepted or refused by the FIRS[955] subject to subsection (3).[956]

524. Additional assessments may become necessary where the FIRS discovers or is of the opinion at any time that, hydrocarbon tax has not been charged and assessed upon the company. Additional assessment may also become necessary where a company has been charged and assessed at an amount less than that which ought to have been assessed and charged for any accounting period. Where this occurs, the law directs that the FIRS may within six years after the expiration of that accounting period re-assess the company for that accounting period at such amount or additional amount as it ought to have been charged and assessed. The FIRS may also make any consequential revision of the tax charged or to be charged for any subsequent accounting period of the company.[957]

525. By virtue of subsection (2), a revision may result in a greater amount of tax charged. Where a revision results in a greater amount of tax to be charged than has been charged, an additional assessment or an assessment for any such subsequent accounting period shall be made and the provisions of the Act as to notice of assessment, objection, appeal and other proceedings shall apply to any such assessment or additional assessment and to the tax charged.[958] Where any form of fraud, wilful default or neglect has been committed by or on behalf of any company in connection with hydrocarbon tax imposed under the Act, the FIRS may, at any time and as often as may be necessary, assess the company on such amount as may be necessary for the purpose of recovering any loss of tax attributable to fraud, wilful default or neglect.[959]

X. Making Assessments and Assessment Notices

526. The PIA stipulates the forms and contents of an assessment. An assessment of a company for purposes of hydrocarbon tax shall be made in such form and in such manner as the FIRS shall authorize. An assessment shall contain the names and addresses of the companies assessed to tax or of the persons in whose names any companies have been assessed to tax, provided that the names of the represented companies are indicated. It shall also state the particular accounting period and the

955. *See* s. 282(1) and (2)(a–c) of the PIA.
956. *Ibid.*, subs. (3)(a–b).
957. Section 283(1)(a–b) of the PIA.
958. *Ibid.*, subs. (2). However, the Act provides in subs. (3) that:

> for the purpose of computing under subsection (1) the amount or the additional amount of tax for any accounting period of a company which ought to have been charged, all relevant facts consistent with section 289 (4) of this Act shall be taken into account even though it is not known when any previous assessment or additional assessment on the company for that accounting period was made or could have been made.

959. *Ibid.*, subs. (4).

amount of chargeable profits and chargeable tax for that period for each of its accounting periods.[960] Any amended or revised assessment shall reflect the original form and a copy of each assessment or an amended or revised assessment shall be filed in a list which shall constitute the assessment.[961]

527. Notices of assessment shall be personally served on or sent by courier to a company which is liable to hydrocarbon tax by the FIRS. The notice of assessment shall indicate the accounting period and the amount of its chargeable profits and chargeable tax assessed and charged upon the company. It shall also indicate the place at which payment of the tax should be made as well as the rights of the company under subsection (2) which enable a company that disputes the assessment to serve a notice of objection. For the avoidance of ambiguity, it provides that:

> Where any person in whose name an assessment was made in accordance with this Act, disputes the assessment, the person may apply to the Service by notice of objection in writing, to review and revise the assessment made on him and the application shall be made within 30 days from the date of service of the notice of the assessment, stating the amount of chargeable:
>
> (a) profits of the company of the accounting period in respect of which the assessment is made; and
> (b) tax and the tax which such person claims should be stated on the notice of assessment.

528. Upon being satisfied that due to absence from Nigeria, sickness or other reasonable cause, the person in whose name the assessment was made was prevented from making the application within such period of thirty days, the FIRS shall extend the period as may be reasonable in the circumstances.[962] Where a notice of objection is received pursuant to subsection (2), the FIRS may require the person giving the notice of objection to furnish such particular as it may deem necessary. It may also require any other person, by notice, to give evidence orally or in writing in respect of any matter necessary for the ascertainment of the hydrocarbon tax payable. In appropriate cases, the FIRS may further require that such evidence be given orally or on oath in writing in the form of an affidavit.[963]

529. Amendment of assessment may be made on the concurrence of the FIRS and the party, and the assessment shall be amended accordingly and notice served upon the person. Where there is no concurrence, the FIRS shall give such applicant notice of refusal to amend the assessment. It may also revise the assessment to such

960. Section 284(1)(a–b) of the PIA.
961. *Ibid.*, subs. (2) and (3).
962. *Ibid.*, subs. (3).
963. *Ibid.*, subs. (4)(a) and (b)(i–ii).

amount as it may determine and give the applicant notice of the revised assessment and tax payable. It may serve any such amendment together with notice of refusal.[964]

530. Any errors or defects in assessment and notice shall not render it to be quashed or deemed to be void or voidable by reason of any such mistake, defect or omission where the substance and effect of the assessment are in conformity with the provisions of the Act and the company assessed or intended to be assessed or affected is designated according to common intent and understanding.[965] This necessarily means that, by virtue of the provisions of the PIA, an assessment made by the FIRS shall not be invalidated or become defective by reason of a mistake as to the name of a company liable or of a person in whose name a company is assessed, or amount of the tax. The Act treats any variance between the assessment and the notice as a misnomer that does not go to the root, and is deemed not to affect the validity of such assessment where the same is validly made on a company, provided such notice contains the particulars on which the assessment is made.[966]

531. The tax computation is denominated in US dollars. The basis of seeming dollarization is not unconnected with the fact that crude oil is an international commodity. It is, therefore, not out of place for the PIA to provide that:

> Notwithstanding anything to the contrary in any law:
>
> (a) all hydrocarbon tax computation made under this Act shall be in US Dollars; and
>
> (b) any assessment made under section 284 of this Act shall be in US Dollars.[967]

XI. Tax Appeals

532. The PIA grants rights to any company or taxpayer, who does not agree with an assessment made under section 285 (6) of the Act to appeal against the assessment to the Tax Appeal Tribunal (TAT) established under the provisions of section 59 of the Federal Inland Revenue Service (Establishment) Act. The right of appeal to TAT has been tested in a number of cases under the repealed Petroleum Act, including in the case of *OandO Supply & Trading Limited v. Federal Inland Revenue Service (FIRS)*,[968] where the TAT held that a non-exploration and non-production company could validly appeal to the TAT against a tax assessment by FIRS without waiting indefinitely for a Notice of Refusal to Amend (NORA) from the latter.

---

964. *Ibid.*, subs. (5) and (6).
965. *See* the provision of s. 286(1)(a–b) of the PIA.
966. *Ibid.*, subs. (2)(a)(i–ii) and (b).
967. *See* s. 287 which provides for tax computation, assessment and payment in UD Dollars.
968. Appeal No. TAT/LZ/041/2010.

533. Assessment of tax by the FIRS will be final and conclusive where no valid objection or appeal against an assessment as regards the amount of the hydrocarbon tax assessed, has been lodged within the time limited by section 285 of the Act or the rules of the relevant tribunal or court. The assessment shall also be final and conclusive where the amount of the tax has been agreed or the tax has been determined on objection or revision of the assessment made.[969] Failure to pay the full amount of the final and conclusive assessment shall form the basis for the crystallization of provisions of the Act relating to the recovery of tax. The penalty under section 292 of the Act for non-payment of tax and enforcement of payment, shall apply.[970]

534. The fact that an assessment is final and conclusive does not preclude repayment for overpayment of tax, which shall be refunded or credited in favour of the assessed party.[971] Irrespective of the notice of assessment under section 285 of the PIA, the FIRS may make an assessment or additional assessment to hydrocarbon tax for any accounting period which does not involve re-opening any issue on the same facts which have been determined for that accounting period, under section 285 (5) and (6) of the Act by agreement or otherwise on appeal.[972]

XII. Collection, Recovery and Repayment of Tax

535. By virtue of the procedure under part VIII of Chapter 4 of the PIA, collection of hydrocarbon tax shall remain in abeyance where notice of an objection or an appeal has been given. No hydrocarbon tax shall be collected pending proceedings for any payment in instalments until the objection or appeal is determined. FIRS is not inhibited from enforcing payment of that portion of the tax which is not in dispute by an application to the tribunal or court.[973]

536. The time within which payment of hydrocarbon tax is to be made is a matter of statutory provisions and shall be payable in equal monthly instalments together with a final instalment as provided in subsection (4).[974] The first monthly payment shall be due and payable not later than the third month of the accounting period. The quantum due at this stage shall be in an amount equal to one-twelfth or where the accounting period is less than a year, in an amount equal to the monthly proportion of the amount of tax estimated to be chargeable for such accounting period in accordance with section 280 (1) of the Act on return of estimated tax.[975] The remainder of monthly payments shall be due and payable not later than the last day of the month in the amount equal to the tax estimated to be chargeable for such

969. *See* s. 289(1)(a–c) of the PIA.
970. *Ibid.*, subs. (2).
971. *Ibid.*, subs. (3).
972. *Ibid.*, subs. (4).
973. Section 290 of the PIA.
974. Section 291(1) of the PIA.
975. *Ibid.*, subs. (2).

period while the final instalment of tax shall be due and payable on or before the due date of filing of the self-assessment of tax for such accounting period.[976]

537. The PIA provides punitive measures for defaulters of hydrocarbon tax. Penalty for non-payment of tax includes charging of interest at the prevailing LIBOR rate.[977] The Act further stipulates penal consequences for failure to pay hydrocarbon tax. It criminalizes failure to comply, stating that any person who without lawful justification or excuse fails to pay hydrocarbon tax within the period of one month prescribed in subsection (1) (c), commits an offence and the provisions of subsection (1) (a) to (c) shall apply.[978]

538. The FIRS may recover hydrocarbon tax from defaulters by a lawsuit filed in a court of competent jurisdiction at the place where payment shall have been made. The PIA provides that the production of a certificate signed by any person duly authorized by the FIRS giving the name and address of the defendant and the amount of tax due by the defendant shall be sufficient evidence of the amount due. This shall form the basis of the suit for the purpose of claiming appropriate reliefs by FIRS.[979]

539. The Act provides relief in respect of error or mistake leading to excessive payment by reason of some error or mistake in the accounts, particulars or other written information supplied to the FIRS. The affected person shall make an application in writing to the FIRS, not later than six years after the end of the accounting period in respect of which the assessment was made, for relief or to set off the credit against the liability of a similar tax payable to the FIRS.[980]

XIII. Offences and Penalties

540. The PIA provides for tax-related offences and specific penalties for such offences under Part IX of Chapter 4. Default is a criminal offence under the PIA. A person who fails to comply with the requirements of a notice of hydrocarbon tax served on him or fails to comply with section 277 on the preparation and delivery of accounts and particulars, commits an offence under the Act. Also falling within the category is a person who without sufficient cause fails to answer a notice or summons served on him or having attended fails to answer any question lawfully put to him, or fails to submit any return required to be submitted under section 277 or 281 of the Act, commits an offence.[981]

976. *Ibid.*, subs. (4).
977. *See* s. 292(1)(a–d) of the PIA which provides for penalties for non-payment of hydrocarbon tax.
978. *Ibid.*, subs. (2). The Act further provides under subs. (3) that the Service (FIRS) may, for any good cause shown, remit the whole or any part of the additional 10% penalty and interest on the tax due under subs. (1).
979. Section 294(1) and (2) of the PIA.
980. *See* generally s. 295(1) on reliefs in respect of overpayment to the FIRS.
981. *Ibid.*, subs. (3)(a–d) of the PIA.

541. Filing, making or furnishing incorrect accounts also constitutes an offence under the PIA. A person who without reasonable excuse makes up or causes to be made up any incorrect accounts by omitting or understating any profits or overstating any losses of which he is required under the Act to make up accounts commits an offence. Similarly, a person who prepares or causes to be prepared any incorrect schedule or statement required to be prepared under section 277 of the Act by overstating any expenditure or overstating any royalties or other sums or by omitting or understating any amounts repaid, refunded, waived or released, commits an offence.[982]

542. A person who gives or causes to be given any false or misleading information in relation to any matter or thing affecting his liability to hydrocarbon tax is liable to an administrative penalty of the sum of NGN 15,000,000 or 1% of the amount of tax which has been undercharged in consequence of such incorrect account, schedule, statement or information or would have been so undercharged if the account, schedule, statement or information had been accepted as correct, and is also liable for the appropriate tax which would have been charged.[983]

543. False statements and returns are also similarly punished under the PIA. A person who for the purpose of obtaining any deduction, refund, rebate, reduction or repayment in respect of hydrocarbon tax for himself or for any other person knowingly makes any false statement or false representation or forges or fraudulently alters or uses or fraudulently lends or allows to be used by any other person any receipt or token as evidence for payment of the tax commits an offence.[984] Similarly, anyone who aids, abets, assists, counsels, incites or induces any other person to make or deliver any false return or statement or to keep or prepare any false accounts or particulars affecting tax, or unlawfully refuses or neglects to pay tax, commits an offence.[985]

544. A person who commits any or all of the above-listed offence(s) shall be liable on conviction to a fine of NGN 15,000,000 or 1% of the amount of tax for

---

982. Section 298(a) and (b).
983. *Ibid.*, subs. (c). The Act provides penal consequences under subs. (2) and (3) for giving false or misleading information, thus:

> (2) Notwithstanding the provisions of subsection (1) (c), a person who gives or causes to be given any false or misleading information in relation to any matter or thing affecting his liability to hydrocarbon tax, commits an offence and on conviction is liable to a fine of N15,000,000 or 1% of the amount of tax which has been undercharged in consequence of such incorrect account, schedule, statement or information, or would have been so undercharged if the account, schedule, statement or information had been accepted as correct and is also liable for the appropriate tax which would have been charged.
>
> (3) The Service may compound any offence under this Act by accepting a sum of money not exceeding the maximum fine specified for the offence and shall issue an official receipt for any money so received.

984. Section 299(1)(a) of the PIA.
985. *Ibid.*, para. (b)(i–iii).

which the person assessable is liable for the accounting period in respect of or during which the offence was committed, or to imprisonment for six months or to both the fine and imprisonment. He shall also be liable for the appropriate hydrocarbon tax which would have been assessed and charged.[986] The Act likewise punishes any acts or omissions for offences described in subsection (1).[987]

545. The PIA balances the 'demand' side of false or misleading information for purposes of conferring undue hydrocarbon tax benefits in a company engaging in upstream petroleum operations. It imposes very stiff penal consequences on authorized and unauthorized persons, who is a member of the FIRS charged with administrative functions or any assistant employed in connection with the assessment and collection of the hydrocarbon tax. It makes it an offence for such person to demand from any person an amount in excess of the authorized assessment of the tax payable; withhold for his own use or otherwise any portion of the amount of tax collected; render a false return, whether verbal or in writing of the amounts of tax collected or received by him, or defraud any person, embezzles any money or otherwise uses his position to deal wrongfully with the FIRS or any other individual.[988]

546. The PIA also criminalizes the act of a person who, not being authorized, collects or attempts to collect the tax.[989] All categories of persons listed above commit an offence and are liable on conviction to a fine equivalent to 200% of the sum in question or to imprisonment for a term not exceeding three years or to both such fine and imprisonment.[990] The Act makes an important clarification as to the essence of recovery proceedings and pending liability amidst invocation of the principle of double jeopardy under the Constitution which forbids being punished twice for the same offence.[991] The PIA states that the institution of proceedings for or the imposition of a penalty, fine or term of imprisonment under shall not relieve any person of liability as to payment of any hydrocarbon tax for which he is or may become liable.[992]

---

986. *Ibid.*

987. *Ibid. See* subs. (2) which provides that:

> Notwithstanding the provisions of subsection (1), any person who does any of the acts or makes the omissions contained in subsection (1), may be liable to an administrative penalty of N15,000,000 or 1% of the amount of hydrocarbon tax for which the person assessable is liable under this Act for the accounting period in respect of or during which the act or omission occurred and shall still be liable for appropriate tax which would have been assessed and charged.

988. *See* s. 300(a)(i–iv) of the PIA.

989. *Ibid.*, para. (b).

990. *Ibid.*

991. Double jeopardy is age-long fundamental principle law that has become part of under the Constitutional law and criminal law and procedure in Nigeria, and elsewhere. Section 36(9) of the Constitution of the Federal Republic of Nigeria provides that:

XIV. Application of Companies Income Tax to Petroleum Operations

547. The provisions of the *Companies Income Tax Act* (CITA)[993] is made expressly applicable to petroleum operations by Part X of Chapter 4 of the PIA. Generally, the incomes of Nigerian companies are taxed under CITA. A separate tax regime governs the income of companies engaging in petroleum operations. For companies that engage in petroleum operations, a separate regime of tax law governs their income and taxation. The PIA provides that:

> Without prejudice to Companies Income Tax Act and any other applicable law, the provisions of this Act shall apply and any company, concessionaire, licensee, lessee, contractor or subcontractor involved in the upstream, midstream or downstream petroleum operations under this Act, shall also be subject to the Companies Income Tax Act.
>
> For the purpose of determining the value of chargeable crude oil or chargeable gas, in relation to any accounting period, the crude oil and gas revenue of a company for that period shall be the value of any chargeable oil or chargeable gas adjusted to the measurement points, based on the:
>
> (a) proceeds of all chargeable oil or gas sold by the company; and
> (b) value of all chargeable oil or gas disposed of by the company.[994]

548. The PIA provides leeway for avoiding higher tax implications by companies engaged in petroleum operations. Thus, subject to sections 142(2) and 197 (2) of the Act, a person intending to be involved in more than one stream, that is upstream, midstream or downstream petroleum operations shall register and use a separate company for each stream operation. However, for companies with petroleum mining leases selected under sections 93 (6) (b) and (7) (b) of the Act, no stamp duties and capital gains tax shall be levied by the government on such segregation.[995]

549. One of the innovative provisions of the PIA is Integrated Strategic Projects (ISP), and the exclusion of such ISPs from payment of hydrocarbon tax by determining their income pursuant to the Companies Income Tax Act.[996] Domestic supplies of gas are incentivized by the PIA. It provides that all companies engaged in

---

> No person who shows that he has been tried by any court of competent jurisdiction or tribunal for a criminal offence and either convicted or acquitted shall again be tried for that offence or for a criminal offence having the same ingredients as that offence save upon the order of a superior court.

992. *See* s. 301 of the PIA.
993. *See* generally Companies Income Tax Act (CITA), *Cap C21*, LFN 2004 (as amended) (CITA).
994. *See* s. 302(1) and (2)(a–b).
995. *Ibid.*, subs. (3).
996. *Ibid.*, subs. (5).

domestic midstream petroleum operations, downstream gas operations and large-scale gas utilization industries shall be entitled to benefit from the incentives provided under section 39 of the Companies Income Tax Act. Similarly, investors in gas pipelines are entitled to an additional tax-free period of five years under the PIA at the expiration of the tax-free period granted in section 39 of the Companies Income Tax Act.[997]

550. Natural gas transferred or disposed from the upstream to the midstream or downstream as well as natural gas liquids and liquid petroleum gases derived from natural gas shall all be subject to companies income tax.[998] A similar incentive is provided for the acquisition costs of petroleum rights. The Act states that it shall be eligible for annual allowance at the rate of 20% with a retention value of 1% in the last year until the asset is disposed of. It further provides that capital allowances for other assets shall be granted for upstream petroleum operations assets in accordance with the Fifth Schedule to the Act while that of midstream and downstream operations shall be in accordance with the Second Schedule to the Companies Income Tax Act.[999]

551. The PIA incorporates the provision of CITA by reference and directs adoption in a few instances. For the purpose of companies engaged in petroleum operations and related tax implications, the PIA also provides that section 27 of the Companies Income Tax Act shall be read in conjunction and in consonance with specific subjects and related issues under the PIA. Similar to section 24 of CITA, the PIA specifically states that section 27 of CITA shall be read subject to the following provisions of the Act (PIA).

552. A general obligation is imposed on any company involved in upstream petroleum operations to apply the accounting periods established for hydrocarbon tax on an actual year basis for its company's income tax in accordance with sections 277, 280 and 291 of the Act. Failure of a company involved in upstream petroleum operations to comply with the provisions in relation to filing of companies' income tax returns, shall render it liable to pay a penalty for late filing of NGN 10,000,000 on the first day the failure occurs and NGN 2,000,000 for each and every subsequent day in which the failure continues; or other sum as may be prescribed by the Minister of Finance by order published in the Federal Government Gazette.[1000]

553. The tax due from a company involved in upstream petroleum operations shall in the case of Naira remittances, carry interest at the prevailing NIBOR plus

997. *Ibid.*, subs. (6).
998. *Ibid.*, subs. (7) and (8).
999. *Ibid.*, subs. (9) and (10)(a–b).
1000. *Ibid.*, subs. (14) of the PIA. By virtue of subs. (15), offences and penalties specified under Part IX of this chapter shall be applicable to companies income tax of upstream petroleum companies.

10% from the date when the tax becomes payable until it is paid. In the case of foreign currency remittances, it shall incur interest at the prevailing LIBOR or any successor rate plus 10% from the date when the tax becomes payable until it is paid.[1001] The PIA lists and imposes additional basis and conditions for purposes of calculating or determining the applicable chargeable tax of upstream petroleum operations under subsection (17).

§2. Taxes Applicable to Both Exploration and Non-exploration Companies

554. For the avoidance of doubt, certain taxes are applicable to both exploration and production companies and non-exploration and production companies in Nigeria. These include Value Added Tax (VAT), Capital Gains Tax (CGT), Education Tax (ET), WHT and others as further explained below.

I. Value Added Tax

555. VAT[1002] is a tax on spending. The tax is borne by the final consumer of goods and services and it is invoice-based. The VAT element is to be separately indicated in the tax invoice. The tax is at a flat rate of 5%. The tax is collected on behalf of the government by businesses and organizations which have registered with the FIRS Integrated Tax Office for VAT purposes nearest to them or operating basis or branches of such businesses or organizations that have registered independently in their own areas of operation. For the purpose of VAT, they are classified as registered persons. A consumer will pay 5% on goods and services purchased but can claim credit for input tax when sold.

556. VAT returns and payments are normally made monthly for the integrated Tax Office where registered on or before the thirtieth day of the month following that in which the supply was made through proper keeping of records and accounts of all business transactions. No individual, business organization or government agencies are exempted from the tax, except goods and services so specified as exempted activities.

II. Capital Gains Tax

557. CGT[1003] is a tax chargeable at the rate of 10% on capital gain arising from the disposal of capital assets which is assessable on a current-year basis. In other words, the assessment is based on the year the asset is disposed of. It mainly represents the excess of disposal realized over the cost of the particular asset. Capital

1001. *Ibid.*, subs. (16(a–b).
1002. Payable under s. 4 of the *Value Added Tax Act*, Cap V1, LFN, 2004.
1003. Payable under s. 2 the *Capital Gains Tax Act*, Cap C1, LFN, 2004.

losses on the disposal of any assets are not deductible from the capital gains on the disposal of any other asset even if both are of the same nature or type. However, rollover relief is available to any company acquiring a new asset to be used for the purpose of the trade-in replacement of an old one. The production of evidence of payment of applicable capital gain tax is a condition for effecting changes of ownership.

III. Education Tax

558. Education Tax[1004] is imposed on companies registered in Nigeria that are liable to pay tax on their assessable profit as defined in CITA or PPTA as the case may be. The rate of the tax is 2% of the assessable profit. The assessment of the education tax and that of the CITA are done concurrently. The due date of payment of education tax is sixty days after the notice of assessment has been served. Any tax outstanding after the tax date will attract a penalty of 5% plus interest at commercial rate. It is deductible for tax purposes in the determination of PPTA.

IV. Withholding Tax

559. Nigerian law subjects certain activities and services to WHT. This basically means that where for transactions in any of the specified activities or services a payment is due from one person to another, the person making the payment is expected to deduct tax at the applicable rate and remit it to the relevant tax authority. This should be done not later than thirty days after the deduction. This provision can be found in sections 60–64 of the CITA (as amended), and section 54 of the Petroleum Profits Tax Act (as amended).

V. Other Petroleum Production Revenues

560. Apart from the foregoing taxes, the Federal Government of Nigeria also levies and collects certain oil production revenues. These are royalties, bonuses and rents. Under the *Oil Terminal Dues Act*, government derives a kind of revenue which is however not paid by oil-producing companies but by the shipowner or master evacuating crude oil. Royalties on the contrary are amounts payable to the owner of a natural resource as compensation for the exploitation of a renewable and irreplaceable natural resource. In the PPTA, it is provided that 'royalties' means and includes: (a) the amount of any rent as to which there is provision for its deduction from the amount of any royalties under an OPL or oil mining lease to the extent that such rent is so deducted; and (b) the amount of any royalties payable under any such licence or lease less any such rent deducted from those royalties.

1004. Payable under s. 1(2) of the *Education Tax Act*, Cap E4, LFN, 2004.

561. The rates of royalties applicable to deep offshore crude oil production are provided for in the Petroleum (Drilling and Production) Amendment Regulations 1995 and in section 4 of the Deep Offshore and Inland Basin Production Sharing Contracts Act of 1999 as amended:

- Onshore 20%.
- Offshore 0–100 metres 18.5%.
- 100–200 metres 16.67%.
- 201–500 metres 12.00%.
- 501–800 metres 8.00%.
- 801–1000 metres 4.00%.
- 1000 metres 0%.

562. Variation in royalties is to reflect the increased difficulties and higher technology and expertise needed for deepwater production. The regime of royalties has also taken into account other inbuilt incentives for deepwater petroleum production, among others.

563. Bonuses: A bonus is a payment made by a company to the State at agreed designated periods. Invariably, bonus payments are made when the contract has been signed. Such a bonus is known as a signature bonus. Signature bonuses are sometimes regarded as onerous by the companies because they are additional pre-discovery costs that increase initial expenditure. Another common payment is the production bonus, which is paid by the contractor to the State when production reaches mutually agreed levels. The company's accession to both signature and production bonuses depends on the type of discovery anticipated or made and the prevailing economic climate.

564. Rents: rents are amounts paid in exchange for the OPLs and oil mining leases granted. They are as specified in paragraph 31, Schedule 1 and Regulation 59(2) of the *Petroleum (Drilling and Production) Amendment Regulations 1995*. Rents paid for non-producing areas are credited 100% against petroleum profits tax while rents paid for producing leases are credited 85% against royalty payments.

§3. Abandonment and Restoration Costs

565. Abandonment relates to activities involved in giving up further exploration activities in a well or field in which oil or gas has not been found in commercial quantity. The cost incurred in the dismantling of production facilities on abandoning the oil well, as well as those incurred in restoring the well to its original ecological state, are called restoration and abandonment costs. Abandonment can also occur when the operators are of the view that oil or gas is exhausted and can no longer be profitably produced. On the contrary, restoration involves bringing the exploration site to its original ecological state.

566. Due to the size and complex nature of oil wells, the costs could run into several millions of dollars. The ability to cover such costs by insurance is severely restricted. Therefore, tax treatment is imperative for any E&P company. E&P companies may, however, be able to obtain a tax deduction for this item, if they execute a plan for restoration and abandonment. Such a plan should provide for a fund, to which any provision for this cost can actually be paid into, and managed by an external fund manager. On commencing an abandonment and restoration programme, the company can draw down on the fund (together with any accrued interest income) to finance the cost. It is believed that if this approach is adopted, the yearly expenditure, involving actual physical cash payment, should be deductible for the E&P Company's PPT purpose.

§4. Taxation of Marginal Fields

567. In recent times, the FG has come under great pressure to increase indigenous participation in the oil and gas industry by relocating marginal fields, belonging to multinational companies, to indigenous concession holders. In response to this call for increased participation, the government, in 1996, promulgated the Petroleum (Amendment) Act No. 23 on the development of marginal fields. The Act does not define marginal fields. It however provides the criteria for determining which fields are marginal. Section 16A(2) of the first schedule provides that:

> the Head of State, Commander-in-Chief of the Armed forces may cause the farm-out of marginal field if the marginal field has been left unattended for a period of not less than ten years from the date of the first discovery of the marginal field.

568. The above suggests that where non-producing fields have been *left unattended* for not less than ten years, they qualify as marginal fields, and therefore can be compulsorily assigned by the government without the consent of the concession holder. The DPR's *'Draft Guidelines for Farm-out of Marginal Fields'* also mandates all oil companies to update their portfolio of underdeveloped fields and report to the DPR on a periodic basis. A Marginal Field is thus, *any field that has reserves booked and reported annually to the DPR and has remained unproduced for a period of over ten years.*

§5. Taxation of Natural Gas

569. The level of natural gas is about 22 billion barrels of its crude oil equivalent. One of the reasons put forward for the underutilization of gas is the absence of a ready market for gas internally and inappropriate pricing locally. To enhance the development of the gas industry, especially for export, the government has put in place specific export-oriented gas utilization initiatives as well as other fiscal incentives that would act as stimuli for the development and utilization of Nigerian gas. The following are the incentives granted to companies involved in gas utilization projects:

(i) an initial tax holiday period of three years, which may, subject to the satisfactory performance of the business, be renewed for an additional period of two years;
(ii) as an alternative incentive to the initial tax-free period, gas utilization companies may claim an additional investment allowance (IVA) of 35%, which will not reduce the value of the asset. However, if the company claims the IVA, as opposed to the tax-free holiday, it will not be able to claim the accelerated capital allowances which are provided in (iii) below;
(iii) accelerated capital allowances after the tax-free period which includes an annual allowance of 90% with 10% retention for investment in plant and machinery, and an additional investment allowance of 15% which shall not reduce the value of the asset;
(iv) tax-free dividends during the tax-free period, where the investment was in foreign currency, or the introduction of imported plant and machinery was not less than 30% of the company's equity share capital; and
(v) interest payable on any loan obtained for a gas project, with the prior approval of the Minister of Finance shall be tax deductible.

570. Gas income is taxed at the rate of 30%. Also worthy of note are the special incentives granted to Nigeria LNG Limited under the Nigeria LNG (fiscal incentives, Guarantees and Assurances) Act. A few of these incentives include a ten-year tax relief period for the company and the exemption of the company and its contractors and subcontractors from all customs duties, taxes, levies and imposts of a similar nature in respect of imports pertaining to plant, machinery, goods and materials for use in the construction of, or incorporation to the project.

I. Upstream Gas Operations

571. Upstream gas operation involves all operations necessary to separate gas from the reservoir into usable form at utilization or designated custody transfer points, either through pipelines or tankers. The capital allowances, operating expenses and assessment of companies engaged in upstream gas operations are subject to the provisions of the PPT Act and fiscal incentives under the revised MOU.

II. Downstream Gas Operations

572. Downstream gas operation involves the marketing and distribution of gas and its industrial uses. This would include power generation, liquefied natural gas (LNG), and household factory consumption. Companies engaged in downstream gas operations are subject to the provisions of the CITA.

III. Review of the OGEFZ Act

573. The OGEFZ Act governs the operations of Tax Free Zones (TFZ) that are designated for oil and gas activities. Approved enterprises operating in TFZ in Nigeria are exempted from all Federal, State and Local government taxes, levies and rates by virtue of section 8 of the Act. For the exemption to apply to a company operating in the zone, the company must deal in approved activities and must apply for, and obtain the approval of, the free zone authority to operate within the zone.

IV. Incentives for Investing in the Onne Oil and Gas Free Zone

574. The Onne Oil and Gas Free Zone aims to provide investors with a perfect platform to support the Nigerian Oil and Gas Industry and the entire West Africa Oil and Gas Market. The following are some of the incentives enjoyed by companies that operate in the free trade zone; easy registration to enter the Nigerian Oil and Gas Market; bureaucracy limited to a minimum; delays of imports into Nigeria will be drastically reduced; possibility to sell products and services into the entire West Africa Region; 100% repatriation of capital and profit; no foreign exchange regulation; no pre-shipment inspection for goods imported into the export Free Zone; first-class port facilities; supported by an efficient Oil Service Centre.

575. With the possibility of 100% ownership, foreign investors do not need any local partners. Furthermore, they are free to employ anyone they choose to do so with no limitation of expatriate quota. With no taxes, either personal or corporate, and 100% repatriation of capital and profit, the risk of investment is minimum. The absence of import and export duties combined with no pre-shipment inspection for goods imported into the free zone creates the perfect location to use Onne as a Distribution Centre for goods and services in the sub-Sahara West Africa region. Onne offers business opportunities to investors to take part in an impressive number of projects which already exist under construction or are planned in this area. Though these projects require huge investments, the Onne Free Zone provides a cost-effective solution for every company involved in drilling, technical assistance, construction, maintenance, coating of pipe, machine shop, ship repair activities, etc. Furthermore, the huge availability of oil resources in this area combined with the incentives provided by Onne Free Zone create incomparable opportunities for downstream industries such as refineries, petrochemical and fertilizer plants.

V. Petroleum Operations and Host Communities Development

576. One of the most innovative provisions of the *Petroleum Industry Act (PIA), 2021*[1005] is contained in Chapter 3 which deals comprehensively with 'Host

---

1005. *See* the *Petroleum Industry Act, (PIA) No. 6 of 2021.* According to the Long Title to the PIA, it is 'An Act to Provide Legal, Governance, Regulatory and Fiscal Framework for the Nigerian

Community Development'.[1006] This is a clear acknowledgement of the ugly past and a determination to depart from the old norms of reckless and unhealthy relationships that had existed between resource-bearing communities and companies engaging in petroleum operations, particularly in the Niger Delta.

VI. Objectives of Host Communities' Development under the PIA

577. The PIA sets clear objectives as the basis for the new regime and a much more proactive paradigmatic approach to the issue of host communities' development under the Act. According to the PIA, objectives are to: (a) foster sustainable prosperity within host communities; (b) provide direct social and economic benefits from petroleum operations to host communities; (c) enhance peaceful and harmonious co-existence between licensees or lessees and host communities; and (d) create a framework to support the development of host communities.[1007]

578. The PIA gives both the Commission and Authority powers to make regulations in respect of host communities' development, including a grievance mechanism to resolve disputes between settlors and host communities.[1008] The regulations also include the ability of the settlor to make adjustments to reduce expenditures. This applies to situations where the available funds for administration under section 244 (c) of the Act[1009] are insufficient to fund the ongoing operations. The Act enables a settlor to make necessary adjustments to: (a) reduce the number of members of the Board of Trustees and frequency of meetings; (b) not fund the reserve fund under section 244 (b) and not hire the respective fund manager under section 246; (c) reduce the number of members of the management committee under section 247 and the frequency of meetings; and (d) reduce the frequency of meetings of the host communities advisory committee under section 249.

Petroleum Industry, the Development of Host Communities; and For Related Matters'. The PIA commenced on the 16 Aug. 2021.

1006. *See* generally Ch. 3, ss. 244–257 of the PIA, *ibid.*
1007. *See* generally s. 234(1)(a–d) of the PIA.
1008. *Ibid.*, subs. (2) and (3).
1009. Section 244(c) states in respect of 'Allocation of funds' that:

> The Board of Trustees shall in each year and under section 240 of this Act allocate from the host communities development trust fund, a sum equivalent to:
>
> (c) an amount not exceeding 5% to be utilised solely for administrative cost of running the trust and special projects, which shall be entrusted by the Board of Trustee to the settlor, provided that at the end of each financial year, the settlor shall render a full account of the utilisation of the fund to the Board of Trustees and where any portion of the fund is not utilised in a given year, it shall be returned to the capital fund.

VII. Incorporation of Host Communities' Development Trusts

579. The law requires that a settlor[1010] shall incorporate host communities' development trust ('the trust') for the benefit of the host communities for which the settlor is responsible.[1011] In case of joint or collective of settlors operating under a JOA with respect to upstream petroleum operations, the operator appointed under the agreement shall be responsible for compliance with the provisions of Chapter 3 of the PIA relating to host communities' development on behalf of all the settlors under such joint operating arrangement or agreement.[1012] Where settlors operate in shallow water and deep offshore, the littoral communities and any other community determined by the settlors shall be host communities for the purposes of the provisions of the Act regarding host communities' development.[1013]

580. The Act provides that the settlor shall for the purpose of setting up the trust, in consultation with the host communities, appoint and authorize a board of trustees ('the Board of Trustees'), which shall apply to be registered by the Corporate Affairs Commission as a corporate body containing the phrase 'host communities' development trust' under the CAMA[1014] in the manner provided under the Act.[1015] The Commission or Authority shall make regulations on the administration, guide and safeguard the utilization of the trust fund as well as exercise oversight functions and responsibilities for ensuring that the projects proposed by the Board of Trustees are implemented. This is subject to prior needs assessment undertaken by the settlor which may be adopted into the community development plan for the purpose of determining the projects to be undertaken by the host communities development trust.[1016] The Act imposes a timeline on the settlors for incorporation of host communities' development trust. It states that:

> The host communities' development trust shall be incorporated:
>
> (a) within 12 months from the effective date for existing oil mining leases;
> (b) within 12 months from the effective date for existing designated facilities;
> (c) within 12 months from the effective date for new designated facilities under construction on the effective date;
> (d) prior to the application for field development plan for existing oil prospecting licences;
> (e) prior to the application for any field development plan under a petroleum prospecting licence or petroleum mining lease granted under this Act; and

1010. By virtue of s. 318 of the PIA ('Interpretation' section), a 'Settlor' is a holder of an interest in a petroleum prospecting licence or petroleum mining lease whose area of operations is located in or appurtenant to any community or communities.
1011. *See* s. 235(1) of the PIA.
1012. *Ibid.*, subs. (2).
1013. *Ibid.*, subs. (3).
1014. *See* the *Companies and Allied Matters Act*, 2020.
1015. *See* s. 235(4) and (5) of the PIA.
1016. *Ibid.*, subs. (6) and (7).

(f) prior to commencement of commercial operations for licensees of designated facilities granted under this Act.[1017]

VIII. Transfer of Settlor's Interest and Obligations

581. The PIA provides for the transfer of settlor's interest and obligations subject to its host communities' development trust obligation under the law where the whole or part of an interest in a licence or lease is assigned, novated or otherwise transferred to another party. Therefore, the legal and equitable interest, rights and obligations of the transferor in relation to any associated host communities' development plan and host communities' development trust, shall be deemed to attach to the property to be transferred to the transferee, the legal and equitable interests, rights and obligations of the transferor shall be deemed to become the interests, rights and obligations of the transferee.[1018]

582. The Act provides that where the whole or part of a licence or lease is surrendered, the holder or holder nominee will continue to discharge its surviving obligations, notwithstanding that the area that is surrendered may be granted to a new lessee or licensee. However, where the surviving obligations have been complied with the holder shall have no further obligations relating to the part that was surrendered or the whole of the licence or lease where the entire licence or lease was surrendered.[1019] But in case of revocation, termination or expiration, the holder will continue to discharge its surviving obligations, notwithstanding that the area is revoked, terminated or expired.[1020]

583. The obligation to incorporate host communities' development trust is a very strict one under the PIA. This further confirms the seriousness attached to host communities' issues under the new regime under the PIA and the regulations made pursuant to the Act under the direction of the Commission and Authority. In very clear and definitive terms, the PIA provides that failure by any holder of a licence or lease to comply with its obligations to incorporate host communities' development trust after having been informed of such failure in writing by the Commission or Authority, may be a ground or form part of the grounds for revocation of the applicable licence or lease.[1021]

IX. Objectives of Host Communities' Development Trust

584. The constitution of the host communities' development trust must be drawn up in such a way as to allow the trust to manage and supervise the administration

1017. *See* s. 236(a–f) of the PIA.
1018. Section 237(1) of the PIA.
1019. *Ibid.*, subs. (2).
1020. *Ibid.*, subs. (3).
1021. *See* s. 238 of the PIA.

of the annual contribution of the settlor contemplated and any other sources of funding.[1022] The objectives of the trust shall be specified in the constitution and shall include without limitation to: (a) finance and execute projects for the benefit and sustainable development of the host communities; (b) undertake infrastructural development of the host communities within the scope of funds available to the Board of Trustees for such purposes; (c) facilitate economic empowerment opportunities in the host communities, and (d) advance and propagate educational development for the benefit of members of the host communities.[1023]

585. The PIA lists other objectives of the fund to include issues such as: (e) support healthcare development for the host communities; (f) support local initiatives within the host communities, which seek to enhance the protection of the environment; (g) support local initiatives within the host communities which seek to enhance security; (h) invest part of the available fund for and on behalf of the host communities; as well as (i) assist in any other developmental purpose deemed beneficial to the host communities as may be determined by the Board of Trustees.[1024]

586. Notwithstanding the above, funding of the trust fund shall not preclude the host communities from their entitlements under any other law.[1025] The essence of this provision is to preclude the licensee or lessee from backing down from its statutory obligations to fund host communities' development initiatives or programmes on the ground that other entities or bodies that are under similar obligations to the host community had undertaken the project or made available similar or same benefits it intended under another law or related host community development initiatives or policies.

X. Sources of Funding for Petroleum Host Communities' Development Trust

587. Sources of funds for the trust must be stipulated by its constitution. The Act specifically states that the constitution of each host communities' development trust shall establish a fund comprising of one or more accounts ('host communities' development trust fund') to be funded by the licensee or lessee. Each settlor makes an annual contribution to the applicable host communities' development trust fund of an amount equal to 3% of its actual annual operating expenditure of the preceding financial year in the upstream petroleum operations affecting the host communities for which the applicable host communities' development trust fund was established.[1026]

1022. *See* s. 239(1) of the PIA.
1023. *Ibid.*, subs. (2) and (3)(a–d).
1024. *Ibid.*, para. (e–i).
1025. *Ibid.*, subs. (4).
1026. *See* s. 240(1) and (2) of the PIA.

588. The trust's sources of funds may also include donations. The Act allows each host communities' development trust to receive donations, gifts, grants or honoraria that are provided to such host communities' development trust for the attainment of its objectives. The trust's profits and interest accruing to the reserve fund are also contributed to the applicable sources of funds of the host communities' development trust fund.[1027] In practical sense, the trust may also create other sources of funds for its objectives provided such is within the confines of its objectives and constitution. The constitution of each host communities' development trust shall further provide that the trust fund shall be used exclusively for the implementation of the applicable host communities' development plan.[1028]

XI. The Board of Trustees, Management, Duties and Functions

589. The constitution of the trust shall contain provisions requiring the settlor to set up a Board of Trustees and determine its membership subject to the approval of the Commission or Authority. Membership of the Board of Trustees shall include persons of high integrity and professional standing, who shall come from the host communities. The members of the Board shall elect a Chairman from among themselves.[1029]

590. The law allows the settlor to determine the selection process, procedure for meeting, financial regulations and administrative procedures of the Board of Trustees as well as the remuneration, discipline, qualification, disqualification, suspension and removal of members of the Board of Trustees and for other matters relating to the operation and activities of the Board of Trustees.[1030] Each member of the Board of Trustees shall serve a term of four years in the first instance and may be reappointed for another term of four years and no more. The Board shall have a secretary, who shall be appointed by the settlor to keep the books of the Board.[1031]

591. The duties of the Board are clearly spelt out by the PIA to include determining the criteria, process and proportion of the host communities' development trust fund to be allotted to specific development programmes; approving the projects for which the host communities' development trust fund shall be utilized and providing general oversight of the projects for which the host communities' development trust fund shall be utilized. The board's duties also include approving the appointment of fund managers for purposes of managing the reserve fund; setting-up of the management committee of the host communities' development trust and appointing its members as well as determining the allocation of funds to host communities based on the matrix provided by the settlor.[1032]

1027. *Ibid.*, subs. (3–4).
1028. Section 241 of the PIA.
1029. *Ibid.*, s. 242(1–2).
1030. *Ibid.*, subs. (3)(a–c).
1031. *Ibid.*, subs. (4–5).
1032. *See* generally s. 243 (a–f) of the PIA.

XII. Allocation of Funds

592. The PIA makes definite provisions for the allocation of funds from the host communities' development trust fund. A sum equivalent to 75% shall be set out for capital fund out of which the Board of Trustees shall make disbursements for projects in each of the host communities. Any sum not utilized in a given financial year shall be rolled over and utilized in the subsequent year. An amount equivalent to 20% of the reserve fund shall be invested for the utilization of the host communities' development trust whenever there is a cessation in the contribution payable by the settlor. The balance, being an amount not exceeding 5% shall be utilized solely for the administrative cost of running the trust and special projects. This shall be entrusted by the Board of Trustees to the settlor, and the settlor shall render a full account of the utilization of the fund to the Board of Trustees. Any portion of the fund not utilized in a given year shall be returned to the capital fund.[1033]

593. For the above purpose, the settlor shall provide to the Board of Trustees a matrix for the distribution of the trust fund to the host communities and the Board shall utilize the matrix provided for the distribution of the funds in the host communities' development trust fund to each of its host communities.[1034] To further strengthen financial prudence and efficiency, the Board of Trustees shall engage a fund manager to invest the reserve fund as the fund accrues. The Board shall have responsibilities for managing the interest and profits accruable from the investment of the reserve fund and allocate the gain in accordance with the provisions of section 244 of the Act.[1035]

XIII. Management Committee, Composition and Powers

594. Like the board, the constitution of the host communities' development trust shall contain provisions requiring the Board of Trustees to set up a management committee for the host communities' development trust. The membership of the management committee shall comprise one representative of each host community, who shall be nominated by the host community as a non-executive member. Executive members selected by the Board of Trustees shall be Nigerians of high integrity and professional standing, and may not necessarily be members of the host communities.[1036]

595. Members shall serve a term of four years in the first instance and may be reappointed for another term of four years and no more.[1037] The Board of Trustees shall in accordance with the host communities' development trust determine the selection process, procedure for meetings, financial regulations and administrative

1033. *Ibid.*, s. 244(a–c).
1034. Section 245(1–2) of the PIA.
1035. Section 246(1) and (2) of the PIA.
1036. Section 247 (1) and (2)(a–b).
1037. *Ibid.*, subs. (3).

procedures of the management committee; the remuneration, discipline, qualification, disqualification, suspension and removal of members of the management committee; and any other matter relating to the operations and activities of the management committee. Like the Board of Trustees, the management committee shall also have a secretary, who shall be appointed by the Board of Trustees to keep the books of the committee.[1038]

596. The management committee is saddled with a number of statutory duties and functions, including the general administration of the host communities' development trust on an ad hoc basis as well as the preparation of the budget of the trust for approval of the Board of Trustees.[1039] It shall also be responsible for the development and management of the contracting process for project award on behalf of the trust subject to the approval of the Board of Trustees as well as the determination of project award winners and contractors to execute projects through a transparent process subject to the approval of the Board of Trustees.[1040]

597. The management committee is also saddled with the responsibility of: supervising projects execution; nominating fund managers for appointment by the Board of Trustees for approval, to manage the reserve fund; reporting on the activities of the management committee, contractors and other service providers to the Board of Trustees; and undertaking of any other function and duty that may be assigned to it by the Board of Trustees to enhance the performance of the trust.[1041]

598. The PIA also provides that the constitution of the trust shall provide for an advisory committee of the trust, which shall contain at least one member of each host community.[1042] The management committee shall determine the selection process, procedure for meetings, financial regulations and administrative procedures of the host communities' advisory committee. It shall also determine the remuneration, discipline, qualification, disqualification, suspension and removal of members of the host communities' advisory committee as well as any other matter relating to the operations and activities of the host communities' advisory committee. However, decisions of the management committee on the above-listed issues shall be subject to the approval of the Board of Trustees.[1043]

599. The duties and functions of the host communities' advisory committee shall include: nominating a member to represent the host communities on the management committee; articulating community development projects to be transmitted to the management committee; and monitoring and reporting the progress of projects being executed in the community to the management committee. It shall also advise

1038. *Ibid.*, subss. (4)(a–c) and (5).
1039. Section 248(a) of the PIA.
1040. *Ibid.*, para. (b–c).
1041. *Ibid.*, para. (d–g).
1042. *See* s. 249(1) of the PIA.
1043. *Ibid.*, subs. (2)(a–c) and (3).

the management committee on activities that may lead to the improvement of the security of infrastructure and enhancement of peace-building within the communities and the entire area of operation.[1044]

XIV. Host Communities Needs Assessment, Development Plan and Others

600. The settlor shall conduct a needs assessment ('host communities needs assessment') upon being granted a licence or lease. Host communities needs assessment shall contain social, environmental, and economic perspectives as determined by the specific needs of each affected host community. It shall also ascertain the effect that the proposed petroleum operations might have on the host communities as well as provide a strategy for addressing the needs and effects identified.[1045]

601. Each community need assessment shall indicate that the settlor has engaged with each affected host community to understand the issues and needs of such host communities and that it has consulted with and considered the reasonable concerns of women, youth and community leaders. It shall also reflect the fact that it has engaged with each affected host community in developing a strategy to address the needs and effects identified in the applicable host communities needs assessment.[1046] The settlor shall submit the needs assessment to the Commission or Authority, based on the findings for the regulator to undertake its oversight function preparatory to the establishment of the trust.[1047]

602. The host communities' development plan shall be based on the matrix provided in section 245 for the distribution of trust funds. It shall specify the community development initiatives required to respond to the findings and strategy identified in the host communities needs assessment. It shall also determine and specify the projects to implement and the specified initiatives, as well as provide a detailed timeline for projects. The host communities' development plan shall also determine and prepare the budget of the host communities' development plan; set out the reasons and objectives of each project as supported by the host communities needs assessment. It shall conform with the Nigerian content requirements provided in the Nigerian Oil and Gas Industry Content Development Act and provide for ongoing review and reporting to the Commission.[1048]

603. By its constitution, the trust shall require the management committee to submit a mid-year report of its activities to the Board of Trustees not later than 31 August of the particular year. It shall also submit an annual report accompanied by its audited account to the Board of Trustees not later than 28 February of the succeeding year. The Board of Trustees shall submit an annual report of the activities

1044. *See* s. 250 (a–d) of the PIA.
1045. Section 151(1) and (2)(a–c) of the PIA.
1046. *Ibid.*, subs. (3)(a–c).
1047. *Ibid.*, subs. (4).
1048. *See* generally s. 252(a–g) of the PIA.

of the trust accompanied by its audited account to the settlor not later than 31 March of the particular year. Upon receipt of the annual report, the settlor shall then submit an annual report of the activities of the host communities' development trust accompanied by its audited account to the Commission or Authority, as the case may be, not later than 31 May of the particular year.[1049]

604. The funds of the host communities' development trust shall be exempted from taxation,[1050] but payment made by the settlor under section 240 (2) of the Act,[1051] shall be deductible for the purposes of hydrocarbon tax and companies income tax as applicable. However, where in any year, an act of vandalism, sabotage or other civil unrest occurs causing damage to petroleum and designated facilities or disrupting production activities within the host communities, the community shall forfeit its entitlement to the extent of the costs of repairs of the damage that resulted from the activity with respect to the provisions of the Act within that financial year. This will not be applicable where the interruption is caused by technical or natural causes.[1052]

1049. *See* generally s. 255(a–d) of the PIA.
1050. *Ibid.*, s. 256.
1051. Section 240(2) of the PIA states that:

> Each settlor, where applicable through the operator, shall make an annual contribution to the applicable host communities development trust fund of an amount equal to 3% of its actual annual operating expenditure of the preceding financial year in the upstream petroleum operations affecting the host communities for which the applicable host communities development trust fund was established.

1052. *See* s. 257(1–2) of the PIA. Subsection (3) specifically provides that the basis for computation of the trust fund in any year shall always exclude the cost of repairs of damaged facilities attributable to any act of vandalism, sabotage or other civil unrest.

Selected Bibliography

Journals/Papers

Agbonifo E., 'Opportunities and Obstacles to Economic Growth and Sustainable Development through Natural Gas in Nigeria' (2015) 17:5 *Journal of Sustainable Development in Africa*.

A.W. Reitze, 'Federal Control of Carbon Dioxide Emissions: What Are the Options?' (2009) 36:1, *Boston College Environmental College Law Review* pp. 1–79.

Arnosti, D. and Abbas, D. 'Harvesting Fuel: Cutting Cost and Reducing Forest Fire Hazards through Biomass', (2008) *Institute for Agriculture and Trade Policy*, at p. 1.

Babarisa A., *NNPC: 30 Active Years, 1970–2007* (Lagos: Octopus Communications Company, 2007) at p. 61.

Baghebo, M. and Atima, T.O. 'The Impact of Petroleum on Economic Growth in Nigeria' (2013) 2:5 *Global Business and Economics Research Journal*, p. 103.

Bagudu, I. et. al., *Oil and Gas Exploration: Reconciling Contending Issues* in Simpson & Fagbohun (Eds,) *Environmental Law and Policy* (Lagos: Law Centre, 1998) at 310.

Baghebo, M. and Atima, T.O. 'The Impact of Petroleum on Economic Growth in Nigeria' (2013) 2:5 *Global Business and Economics Research Journal*, p. 103.

Banigo, I., *The Development of a Downstream (Domestic) Gas Market in Nigeria: Barriers and Reforms?* (Unpublished Dissertation submitted to CEPMLP, University of Dundee, 2005) p. 45.

Brown, L.R. 'Plan B: Mobilizing to Save Civilization'. *(2008) Earth Policy Institute*, W.W. Norton and Company, New York, p. 398.

Christopher Carr, 'Structuring and Financing Projects' in Paul O. Watchman (ed.) *Climate Change: A Guide to Carbon Law and Practice* (London, Globe Business Publishing, 2008), at 39.

D.C. John, 'A Critical Analysis of the Petroleum Tax Act (PPTA) of 2004 and the Petroleum Industry Bill (PIB)' (2012) *Tax Law Journal of Nigeria*, p. 130 at 135.

Deunden Nikomborirak and Wanwiphang Manachotphong, 'Electricity Reform in Practice: The Case of Thailand, Malaysia, Indonesia and the Philippines "*Intergovernmental Group of Experts on Competition Law and Policy*"', Geneva, 17–19 2007, at 1–3.

Selected Bibliography

E. Gnansonuou, 'Boosting the Electricity Sector in West Africa: An Integrative Vision' (2008) *International Association of Energy Economies, Third Quarter*, at 23.

E.I. Kachikwu, 'Legal Issues in Oil and Gas Industry' (1989) Gravitas, Vol 2, No. 34 at 39.

Eweje Gabriel. 'Environmental Costs and Responsibilities Resulting from Oil Exploitation in Developing Countries: The Case of the Niger Delta of Nigeria'. (2006) 69:1, *Journal of Business Ethics*, p. 30.

Federal Republic of Nigeria, 'National Energy Policy', the Presidency- Energy Commission of Nigeria, April 2003, at p. 1.

Freling, R. & Lahl, J. *Renewable Energy Technology: Optimizing Energy Sources for the Development of Millennium Project Villages*; Solar Electric Light Fund (SELF): Washington, DC, USA, 8 July 2005.

J.J. Fialka, 'World Bank Emissions-Trading Venture May Expand to Accommodate Interest' *Wall Street Journal*, 24 April 2000 at A18.

J.R. Nash, 'Too Much Market? Conflict Between Tradable Pollution Allowances and the Polluter Pays' Principle' (2000) 24 *Harvard Environmental Law Review*, 465 at 466.

Julia Kennedy-Darling, Nick Hoyt, Kyle Murao and Allison Rose, 'The Energy Crisis of Nigeria' -An Overview and Implications for the Future, (LL.M Thesis, The University of Chicago, 6.3.2008), pp. 2–5.

L. Justin. 'Rooting the Concept of Common But Differentiated Responsibilities in Established Principles of International Environmental Law'. (2015) 17:1 *Vermont Journal of Environmental Law*, pp. 27–50.

Manafa, N.: Electricity Development in Nigeria, Rasheen Publisher, Lagos, 1995, pp. 37–1.

Miller Alan and Serchuk Adam, 'The Environmental Imperative: A Driving Force in the Development and Deployment of Renewable' (1996) No. 1 *REPP Issue Brief*, p. 5.

M. Battiste & J.Y. Henderson, *Protecting Indigenous Knowledge; A Global Challenge* (Saskatoon: Purich Publishing, 2000) at 13.

M.M. Gidado, 'Fiscal Provisions for Gas Development and Commercialisation under the Petroleum Industry Bill (P.I.B.)' 2009 *NIALS Journal of Business Law*, p. 27.

M.M. Ologundudu, '*The Epileptic Nature of Electricity Supply and Its Consequences on Industrial and Economic Performance in Nigeria*', (2014) Vol. XIV, issue IV, version 1, *Global Journal of Research in Engineering*.

Nkiruka, C.M., 'Unbundling and Privatisation of the Nigerian Electricity Sector: Reality of Myth? (LL.M paper, CEPMLP, University of Dundee)', 2010 at p. 2.

Niger Power Review: 'Development of Electricity Industry in Nigeria (1960–1985), 1985, pp. 1–6.

O. Fagbohun, 'The Law of Oil Pollution and Environmental Restoration: A Comparative Review', (Odade Publishers, Lagos: 2010) p. 303.

Oladele M. Oladunjoye, 'Incorporated Joint Ventures in the Nigeria Petroleum Industry: Examining the Legal Implications & Regulatory Risks', (2013) 11:2 *OGEL*, at p. 2.

Orji Ogbonnaya, 'How Major Oil and Gas Firms Defraud Government of Revenues', Guardian Newspaper Vol. 30. No. 12, 947, Tuesday, 10 June 2014.

Oscar Arricta's report that the first commercial oil well was successful drilled in Peru in 1863 in Arricta, O.E., 'New Petroleum Law of Peru' (1996) 14:4 *Journal of Energy & Natural Resources Law*, 424 at 425.

Oyewunmi, O.A. & Oyewunmi, A.E, 'Managing Gas Flaring and Allied Issues in the Oil and Gas Industry: Reflections on Nigeria', (2016) 7:4 *Mediterranean Journal of Social Sciences* (MCSER Publishing, Rome-Italy, p. 643.

Policy Guidelines on Renewable Electricity in Nigeria, December 2006, paragraph 2.0.

Presidential Power Reform Transaction signing Summit, *The Punch Newspaper*, Friday 19 April 2013, at 36.

R.H. Acker, 'The Quiet (Energy) Revolution: Analysing the Dissemination of Photovoltaic Power Systems in Kenya' (1996) 24:1 *Energy Policy*, pp. 81–111 at 81.

Tolupe, A. O, 'Oil Exploration and Environmental Degradation: the Nigeria Experience' (2004) 4 *International Society for Environmental Information Science*. pp. 34–36.

Tunde Oyesina, 'Implications of the Petroleum Industry Bill on the Nation', *The Nigerian Tribune Newspaper*, 3 May 2010.

Ukpebor, E.T.O, *Nigerian Gas Master Plan: Strengthening the Nigeria Gas Infrastructure Blueprint as a Base for Expanding Regional Gas Market*, presented at the 24th World Gas Conference, October, 2009, p. 9.

U. Udok & E.B. Akpan, 'Gas Flaring in Nigeria: Problems and Prospects', 5:1 (Global Journal of Politics and Law Research (European Centre for Research Training and Development, UK: March 2017) p. 26.

Volk, T.A. *Developing a Willow Biomass Crop Enterprise for Bioenergy and Bioproducts in United States*, (Buffalo Press, New York, 2000), at 15.

Yemi Oke, '*International Criminal Court, Crimes Against Humanity And The Nigerian Boko Haram Islamist Group: Can Two Wrongs Make A Right?' (2012–13) Vol. XII-XIII, Indian Journal of International Law (The Indian Society of International Law (ISIL)*, Yearbook of International Humanitarian and Refuge Law, New Delhi, India, 2014, at 156–188.

Yemi Oke, 'Impacts of International Law and Global Best Practices on Energy Resources Governance in Nigeria' (2012) 8 *University of Ilorin Law Journal*, 156–180.

Yemi Oke, 'Beyond Power Sector Reforms: The Need for Decentralized Energy Options (DEOPs)' (2012) 18:1 *Nigerian Journal of Contemporary Law, University of Lagos*, 67 at 68–71.

Yemi Oke, 'National Grid or National Greed', The Punch Newspaper (7 December 2011) 14 and (8 December 2011) 16.

Yemi Oke, 'Adapting to Climate Change: Sustainable Mitigation Options for Developing Countries in Sub-Saharan Africa' (2011) 1 *NAILS Journal of Environmental Law* (Nigerian Institute of Advanced Legal Studies), at pp. 59–101.

Yemi Oke, 'Impacts of International Law and Global Best Practices on Energy Resources Governance in Nigeria' (2012) 8 *University of Ilorin Law Journal*, 156–180.

Selected Bibliography

Yemi Oke, 'Manitoba Hydro and Electricity Undertakings in Developing Countries: The Case of Nigeria' (2012) 36: 1 *Manitoba Law Journal*, at 37–65.

Yemi Oke, 'Rural Electrification and Captive Power Generation' (2013) 3 *Nigerian Lawyers' Journal, Law Digest* (UK), summer 2013, at 51–52.

Yemi Oke, 'Compulsory Purchase as an Alternative to Revocation of Title to Land for Electricity Purpose in Nigeria' (2013) *Journal of Private and Property Law*, University of Lagos, at pp. 36–59.

Yemi Oke, 'Relevance of Derivatives and Related Debt Instruments to Public-Private Sector Financing of Energy Resources in Nigeria' (2012) 1 *NIALS Journal of Law and Public Policy*, p. 185.

Yemi Oke, 'Multi-Jurisdictional Evaluation of the Nigerian Oil & Gas (Industry and Content Development) Act, 2010' (2012) Vol. 2, No.1, *University of Ibadan Law Journal*, at 153–179.

Yemi Oke, 'Impacts of International Law and Global Best Practices on Energy Resources Governance in Nigeria' (2012) 8 *University of Ilorin Law Journal*, 156–180.

Yemi Oke, 'Developing Countries and the Global Trends in Natural Resources Management' (2009) 19, *NLA Journal* (New York), at 19–22.

Yemi Oke, 'Africa and the Quest for Mining Sustainability: A Comparative Evaluation of the Mineral Law of Nigeria with South Africa and Ghana' (2008) 15 *South African Journal of Environmental Law and Policy* [SAJELP], 183–215 at 183.

Yinka Omorogbe, 'Oil and Gas Law in Nigeria *simplified*', (Malthouse Press Ltd., Lagos: 2001) p. 58.

Books

Akanle, O., *Nigerian Income Tax Law and Practice* (Centre for Business and Investment Studies Limited, Nigeria, 1991), pp. 4, 5.

Akinrele, A. *Nigeria and Oil and Gas Law* (OGEL-Oil, Gas & Energy Intelligence, 2005) at 5.

Atsegbua L., *Oil and Gas Law in Nigeria, Theory and Practice*, Second Edition, (New Era Publication, Benin City: 2004), at 42.

Atsegbua L. Akpotaire, V. Dimowo F., Environmental Law in Nigeria: Theory and Practice, Lagos; Ababa Press Ltd., 2004, p. 3.

Barry Denyer-Green, *Compulsory Acquisition and Compensation* (8th ed.) (EG Books, London: 2005), at 168.

Garner, Bryan A. (ed.), *Black's Law Dictionary* (8th Edition) (West Publishing Company, St. Paul, Minn, 2004), p. 1496.

International Websters Encyclopedic Dictionary of the English Language. 2003 Edition.

Martin M Olisa *Nigerian Petroleum Law and Practice* 2ed (Jonia Ventures Limited, Lagos: 1997).

Micheal A.G. Bunter, *The Promotion and licensing of Petroleum Prospective Acreage* (Kluwer Law International, 2001) p. 379.

O.A. Osunbor, 'Environmental Law and Policy', in in Simpson & Fagbohun (Eds,) *Environmental Law and Policy* (Law Centre, Faculty of Law, Lagos State University: 1998) p. 312.

T. Daintith, *The Petroleum Production License in the United Kingdom*, in Daintith, T., ed., The Legal Character of Petroleum Licenses: A Comparative Study, (1981), p. 216.

U.B. Akuru, O.I. Okoro, 'Renewable Energy Investment in Nigeria: A Review of the Renewable Energy Master Plan', J. Energy South, Afr. 25, 3 (2014).

Yemi Oke, 'Intergenerational Sustainability and Traditional Knowledge in Africa: Natural Resource Management Perspective' in Sustaining Life on Earth: Environmental and Human Health Though Global Governance (C.L. Soskolne, et al., eds) Lexington Books Maryland, USA. (2007) at pp. 227–239.

Yemi Oke, *Nigerian Energy Resources Law and Practice*. Princeton Publishers, Lagos, 2019, 1320 pp.

Yemi Oke, *Nigerian Electricity Law and Regulation*. LawLords Publications, Abuja/Lagos, 2013, 500 pp.

Yemi Oke, *Nigerian Energy and Natural Resources Law (Notes & Materials)*. Princeton Publishers, Lagos, 2016, 200 pp.

Yemi Oke, *Essays on Nigerian Electricity Law*. Princeton Publishers, Lagos, 2016, 160 pp.

Internet Sources

Adenike Boyo, 'Development of Solar Energy in Lagos State, Nigeria' online at: http://www.wcpsd.org/posters/environment/Boyo_Adenike_2.pdf, accessed 15 October 2015.

Adeoye Adefule 'Fundamental Legal Issues in Oil and Gas Industry', online at: http://www.scribd.com/doc/6412031/Paper-6-Fundamental-Legal-Issues-in-the-Oil-and-Gas-Industry-II, assessed 22 August, 2023.

Alex O. Awiti, <Rio=20 Must Focus on Local Action', <http://www.mwanabidii.com/showthread.php?1502-Rio-20-Must-Focus-On-Local-Action>, accessed 28 April, 2018.

Aluko & Oyebode, 'Overview of The Petroleum Industry Bill' pp. 1–12, p. 3, available online at http://www.aluko-oyebode.com/files/overview-of-the-petroleum-industry-bill.pdf, accessed on 1 November 2016.

Amanze R. Ejiogu, 'Gas Flaring in Nigeria: Costs and Policy' (2013) 24:6 *Energy & Environment Journal*, (2013), pp. 983–998 online at: http://www.jstor.org/stable/43735213 accessed 16 July 2017.

Babatunde Adeyemo 'West African Power Pool' *South Asia Regional Workshop on Competitive Electricity Markets*, Colombo, Sri Lanka: 18 March 2014; International Renewable Energy Agency, 'West African Power Pool: Planning and Prospects for Renewable Energy', online at: https://www.irena.org/DocumentDownloads/Publications/WAPP.pdf, accessed 13 June 2017.

Banwo & Ighodalo, 'Synopsis of the 2017 National Gas Policy' http://www.banwo-ighodalo.com/resources/synopsis-of-the-2017-nationalgas-policy, accessed 29 August 2018. *See also* online at: http://www.eia.gov/countries/cab.cfm?fips=NI, accessed 14 June 2013.

BusinessDay, 1 December 2008, online at: http://www.businessdayonline.com/index.php?option=com_content&view=Article&id=1606:gaslink-completes-n7bn-pipeline-expansion&catid=85:national&Itemid=266, accessed 18 March 2016.

Selected Bibliography

Chigbue, I.N., 'Electric Power Sector Reform: Privatization, Regulation and Other Challenges' a presentation at the National Workshop on Electric Power Sector Liberalization, Abujam 30 March 2006, online at: http://worldstagegroup.com/truecolour/media/11152404.ppt, accessed 18 April 2010.

Donna Obaseki-Ogunnaike, 'Understanding the Petroleum Industry Governance Bill 2016', published in the 'West Africa Energy' segment of Business Day Newspaper, 13 July 2016, pp. 1–5, p.1, available online at: http://www-acas-law.com/assets/opinion-piece-as-written-by-donna-obaseke-understanding-petroleum2.pdf/, accessed on 3 February 2017.

Duru O. W., 'An Appraisal of the Legal Framework for the Regulation of Nigerian Oil and Gas Industry, with Appropriate Recommendations' available at http://ssrn.com/abstract=2137979 accessed on 1 January 2014.

Energy Policy of Nigeria, 2003, available online at: www.onlinenigeria.com/geology/?blurb=514, accessed viewed on 12 July 2017.

Environmental Law Alliance Worldwide, https://elaw.org/af-akpan-v-royal-dutch-shell, accessed 12 July 2017.

Environmental Policy online at: http://www.unece.org/environmental-policy/conventions/envlrtapwelcome/the-air-convention-and-its-protocols/the-convention-and-its-achievements.htm, accessed 8 July 2017.

Federal Ministry of Power and Steel, Federal Republic of Nigeria: 'Renewable Electricity Policy Guidelines' December 2006, (International Centre for Energy, Environment and Development (ICEED), online at www.iceednigeria.org, accessed 20 May 2014.

F.T. Sparrow; William A. Masters and Brian H. Bowen, 'Electricity Trade and Capacity Expansion Options in West Africa' Purdue University Institute for Interdisciplinary Engineering, online at: http://www.ecn.purdue.edu/IIES/SUFG, at p. 5, accessed 15 April 2015.

Freedom Daily http://www.fff.org/freedom/fd0410d.asp, accessed December 2015.

Gidado M. *Petroleum Contract with Multinational Oil Firm – The Nigerian Experience.* A Thesis Submitted for the Degree of Phd at the University of Warwick http://wrap.warwick.ac.uk/4320/1/WRAP_THESIS_Gidado_1992.pdf, p. 66.

Gigi Nwagbo, 'Renewable Energy in Nigeria' 12 December 2017, available online at: http://large.stanford.edu/courses/2017/ph240/nwagbo2/, accessed 12 January 2019.

http://www.worldenergy.org/documents/congresspapers/135.pdf, accessed 15 October 2012.

International Convention on Civil Liability for Oil Pollution Damage (Civil Liability Convention), 1996, online at: www.imo.org/.../Conventions/ListOfConventions/.../International-Convention-on-Civi, and treaties.fco.gov.uk/docs/pdf/1996/TS0086.pdf, accessed 29 August 2018.

International Convention for the Establishment of an International Fund for Compensation for Oil Pollution Damage Caused by Sea Going Vessels Carrying Oil as its Cargo, online at www.cep.unep.org/meetings-events/11th-igm/oil-spill-compensation-funds.../file, accessed 29 August 2018.

List of available pipelines run by the Nigerian gas company available online at: http://www.nnpcgroup.com/NNPCBusiness/Subsidiaries/NGC.aspx, accessed on 24 May 2016.

Mourad Belguedj 'Strategic Gas Plan for Nigeria' Publication of Joint UNDP/ World Bank Energy Sector Management Assistance Programme (ESMAP) available at: www.esmap.org/esmapsites/esmap.org/files/FR58200861713_Nigeria_strategicgasplanfornigeria.pdf, accessed on 10 October 2015.

Muhammed Ladan, 'Access to Environmental Justice in Oil Pollution and Gas Flaring Cases as Human Right Issue in Nigeria', Paper Presented at a Training Workshop for Federal Ministry of Justice Lawyers Organized by the Institute for Oil and Gas Law, Abuja, Nigeria, 28–30 November 2011, http://papers.ssrn.com/sol3/papers.cfm?abstract_id=2336093, accessed 12 December 2016.

Nigerian National Petroleum Corporation (NNPC) Group- Gas; Nigerian Gas Company), online at: http://www.nnpcgroup.com/nnpc-group/ngc, accessed 24 March 2016.

NNPC Business Information, online at:http://www.nnpcgroup.com/NNPCBusiness/BusinessInformation/OilGasinNigeria/IndustryHistory.aspx last viewed on 24/05/14, accessed 24 June 2017.

Oyeyemi Oke, 'Marginal Fields In Nigeria: Who Owns the Field?', 4 May 2017, online at: http://www.mondaq.com/Nigeria/x/591234/Oil+Gas+Electricity/Marginal+Fileds+In+Nigeria+Who+Owns+The+Field, accessed 9 June 2018.

P.A. Ilenikhena, 'Sola Energy Applications in Nigeria' WEC, Montreal, Paper No. 135 (Revised), 2010.

PIB Inter-Agency Project Team, 'An Overview of Petroleum Industry Bill' (PIB Consultative forum) July 2009, pp. 1–38, p. 3, available online at: http://nnpcgroup.com/portals/0/pdf/PIBConsultativeforum.pdf, accessed on 1 November 2016.

Renewable Energy and Electricity: 'World Nuclear Association'. Online http://www.world-nuclear.org/info10.html, accessed 13 April 2011, at p. 3.

Rio+20 Summit, 'Little Actual Disappointment over Lack of Progress', online at http://www.pri.org/stories/science/environment/tt-at-rio-20-summit-little-actual-disappointment-over-lack-of-progress-10382.html, accessed 24 June 2012.

Samuel Dinimas, An Analysis of the Nigerian Petroleum Industry Bill 2012', Westpaq, 2013, Vol.1, pp. 1–19, p. 7, available online at: https://www.westpaq.com/wp-content-/uploads/2013/05/An-Analysis-of-the-Nigeria-Petroleum-Industry-Bill-2012_WESTPAQ_v1_Final.pdf, accessed on 1 November 2016.

The Early History of Wind Energy, Global Sources, online at: http://www.brighthub.com/environment/renewable-energy/Articles/71440.aspx, accessed 17 April 2014.

Tristan Edis, 'Climate Spectator: Ignore Rio, Copenhagen and Kyoto', *Business Spectator*, online at http://www.businessspectator.com.au/bs.nsf/Article/Why-you-should-ignore-Rio-Copenhagen-and-KyotoPerp-pd20120622-VH3AC?OpenDocument&emcontent_spectators&src=rot, accessed 24 June 2012.

United Nations Economic Commission for Europe (UNECE) Convention on Long-range Transboundary Air Pollution, (1979) TIAS 10541; 1302 UNTS 217; 18 ILM 1442 (*1979*), online at https://www.unece.org/fileadmin/DAM/env/lrtap/full%20text/1979.CLRTAP.e.pdf, accessed 28 August 2018.

Selected Bibliography

Table of Cases

The bold numbers here refer to paragraph numbers.

Table of Statutes

The bold numbers here refer to paragraph numbers.

Index

The numbers here refer to paragraph numbers.

Index

www.ingramcontent.com/pod-product-compliance
Lightning Source LLC
Chambersburg PA
CBHW071436230926
51846CB00001B/256
* 9 7 8 9 4 0 3 5 3 8 8 7 7 *